Saharan Journey

SVEN LINDQVIST

Translated from the Swedish by Joan Tate

GRANTA

Granta Publications, 12 Addison Avenue, London W11 4QR

First published in Great Britain by Granta Books 2012

This book consists of two previously published volumes: *Desert Divers*, first published by Granta Books 2000, originally published under the title of *Ökendykarna*, by Albert Bonniers Förlag 1990, and '*Exterminate All the Brutes*', first published by Granta Books 1997 by arrangement with The New Press, New York, originally published under the title of *Utrota varenda jävel* by Albert Bonniers Förlag 1992.

A CIP catalogue record for this book
is available from the British Library.

1 3 5 7 9 10 8 6 4 2

ISBN 978 1 84708 232 9

Printed and bound by CPI Group (UK) Ltd, Croydon, CR0 4YY

Contents

Desert Divers

'All is included in transformation. You too are subordinate to change, even destruction. So is the entire universe.'

MARCUS AURELIUS

'The journey is a door through which one goes out of the known reality and steps into another, unexplored reality, resembling a dream.'

MAUPASSANT

Contents

To Tarfaya

1

A large muddy stone is lying in the washbasin of my hotel room.

Carefully, I scrape off the mud and rinse it. The water coming out of the tap is black.

After I have washed the stone clean, it is as pink as the morning sky. It is pink granite and made of two rounded segments resembling the halves of a brain.

Yes, now I can see it – it is my own brain which has arrived before me.

It is so heavy I can hardly lift it out of the washbasin.

I am woken from my dream by the usual charter-flight applause, filled with profound relief that the plane has miraculously landed in one piece at the right airport: Agadir.

Bus to the Hotel Almohades. I rent a room for the night and a car for a month.

I am not drawn to the pool, but to the desert. As a child I read about fire-eaters and well-divers, about sandstorms and desert lakes. I planned a great journey in the Sahara. Now I am here.

I am alone. I have just parted from my volumes of Dostoevsky; with all my notes in them. I have parted from the woman who was once my beloved. I have parted from thirty-three years of my life.

This has one advantage – the period of time before those thirty-three years has suddenly closed in on me.

As long as I remained in my childhood home, I could remember nothing of my childhood. It seemed to have been erased. Nothing but a bunch of anecdotes, no genuine memories.

Nor could I dream.

Now that I have moved, fragments of my childhood often come into my mind. And when I began to train with weights as I did when I was small, then I also began to dream.

Memories and dreams do not allow themselves to be forced. The very intention locks the door you want to open. You can only reach your goal by back ways and sidetracks.

One way I have tried to approach childhood several times is to do now what I so fervently longed to be allowed to do then. Even if it seems childish and unmotivated, sometimes I try what in the impotence of my smallness I dreamt of doing.

'It's like diving into black water,' says Antoine de Saint-Exupéry about a night-landing in the Sahara.

When the mail planes in his novels landed for a stopover in Agadir, the pilots had four hours before they had to go on again. I remember that as if I had read it yesterday. They went on to the town and had dinner, their bodies still singing with the vibrations of the plane.

I eat prawns au gratin at the Water Garden restaurant opposite the hotel and drink a toast to the mail plane pilots in Oulmez fizzy mineral water. Will I find that there, down south, where it really will be needed?

I am not really worried about not finding any there, but just long for it to be necessary.

At about ten in the evening on October 30, it is a little cold around the shoulders to sit outside after dinner. I go to bed early. I lie there, drawing my soul together in the no-man's-land on the borders of sleep. Then the dream interrupted on the plane comes back.

Once again I am washing that stone in black water. Bats whistle around me in the dark of the cave, the breeze from their wings waking others asleep, hanging in the roof with their heads down. Heads? The whole cave is a head, an empty skull full of a whistling darkness, in which I stand with the pink stone in my arms.

The Stravinsky-chatter of sparrows in the bush, the sky blue with light clouds. Early in the morning, I leave the monkey mountain of humanity around the hotel pool, get into my little Renault and drive slowly south.

At first the hollows are still green and glisten with moisture. The fig-cactus is just bearing fruit and bunches of ripe dates hang heavy as udders below the tops of the date palms – yellow, brown, dark red and ready to burst with the sweetness of dates.

Morocco's favourite colour is shocking pink. Instead of the white corners that we have on our red-painted houses, the houses here have reverse-stepped gables, highest in the corners and sinking towards the middle.

But soon the houses become fewer, the ground dryer. The greenery thins out until it looks like the sparse, tender green grass which grew in the sand of our Christmas crib when I was a child.

And as the desert opens up around me, as the sandy colours take over with their million monotonous variations, as the light becomes so intense that it hides shapes, extinguishes colours and flattens out levels – then my whole body hums with happiness and I feel, This is my landscape! This was where I wanted to be!

I stop the car, get out and listen.

A cricket, dark as a splinter of stone, chirps shrilly. The wind whistles in the six telephone wires, a thin, metallic note I haven't heard since childhood.

And then silence, which is even rarer.

Far away over there, the nomads' dark goat-hair tent trembles in the midday heat. Their women and children come walking in the shadow of their burdens.

5

In Tiznit, some of them have camped north of the town wall. They come from the occupied areas in the south to sell their jewellery.

They are not veiled. They have fearless children and fearless eyes. One of them is called Fatima. She has flames painted in henna on her heels, licking her foot from below.

Calmly she spreads a blue cotton cloth out on the ground. Then she starts removing objects from a little chest.

I remember Agadir's shops and their over-decorated leather goods, their rattling metal tray-tables, their thick loose mats in clashing colours – the way smoking-room orientalism has characterized the image of Morocco, perhaps the whole of North Africa.

Fatima's jewellery belongs to another, Saharan, tradition. Eagerly, I ask how much they are. She does not answer.

'This isn't the bazaar,' she admonishes me in Spanish.

I have to wait calmly as the ritual continues. Ornament after ornament is brought out and explained. 'The three tents on the lid of the box are the three tribes in Sahel.' 'This bracelet shows drought and the rains.'

Not until she has finished does she ask which objects I am interested in. She puts those into a dark wooden bowl and packs the others away in the chest.

Then she tells me which families the objects in the wooden

bowl belong to. She is selling them on their behalf. With a gentle naturalness, she gives me the prices in wheat flour.

I had imagined everything beforehand – the sandy mist in the air, the pinch of sunglasses behind my ears, the buzz of flies around military outposts, the perspiration tickling its way from armpit to waistband, everything.

But I had not imagined that only a few hours south of Agadir I would be buying Saharan ornaments for half a ton of wheat flour.

And for whom?

6

The desert road continues south along a green-floored valley.

The water supporting the greenery is nowhere to be seen but is there, beneath the ground. That is how to survive in the desert. Plants exposing themselves to evaporation have failed. The same applies to watercourses. Only those that have made their way below the surface have been able to endure.

Beside the road I see a plant with yellow flowers that leaps forward in a zigzag, covering the ground with squares like wire netting.

I see small, pale pink bell-like flowers on grey bushes and a stonecrop plant with blue star-shaped flowers and long funnels for stems.

Small cacti grow on top of one another in clumps, like coral, and protect themselves not only with spines but also with sharp milk-white juice which spurts out in all directions at the slightest touch.

For an endless half-hour I drive through a cloud of grasshoppers. They are innumerable, as large as small birds, with buzzing, transparent wings. They glisten with moisture, pink as prawns, and with the same crunching sound as when you bite into a prawn's head, they smash against the windscreen.

Something yellow and sticky is left behind and soon obscures my entire field of vision – I have to drive very slowly, until the cloud passes just as suddenly as it came.

7

Tan-Tan is a yellow town with pale blue gates. A garrison town, like Boden in the far, far north of Sweden, a disaster of a posting and where you are afflicted with their equivalent of 'Lapp sickness', *le cafard*.

The town lives off the desert war in the south. This is where the soldiers come on leave. All the small hotels are full of their families who have come to visit.

The Hotel Dakar is by the bus station. Halls and stairways are tiled, which gives an impression of cleanliness and cool. But the bathroom acoustics multiply every sound. The rooms are small and high-ceilinged. Through the closed shutters, my green room is filled with a dim aquarium light.

The sun sets at six. I sit in the twilight outside the hotel listening to the pentatonic music. The Atlantic wind is cool, almost chilly. There is no beer. The tap-water is too salty to drink. Drinking-water comes in tanker carts drawn by small tractors. I no longer long to *need* Oulmez but to drink some.

Inside the café the television blares. The video shop rents out videos. *The Terminator* is on at the cinema. Photocopiers make photocopies. The street lights come on automatically. But the waiter who had said that they have all kinds of vegetables comes back to tell me they have no cauliflower. A moment later he tells me that they have no carrots. When asked what they do have, he suggests tomatoes.

Cats roam hungrily around the table. Everyone shouts for Hasan, apparently because everyone not called Mohammed is called Hasan. When the food comes, the tomatoes, representing 'all kinds of vegetables', turn out to be purée, squeezed out of a tube over the rice.

Before I fall asleep, I see the basket of bloodstained goat hooves, which were for sale in the market. What can they be used for? Maybe to boil down for glue?

In the borderland of sleep, I smell the glue pot from the woodwork room where my father taught, the copper pot with thick layers of congealed glue stuck to its sides . . .

And the workbench from below! I am sitting down there among the sweet-smelling shavings, listening to the tearing sound of the plane, and the shavings come flying down to me, curly, rolled up – the thin fragrant skin of wood . . .

I lie curled up beneath a thick desert blanket of greasy wool. Dogs howl in the night. Perhaps my childhood has not vanished after all. It is true I have virtually not a single memory from that time, but perhaps my memory is only out of sight, like the watercourses in the desert. It has survived by disappearing from the surface and still runs in the depths, where I am heading.

I am buried. But I am far from helpless. Like the pea under the princess's mattresses, I lie under layers of sediment, beneath continents and continental plates. They are forced to shift. My irritating presence is interrupting geological eras and making the continents change direction.

When I get back home, I go and mangle sheets. The old-fashioned hand-driven mangle rolls the washing between polished marble blocks. The upper roller turns out to be the bottom of the Atlantic on its way west to be devoured by the mantle. Suddenly it turns right round so that Boston returns to Casablanca and Rio to the mouth of the Congo.

I persuade myself I am still in control. But soon the movements of the continents become more and more unpredictable. They are dancing to a music I cannot hear. Finally I am leaping in despair between them, as if between ice floes, for a few million years without being able to reach land.

When I have almost got used to living in geological time, short time comes back again, suddenly, like the handle when you step on a rake.

9

Morning urine is thick and sluggish, highly concentrated; dark. Faeces consist of small hard kernels like sheep droppings. I drive out of Tan-Tan between drifts of sand like the heaps of snow in Stockholm at winter and think: sand never melts.

I find it difficult to shake off the geological perspective of my dream. The landscape of the desert has no protective covering – the desert is geology exposed.

One of the few books Darwin had with him on his voyage on the *Beagle* was Charles Lyell's *Principles of Geology*. As he read it, he slowly realized that the earth was much older than he had thought. Not four thousand years but perhaps four thousand *million* years.

Time was given a depth it had never had before. What did Lyell feel, what did Darwin feel, looking down into those depths?

10

The first forty-one hundred million years of the history of the Sahara are still practically unknown today. All we know is that Africa then, as now, was a primaeval mountain plateau of granite.

Our earliest knowledge of the Sahara comes from a period when sedimentary types of rock had just begun to form layers on top of the primary rock. Africa then stood on its head roughly where the Antarctic now lies and the Sahara was covered with kilometre-thick inland ice. The ice left scrape-marks behind in Ordovician sandstone, marks found and interpreted five hundred million years later, in the 1970s.

The continent turned over as it slowly wandered northwards and for a while North Africa bordered on North America. Had the weather been more suitable, it would have been possible to walk dry-shod from Boston to Casablanca.

When the continents were wrenched free of each other, bits of Africa went with America and became eastern Massachusetts and one bit of Pennsylvania stayed behind in the western Sahara.

Four hundred million years ago, the Sahara was under water. Large parts of the oil deposits were formed in the sediment from that period. Three hundred and fifty million years ago, the climate turned warmer and the sea water retreated. Over two hundred million years, the Sahara was alternately land and sea. The last Saharan sea disappeared ten million years ago.

Eight million years ago, the Sahara was an even bigger desert than it is today. The Mediterranean was closed off from its connection with the Atlantic and after a thousand years it had dried out into a desert which lasted for several million years. Salt deposits from the evaporated water still lie on the seabed, found in 1960 and investigated by deep drilling in 1970.

Seventy thousand years ago, the Sahara began to turn green again, with trees and grass. But the same cold snap that made the temperature mild and pleasant in the Sahara turned Central Europe into a treeless tundra and covered North Europe with inland ice for over fifty thousand years.

Twelve thousand years ago, when the inland ice had retreated from Sweden, the Sahara was still green. But about six thousand years BC, a dry spell began and lasted for fifteen hundred years. Then the rains came back for a thousand years. A new dry period occurred between 3300 and 2500 BC. The next rainy period was short – only five hundred years. The present dry period began in about 2000 BC, so has lasted for four thousand years.

Very small changes in the world's average temperature –

only a degree or two – create an ice age in North America or a desert in the Sahara. At this moment, as I arrive, it is one of the hottest periods over the last million years. From a geological point of view, the apparent eternity of the Saharan desert is merely an episode between two European ice ages.

Where the road comes down to the sea there is a small fishing harbour, with screaming gulls swarming around it. The white foaming breakers roll in against sedimentary rock resembling clumps of plasticine. Along the edge of the plateau, often ten or so metres above the surface of the sea, lone fishermen walk with their long fishing rods. Poverty-stricken gatherers of brushwood and roots search for fuel for the night's fire.

People on this coast made their first contact with Europe when the Portuguese Henrique el Navegador sailed past in 1441. His men went ashore and captured twelve nomads to take with them.

Thus the manhunt began. The small fishing villages along the coast had nothing but stones and spears with which to defend themselves. In 1443, Eannes de Azurara relates:

Some were drowned in the sea, others hid in their cabins, yet others tried to bury their children in the sand in order to return later to fetch them. But Our Lord God, who rewards everything well done, decided as compensation for the hard work our men had done in His service that day to allow them to conquer their enemies and take 165 prisoners, men, women and children, not counting those killed or who killed themselves.

At the end of the 1400s, when Portugal and Spain divided up the world between them, the Spaniards were given the Saharan coast, as it lay close to the Spanish Canary Isles. But by the time four hundred Spaniards stepped ashore to take possession of the area, the Saharans had had time to organize resistance. Only a hundred Spaniards escaped with their lives. The hunt for slaves continued all through the 1500s, but for almost four hundred years the Saharans managed to prevent Europeans from gaining a foothold on the coast.

12

At the tip of the Cap Juby headland there is no archipelago, only one small island.

A Scot called Donald MacKenzie opened a store there in 1875. He called it the North West Africa Company and successfully traded cloth, tea and sugar for wool, leather and ostrich feathers.

The Sultan of Morocco disliked the competition. In 1895, he bought the store for £50,000 and closed it.

MacKenzie was also a thorn in the flesh of the Spanish traders on the Canary Isles, where he had a base. They wanted to take over his profitable caravan trade and exploit the rich coastal fishing grounds. In 1884, they sent men to the Sahara

Cap Juby from the air. (*Musée d'Air France*)

and built a fort on the next headland, the Dakla Peninsula, and called it Villa Cisneros.

The Saharans attacked the fort constantly, the caravans never turned up, profits were non-existent and the Spanish state had to take over.

By 1914, the French had subjugated the interior of the Sahara. In the north, they had occupied Morocco. In Europe, the First World War was being fought. Only in the Spanish Sahara was nothing happening. The commanding officer in Villa Cisneros, Fransisco Bens, had been rotting away there for ten years. Now he put his soldiers onto a ship and sailed north to capture Cap Juby.

The Admiralty found out and ordered the ship to return to Villa Cisneros immediately.

But Bens didn't give up. On foot, he marched his men north along the coast.

As they approached Cap Juby, they were overtaken by a Spanish cruiser, ordered to board and were once again conveyed ignominiously back to Villa Cisneros.

Not until 1916 was Bens finally able to occupy Cap Juby, this time at the request of the Saharans, who preferred Bens to the aggressive French, and also of the French, who preferred Bens to the aggressive Saharans.

Of course, by then trade had long gone elsewhere and MacKenzie's island became the Spanish equivalent of Devil's Island, a prison as loathed by the gaolers as it was feared by the prisoners.

Its little fort was surrounded by two kilometres of barbed wire, says Joseph Ressel, the French writer, there on a visit. At night, nowhere was safe outside the walls. It was difficult to tell the difference between soldiers and convicts: all were unshaven, unwashed and in the same ragged uniforms. The officers sat silently in the mess, playing dice, their faces expressionless.

But in the early 1920s, this godforsaken place gained a sudden importance when the French airline Compagnie Latécoère needed it as a stopover on the first Toulouse-Dakar air route.

And in the mid-1920s, when the Germans and the French were competing for the air routes to South America and German agents supplied the Saharans with arms and ammunition to shoot down French planes – then Cap Juby became a focal point.

In the spring of 1927, a new airport chief was appointed to Cap Juby with the task of rescuing shot-down French pilots and creating better relations with the Saharans. His name was Antoine de Saint-Exupéry.

I loved the airmen in Saint-Exupéry's books. The pilots of those days were kind of canoeists of the air, with no more than their lower bodies inside the 'flying machine', as it was called. Flying was shooting the rapids with the propellor as a paddle.

The primitive, single-engined machines flew below the clouds to see their way. In fog or a sandstorm, they were lost. One in six flights between Cap Juby and Dakar ended in a crash or emergency landing in the desert.

And when the pilot in his thick leather overalls, 'heavy and cumbersome as a diver', clambered out of his cockpit – then, if the rescuers did not get to him in time, what awaited him was captivity or death at the hands of hostile nomads. Altogether, 121 pilots were lost.

There was no shortage of exciting adventures in the boys' books of my childhood. But they had one failing – they had no idea what they were talking about.

If you asked Edward S. Ellis how Deerfoot behaved when he 'crept invisibly through the thicket', there would have been a silence. Ellis was not an Indian. He had no idea how it happened. I could see that already from the way he wrote.

Saint-Ex, on the other hand, was a real airman. He knew that the pilot can feel from the vibrations in his own body when fifteen tons of matter has achieved the 'maturity' required to take off. He knew what it felt like to separate the plane from the ground – 'with a movement like picking a flower' – and let it be borne by the air.

His knowledge was no thin veneer concealing massive

ignorance. He was authentic. When he called the desert sun 'a pale soap bubble in the mist', I knew he had seen it. He had been there. It was in his language.

Saint-Ex was the first writer who gave me some sense of what 'style' is.

14

Today, Cap Juby is called Tarfaya. I book in at the Green March hotel. There is no other.

The town is white with blue front doors and flat roofs, a forest of reinforcement rods protruding from the walls – the houses are all prepared for a second floor which has not yet arrived.

The small shops are just holes in the walls, all with an identical assortment of candies, cigarettes, batteries, sewing thread and soft drinks.

I start asking after old people who might have memories of the 1920s. Yes, there should be a few. But while I am waiting for them, a courteous Moroccan policeman comes and asks me to accompany him to the police station.

They already know everything there. The squealing radio with its crackling voices has told them where I have come from, where I have spent the night, which police posts I have passed, all my father's first names, all my mother's first names and her maiden name, and also that claim not to know the names of my father's father or my maternal grandmother.

So I want to talk to old Saharans in Tarfaya, do I? The

chief gendarme is full of goodwill. Tomorrow I am to meet the mayor. He will help me.

I am allowed to see the charming and obliging side of the system of control. Other people get the disappearances and the torture.

15

The front door of the Green March hotel is kept shut with a thick piece of paper folded twice and jammed in between the door and the doorpost. Whenever anyone fails to do this, the door swings open and slams violently in the wind.

There is a café on the ground floor. For dinner, I am served two eggs apparently fried in waste engine oil. I eat the bread with gratitude.

The café has the town's only television set. The news begins with the usual good wishes and other courtesies which Hassan, the King, has exchanged with other heads of state. Then comes what Hassan has done during the day, often with flashbacks to what Hassan had done previously on the same day or in the same genre. It ends with a prediction of what Hassan will do tomorrow, illustrated with film of what it looked like when Hassan last did the same thing.

The few seconds left at the end are devoted to other world news.

Then the screen goes blank. Everyone waits patiently. The landlord gets up, climbs onto a chair and puts in a video.

After ten minutes, the tape breaks. Everyone goes on calmly watching. The landlord runs the tape back and starts it again, the volume higher this time – rather like trying to get through a sandy stretch of road by backing the car, revving the engine and trying it faster.

But it's no use. The tape gives up at exactly the same place in the action.

No one moves a muscle. Everyone stays seated, full of confidence. The landlord goes to fetch another video. This time we go straight into the middle of a quite different story, the beginning missing. No one reacts. Everyone gratefully goes on watching.

All night the door slams violently in the wind blowing off the sea.

16

A man has gasped all his life, then draws his first really deep breath. After 'a life of gasping', as he calls it, he at last, slowly, with great enjoyment, drinks a large glass of cold air.

17

A tall yellow building behind the main street dominates the town. The walls are crowned with watchtowers, with open fields of fire in all directions. This is where Colonel Bens resided in 1925. Now it is the Moroccan mayor's office.

The mayor sits below a preternaturally large photograph of

Hassan and wears an Italian 'camel-hair ulster' made of nylon. With him are some old people in real, smelly camel-hair clothes, among them the son of the interpreter who accompanied Saint-Ex on his flights.

He tells me about an emergency landing in the desert. His father kept the 'bandits' at a distance with his rifle while Saint-Ex repaired the engine. They took off at dusk with bullets whistling round their ears.

'That man saved my life,' said Saint-Ex. Afterwards it was all made into a film so that the whole world could see it.

'Were you there yourself?'

'Not me. But Ahmed was.'

The mayor promises to summon Ahmed the next day.

18

I know which tiles are loose on the steep hotel stairs. Even in the darkness, I can find the footrest of the squatting-toilet. Life in Tarfaya is becoming familiar.

In the mornings, I breakfast on bread and water. Decades old, the bed I am sitting on still has the plastic covering it had been transported in. That probably increases its second-hand value. The bottom sheet is the kind that only goes as far as your knees. There is no top sheet.

Through the little window I can see across the constantly windswept headland to the island with its dark, abandoned prison. Some boys are playing football on the shore, in the wind coming off the sea.

The mayor's office opens at eight-thirty, but there is no

point going there until half-past ten. I sit in the sun outside the hotel and warm up as I wait. The greengrocer puts his wooden boxes out on the pavement. You buy bread from a blue hatch. A Saharan in a white jibba walks past. They are a rare sight here. Uniformed Moroccans are in the majority.

A small girl with a school bag buys some carrots. A man walks past with a large bunch of fragrant mint. His feet are cracked. Fish are being weighed on the corner – some a type of perch, vertically striped or long and silvery with horizontal stripes, glittering in the morning light.

At about half-past ten, I meet Ahmed, aged eighty-five.

'Saint-Ex was different. He tried to learn our language. None of the Spaniards did that. He studied with a teacher of the Koran called Sidi l'Hussein Oueld n'Ouesa. The Spaniards just sat in their fort. They didn't fly. But Saint-Ex was a travelling man, so he had to be able to speak languages. He was a man who knew how to negotiate and often did so over men held for ransom.'

'Is it true that the tribes shot at the French planes?'

'Of course.' He smiles inwardly as though lost in happy memories.

'Why?'

This causes a certain confusion. Naturally they shot, but why?

Gradually the intellectual explanation appears: we were defending ourselves against colonialism. Then comes the current opportune explanation: we were acting on the orders of the Sultan of Morocco. Anyhow, they lived off taking prisoners and demanding ransoms. Why then shouldn't they shoot?

The Moor doesn't defend his freedom, for in the desert
you are always free. No visible treasures, for the desert is
bare. No, the Moor defends a secret realm and that's
why I admire him.

The aristocrat Saint-Ex has a tendency to ennoble everything
that arouses his admiration.

He ennobles the airline pilots as a new aristocracy of the air.
He ennobles their opponents, 'the Moor', as knights of an
exotic realm of pride.

He romanticizes the bearers of a new and unknown technology and a distant unknown people – and so defends old
familiar feudal values, rejected by capitalist Europe.

Saint-Ex could not have known about the invisible treasures
the desert does in fact contain, for phosphates, iron ore and oil
had still not been found in the Sahara. But that it was their
freedom the Saharans were defending – he ought to have
known that.

He had done his military service in conquered Morocco. He
had travelled in conquered Algeria. He knew that freedom is not
something the desert automatically provides. 'The Moors' on the
African Atlantic coast in 1927 were in fact the last unsubjugated
Saharans – a result of the outstanding weakness of the Spanish
colonial powers and the Moors' own bitter resistance.

Perhaps it was natural that Saint-Ex could not support this
struggle for freedom, as it was at him and his friends the
Saharans were shooting with their German Mauser rifles.

But he never even realized what the struggle was about. It
all became romanticism.

White garden furniture dazzles my eyes. I recognize it from previous dreams. Why does it keep coming back? The table and chairs are not spray-lacquered, but their wide boards are painted with layer after layer of thick oil paint. They are not 'creamy white', for there is no tinge of yellow, but the colour has the fat puffiness of whipped cream. The light is reflected from the gleaming white surfaces with a force that makes my eyes smart and everyone squint. Which everyone? Don't know. Their faces are empty, obliterated, wiped out like my whole childhood.

There is no one to ask. They are all dead. But from the depths of the past, this table throws out a sunspot strong enough to wake me up.

The next morning while I sit warming up outside the hotel, the garbage cart comes past, drawn by a mule. The garbage pails are emptied into the open cart, just as used to happen in Älvsjö when I was a child. On the corner they are selling yellow dates on stems, gathered in bunches like the birch sprigs and coloured feathers of Lent at home.

Today's old man points out the exact place where the Frenchman's house stood: right next to the fortress wall on the side facing the airfield. They used to hear music from there at night, notes from an old gramophone he wound up by hand.

For company he had four animals: cat, dog, a chimpanzee and a hyena.

In the evenings I carefully transfer this information from my tape recorder into my notebook. I think I can at last see Saint-Ex fairly clearly in front of me as he sits at his desk, surrounded by his animals.

The light flows from the lamp like oil. I see him dipping his pen into the inkwell, which I used to do when I was learning to write. The sea roars out there in the darkness, the cries of the guards on duty echoing between the walls. A light rain appears to be falling – the sound of the moist night air condensing on the metal roof. Sand crunches between the papers on the desk. Saint-Ex is writing.

When he leaves Cap Juby eighteen months later, he has with him the manuscript of his first novel, *Southern Mail*. And within him he is carrying what are the as-yet-unwritten desert stories in *The Little Prince* and *Wind, Sand and Stars*.

22

What fascinated me as a boy when I read those books was their belief that the airman was a new kind of man.

A person taking off from the ground also elevated himself above the trivialities of life into a new understanding, created by the particular experiences modern technology made possible.

The airman was not yet a captain in the routine trade between tax-free shops of the world's cities. Like the astronaut now, the airman was the most modern man of his day, a

Saint-Exupéry and his best friend, Henri Guillaumet, standing in front of their plane. (*Musée d'Air France*)

representative of the future on a temporary stopover in what was soon to be the past.

That gave him tremendous authority, which Saint-Ex used to ask yet again the great questions.

What is man? What are we for?

Man makes himself, he said.

We aren't born man, we become that.

We become that through solidarity with each other.

We become that by taking responsibility.

I loved his gravity when he said such things, quite shame-lessly, with the same endless trust in his reader as the airman had in the empty air. In that solemnity, he was so close to me, I could lean forward and touch him.

He taught me to demand of a writer not just excitement and adventure, but also knowledge, seriousness and presence. Presence most of all.

If the writer is not there himself in his writing, how can he demand that you should be?

To Smara

23

'Like a pearl-diver, I must immediately return,' wrote Michel Vieuchange in his diary.

Michel read *Southern Mail* when it was published in 1928. He was four years younger than Saint-Ex. He had also read Nietzsche and Rimbaud, and had done his military service in Morocco, and he, too, had dreams of the desert. One September day in 1930, disguised as a woman, he disappeared into the unsubjugated tribal area some miles north of Tiznit. He was on his way to Smara.

Saint-Ex never got that far.

But every morning he did fly one of the off-duty Cap Juby planes to drive the condensation out of the cylinders – planes at that time had to be rested like horses – and sometimes he diverged from the flight path along the coast. Once he flew right into 'the mysterious Smara with its virginal ruins, as forbidden to the white man as Timbuctoo'.

In actual fact, Timbuctoo had been occupied by the French in 1893, and Smara was no more forbidden than that. It was destroyed by French troops in 1913. But the ruins were still defended by the Saharan tribes. Just flying over Smara was a bold, almost foolish act.

Vieuchange was now heading that way. On foot.

24

I go by car.

It is a peculiar day. All week the wind has blown in off the sea but now it is coming from the desert, hot as a hairdryer. The runway in Tarfaya has been shrouded in wet sea mist; today it is shrouded in the hot dry haze of pure dust.

I scrape the sand off the car just as one scrapes snow off a car in a Swedish winter, and as I drive into the white haze it is like driving into a snowstorm. Only slowly does it occur to me that because I am in the desert, this must be a sandstorm.

Twilight descends in the early morning and my field of vision shrinks so that I can see only a few metres ahead. When I stop and get out of the car, I find it difficult to keep my balance. The sand stabs like icy pins at my unprotected face. It is impossible to breathe into the wind. I hurry back into the car and drive on as fast as I dare through the mounting drifts.

The sand is not slippery, but occasionally it is treacherously loose, and sometimes as hard-packed as stone. The dust is finer than snow and penetrates the car so that the air is thick to breathe. The smell is sharply mineral, quite unlike the euphoric fragrance of snow.

Most of all, the physical feeling is different. The body suffocates when it sweats without sweat. Moisture vanishes immediately off the skin, leaving a crackled layer of salt which encloses the body as if in a mould.

When I was small, I often fantasized about sandstorms. Before falling asleep, I surrounded myself with the whistling, biting haze. To be able to breathe, I walked backwards, into the wind. My watch filled with sand and stopped. I drank the last drops from my crumpled water-holder and knew I had to die.

In these sandstorm dreams, there was always a mirror-like lake of clear fresh water which saved my life just before I slipped into sleep.

To believe in water in the desert is not as crazy as it seems. Sometimes it actually rains. At this moment my childish dreams come true, the dreams of desert pools glimmering in hollows and a green veil thrown over the sand. I drive through a green desert gleaming with moisture – although the whole of the Sahara is heading towards me and I am almost suffocated.

No traffic comes towards me. At a turn-off to Boucraa, I am stopped by a military column: open vehicles, dark snow-goggles, on full alert. The Polisario, the Saharan liberation movement, usually strike in the shelter of a sandstorm.

I turn back and spend the night in El Aaiun. Two tank battles are fought that night, one near Boucraa, between Moroccan troops and the still-unconquered Saharans.

25

Vieuchange tried to get to Smara disguised as a woman. His posthumous journal shows him preoccupied with the actual disguise and the conditions his female rôle forces him into.

He shaves his legs. He learns not to show his hands. He always lies curled up like a dog, never on his back – only a Jewess lies on her back. He sits with his knees wide apart, never close together. When he rides, he keeps his heels lower than his toes.

In daytime, he is bathed in sweat inside the blue garment which envelops him like a tent. He longs in vain to feel the wind

Michel Vieuchange, dressed as a Berber woman.

30

on his face, to be able to move freely. He wants to know where he is. He wants to see the great expanses of desert. He wants to see the men coming and going. But all he sees is the ground.

Few accounts of the Sahara deal so much with the actual ground in the desert, the small broken stones, the gravel, the stony riverbeds, the dark tormented soil. That is all he sees.

He doesn't see the sunrise, only a golden wave of light sweeping over the ground, leaving behind it small lakes of night in the hollows.

In the towns, he sees nothing but the room in which he is imprisoned like a criminal: the rough walls that crumble at his touch, the low sooty ceiling and the light let in by deep holes so narrow he can't see out.

In the heat, he pours water over his veiled head so the evaporation will provide him with a little cool. The meat hanging from the ceiling is invisible beneath its carpet of flies. He doesn't eat any of it. He hardly eats anything at all, but lives off sweet mint tea.

On cold damp nights, the women press their bodies against his to seek warmth – or perhaps with other intentions which simply fill him with distaste. Frozen and soaked through, he waits for the golden wave of sunrise finally to sweep over the ground, this ground which is all he sees.

26

I am living in a stable together with a naked gnarled old woman with long breasts hanging down below her waist. She is kind to me. It's only her horse that's pigheaded.

31

She has the horse up in a hayloft with the railing missing. Nothing but its own instinct for self-preservation keeps the horse from falling down.

When I come up to the hayloft, the horse eagerly starts nuzzling my hand and pockets for the sugar it is used to being given. I try to get down again, but the horse bars my way as it nuzzles through my clothes and my body more and more intimately and insistently. Not until the woman comes up and gives the horse some lumps of sugar can I leave.

It strikes me when I see her breasts that perhaps she is my mother and that it is my own greed, greater than the horse's, that has made them so long.

27

The sky is clear again the next morning. The sand-sweeper is already busy sweeping away the drifts. Every tuft has a small train of sand pointing away from the wind.

A few miles outside El Aaiun, a gang of Saudi falconers have their caravan camp. They hunt for partridges over great distances with the aid of sophisticated radar equipment, pursuing them in four-wheel-drive vehicles, then, taking the hood off the specially trained falcons, for a few exhilarating moments experience their own power as the falcon cruises above its prey, strikes, kills and brings back the meat.

'The price per kilo will have been considerable,' say my Saharan hitchhikers dryly.

They are elegant young men with knife-edge creases in their trousers and smart briefcases. At their destination some miles further on, I go with them to two tents by the roadside. The tents smell of milk. Some women live an outfield life there with their goats.

They splash us with lavender water from a litre bottle and call out to the retired soldier in the tent next to them. My hitchhikers and the old man begin the usual ping-pong game of courtesies and mutual exchanges of information. The smart town lads are transformed into scions of herdsmen, and with surprising expertise they carry out the traditional tea ceremony.

'If you were staying any longer, I would have slit the throat of a goat for you,' says the old man.

He is lying on a plaited mat, kneading a large cushion on his stomach. The air is fresh and pleasant under the sky-blue tent, the roof shutting off the sun but giving free rein to the wind. The charcoal glowing in the chafing dish ticks metallically and there is a strong smell of mint and goat's milk.

After the obligatory three cups, I drive on towards Smara through vast flat countryside, punctuated by odd tussocks and groups of heroic tamarisks.

Right out in the dryness, I again meet a large cloud of grasshoppers coming from the south-east, not so much flying as being blown my way by the desert wind, bowling along the ground like a gigantic wavering wheel of insects, some young and pink-winged, but most mature, well-filled, golden-winged creatures which strike the car with a crashing sound and are crushed.

The Hotel Goldsand, the best in Smara, has been requisitioned by the governor. At the Hotel Erraha across the street, I am given the only room with a window. Two beds, and a hook in the wall. A handbasin outside the privy at the end of the corridor. A pound a night.

I go to bathe after the dusty journey. On my way I see a notice: *Club Saquia el Hamra Musculation*. Bodybuilding in the Sahara! Suddenly I feel my muscles aching with a longing for exertion.

The premises have just opened for the day and are still empty. I hang my clothes on the wall and start warming up.

As I lie in the leg-press, an intellectual Moroccan wearing glasses comes and shows me how I can get greater play by pulling out a peg. He is a bookkeeper in the civilian administration and has been here for three years, his family in Casa, as they call Casablanca. Goes home to see them every third month.

We train together and alternate three times fifteen with light weights. There is – he says, in the winter as well, but most of all in the summer when Smara is turned into a reeking hell – there is a yawning chasm between official rhetoric and the reality of war-weariness and longing for home. The Sahara has been designated 'their' country, but it certainly is not their climate or their landscape when they come from northern Morocco . . .

After the long gap in my training, it is wonderful to feel my muscles working again, at first reluctantly, then more and more delighted at being needed. The ego-experience climbs down from my head and out into my limbs. Bit by bit my body comes back and becomes my own again.

After training, we go on to the bath-house. In the innermost of the steaming rooms, we mix hot water from one tap with cold water from another into our black rubber buckets and spend the rest of the afternoon scooping, soaping and scrubbing our newly found bodies while listening to the splash of water against tiles and the murmur of voices under the vaulted ceiling.

There is no wind in there. The light doesn't hurt your eyes. Your nails don't split. You don't get sand in your mouth. The air is not prickly dry in your nose. On the contrary, it is thick with steaming moisture and feels soft and smooth in the hollows of your body. Good water flows. In the desert, that is paradise.

29

The human body has six hundred muscles. You use most of them automatically without experiencing them. The best part of training is finding new muscles which have never been conscious before.

How many muscles has a human life? You're sure to use most of them automatically, without experiencing them. Particularly in long-term relationships, developing a routine is labour saving, and thus enervating. The best part of suddenly encountering solitude is that it provides training: you discover your life when you have to start using its long-since forgotten and atrophied muscles.

I am living on a hillside, the road meandering past. I wake early and go out for a newspaper.

The news on the front page is criss-crossed with thick black lines which make them invalid and partly illegible. There is only one legible and valid item of news. That is printed in microscopic typescript and says that the country has been invaded by a foreign power. The foreign troops can be expected at any moment to pass along this particular road.

Then I suddenly remember that I had a goat as well as a dog when I left. But the dog is too faithful and the goat too rebellious and unmanageable. So I have tied them up in the forest. I was thinking of fetching them later, but forgot them. Are they still alive? Has anyone found them? Have they died of starvation? I must find out before the foreigners get here. But how shall I get there? My wife is already messing about in the garden. The children will soon wake up. So far, I am the only one who knows about the invasion, about the goat, about the dog – and what shall I do?

I go and ask my father. He has put a piece of white paper in front of him on his desk. He takes out his pocket-knife with its mother-of-pearl inlays, slots a nail into the groove and opens the knife. It is the small sharp blade he opens out. Without a word he starts slowly and carefully cutting away the white on his nails.

He isn't cutting his nails. He is trimming them. He prunes them, just as you prune a tree or a bush in the garden. He cuts off just that part of the nail which helped him open the knife.

I say nothing. Father is also silent. With a scraping sound, the slice of nail falls onto the white paper.

The first inhabitants of Smara were black and came from the south. Their rock engravings show a Saharan savanna where elephants and giraffes grazed.

In the millennium before our era, they were driven back south by the drought. Those who stayed behind were subjugated by Berber peoples from the north, who rode horses and had weapons made of iron.

The desert deepened all around them. The horse was followed by the camel, which arrived from the east around the year 100 and made possible the regular caravan trade across the desert.

In the year 1000, there was a gang of Saharans who called themselves the 'Almoravids'. They took over the caravan trade, penetrated northwards and conquered Morocco and Spain. There we got to know them by the name of *Moors*.

In the thirteenth century, all the Saharans who stayed behind in the desert were conquered by a Bedouin tribe, Beni Hassan, emigrating from Yemen. Hassanic Arabic pushed out the Berber language, Znaga. The ruling Arabs accepted tributes from their Znaga vassals who in turn ruled over the black indigenous population: slaves and freed slaves. A council, *djema*, drew up laws and chose a chieftain.

The most famous of these chieftains was Ma Ainin, 'The Water of the Eyes'. He founded Smara in 1895 as the centre for the Saharan tribes and his headquarters in the struggle against the Europeans.

The main enemy was the French, pressing from the south through Mauritania, from the east through Algeria and soon enough from the north through Morocco. That was why

Vieuchange had to travel in disguise. He belonged to the enemy.

Smara was not colonized until 1934 when the Spaniards, with the help of the French, occupied the town.

Decolonization also came late. The Spaniards were not prepared to hand over power to the Polisario until the mid-1970s.

But the King of Morocco had territorial ambitions. He dreamt of a Greater Morocco that would include parts of Algeria, Mali and Mauritania, and on down to the Senegal river. He maintained that Spanish West Sahara belonged to him for historic reasons.

The matter was referred to the international court at the Hague, which replied that there were indeed legal ties between Morocco and West Sahara, but that these ties did not entail territorial supremacy. The principle of the right to self-determination through the free declaration of the will of the people should, the court decided, be applied without restriction.

32

What happened next was extremely peculiar. Only in Smara has anything like it ever happened to me.

One evening, I am sitting in the corridor of the Hotel Erraha, talking to a Moroccan greengrocer. He is from Rabat and has been tempted to Smara with subsidies from the government. Here he has a cheap house, earns good money and likes it. And as evidence that there are no problems in the town, he alleges there are no soldiers there.

'No soldiers, no problems.'

He says this in the Hotel Erraha, which is full of soldiers on leave.

They are sleeping in heaps on the floor of the corridor in front of us.

They have come directly from the fighting at the Wall erected as a defence against the Polisario, sand running off their uniforms, wild-eyed, heads wrapped in cloths and rags. With its music, its lights and occasional women, Smara to them is a paradise compared with the dry dust, the eternal wind and the shadeless heat out there.

Maybe they have no other problems, but they are undeniably soldiers.

Through the hotel window, the greengrocer and I look out over the town. It consists mainly of military installations resembling cartons of eggs with their rows of yellowish-white cupolas. Behind the hotel, army vehicles are lined up in a gigantic military parking lot. In the street below we can see military police walking around in pairs, checking Saharan identity cards. Moroccan conscripts roam in groups along the street, hanging onto each other like teenage girls. A column of army trucks – with their engines running – is ready to depart to the front. The trucks are full of soldiers with closed, sullen, bitter faces.

But the greengrocer maintains they don't exist.

'But hang on a minute,' I say, in appeal. 'You can't even go and have a pee without falling over sleeping soldiers. It's seething with them down there on the street . . .'

I point out through the window. But that makes no impression on the greengrocer.

'Further away maybe,' he says. 'But here in Smara there are no soldiers, no problems.'

Is he saying what the police have told him to say without bothering to make it plausible? Does he wish, while protecting himself, to tell me the exact opposite: 'Many soldiers, many problems'?

I don't know. All I know is that our conversation ceased once it lost touch with reality.

33

On October 16, 1975, when the international court decision was delivered, the Moroccan invasion of West Sahara was already planned in detail. Hassan II was unable to back down. He did the same thing as the greengrocer.

He made a great speech in Rabat, explaining that the international court had upheld Morocco's demands.

To objections that it had done no such thing, he simply declined to answer. Instead he announced a 'peace march' to 'liberate' West Sahara.

At this threat, the Spaniards suddenly broke off all contact with the Saharans. A curfew was proclaimed. The Spanish Foreign Legion erected barbed wire all around Saharan neighbourhoods. Saharan soldiers were dismissed from the army. Petrol stations stopped selling petrol to Saharans. In a week, twelve thousand Spanish civilians were flown out of the country. Even corpses were evacuated. A thousand dead were dug up out of the local cemeteries and flown to the Canary Isles. The animals in the zoo went with them.

The Spaniards persistently denied 'rumours' that they were going to hand over power to the King of Morocco. But in secret they had already done so.

By the time Moroccan troops marched in, the majority of

Smara's Saharan population had fled across the border into Algeria, 150 miles east. Smara, the main centre of the Saharan liberation movement, became the main base for King Hassan's war of conquest in the Sahara.

34

'Problems? In that case, it's the goats,' says the governor.

We are invited to dinner at the governor's palace. A roast sheep with its ribs exposed like a shipwreck is carried in as we sit there on the sofa, all men, all Moroccans, except me and a Saharan poet. Chicken with orange peel and olives comes next, then sweet rice with almonds, raisins and cinnamon completing the meal.

'The nomads make their way from the drought in to the water and electricity of the towns,' says the governor. 'They settle, motorized herdsmen tending their herds from Landrovers and keeping their families wherever there is a school for their children and healthcare for their old.

'It is worst for the women. They know nothing except about goats. The woman belongs with goats. Goats are closer to her than her husband, yes, even closer than her children. Her way of bringing up children is out of date, her cooking primitive, and only goats give her a *raison d'être*. So she can't live without goats. She takes them with her into town. The whole town is full of goats and that creates hygiene problems. It's simply impossible in modern apartments. I have no hesitation in saying that goats are the greatest social problem we have to contend with at the moment.'

'And the solution?'

'I have issued a goat order and appointed one person responsible for goats in each neighbourhood. He sees to it that the neighbourhood is kept free of goats. Each neighbourhood has also been allocated an area outside town, where the goats are allowed. It keeps the women busy – it's a long walk there to do the milking.'

35

The Saharan poet Yara Mahjoub is a handsome man of about fifty with brilliant white teeth and a skipper's wreath of short white hair. He can't write, not even his name. He carries the whole of his repertoire within him.

'Is it ten poems? Or a hundred?' I ask.

'Oh, many many more! I'd be able to recite them to you all night and all the next day and still have many unspoken.'

'What are they about?'

'Give me a subject and I shall sing the praises of it.'

I suggest 'the judgement of the international court' and he is immediately prepared.

> *'Sahara reunited with the mother country*
> *the profound connection*
> *between Saharans and the throne –*
> *the evidence now in the hands of the Hague*
> *where it's been confirmed by the court*
> *so everyone must be convinced.'*

He turns to the assembled company and recites the poem with great bravura, an artist used to performing. Every gesture is part of a stage language, every line in the verse demanding applause.

'When did you compose your first poem?'

'It was during the vaccination year, which is also called the "year of the summer rain". I was eighteen and in love for the first time. This is what it sounded like:

> *'Oh how beautiful it is,*
> *the bridge leading to the hill!*
> *Oh how lovely is the hill's blue*
> *in her eyes!'*

'That was in the days of the Spaniards. Did you compose poems in their honour?'

'I had my camel and my goats. I didn't need the Spaniards. Father was a goldsmith. So am I. That is my profession. Poetry is my vocation. If I don't make poems, I fall ill. All real poetry demands inspiration and the love of the King is the greatest source of inspiration. I made this poem during His visit to the USA:

> *'After your journey to the States*
> *and your visit to the Pentagon*
> *your insignificant neighbours scream,*
> *they who are a thorn in your side,*
> *they who rise against Your Majesty,*
> *they scream as if mad with envy.*
> *But they lack food,*
> *yea, they lack soap!'*

One night on his way to Smara, Michel Vieuchange hears far-distant men singing Saharan songs together in the darkness.

As he listens to the resolute gravity in their voices, he thinks there is something peculiar about his own enterprise. What is he really doing there? Is he going to do violence to a secret which ought to remain untouched?

Justified qualms. But he waves them away and struggles on, drunk with fatigue, exhausted, but upright. Elation pours through him despite his torments. He feels chosen, happy, purified by his own flame.

Sometimes his mouth is so dry he has great difficulty pronouncing the single word 'Ahmed'. He prepares himself for several minutes before attempting it. Only one single word and it seems almost insurmountable.

One of his Saharan companions falls ill and refuses to go on. The little caravan returns to Tiglit. Again Vieuchange is imprisoned in a room with no window, a cloud of flies his only company.

His head is full of one single desire, firm and irrevocable: to complete his journey. He will carry out what he has made up his mind to do. Everything that has been working its way within him since birth is heading towards that goal.

His determination is unyielding. But during the long days of waiting, it changes character.

The thought of Smara no longer gives him any joy. He can no longer find the enthusiasm that has previously borne him along. It has dried out, shrivelled up.

Vieuchange in Tiglit, after his first attempt on Smara.

Decisions are nearly always carried out under different conditions from those under which they are made.

Decisions are made at headquarters. They are carried out in the trenches.

Decisions are made in Paris. They are carried out in the Sahara.

The emotions generated in him by the name 'Smara' have disappeared. Remaining is the decision. The will. The intention. When all the humidity has gone, in the end there is nothing left but defiance.

When desire burns out, it is replaced with lies. Vieuchange begins to pretend.

He writes 'we' about himself. He pretends he is not alone but travelling with his brother.

He pretends they are on an important assignment through unknown country where no one else has ever seen what they see. In reality, he knows who has been there before him and he has no assignment other than to carry out his own intention.

He pretends they are on their way to a living town. In reality, he knows perfectly well Smara is in ruins and that it was his own countrymen who destroyed it.

These false premises make his enterprise utterly artificial. But this artificiality is documented with extreme authenticity.

Step by step, stone by stone, he describes what it means to do something in the Sahara because he 'had wanted it, in Paris'.

On November 1, he finally arrives in Smara. He has spent most of the journey hidden in a pannier, curled up in a foetal position, tormented by unbearable cramps, not even seeing the ground.

He now breaks free and staggers off into town.

The ground is strewn with dark stones. Not a human being in sight. Everything is in ruins.

He buries a bottle with a message in it to show that he and his brother have 'discovered' Smara – a final game of pretence before he crawls back into the pannier and begins the return journey.

Vieuchange in front of Smara.

'I got there,' he writes in his journal. 'But like a pearl-diver, I must immediately return.'

He spent three hours in Smara. The return journey took a month. He died in Agadir on November 30, 1930.

Actual cause of death: dysentery.

Real cause of death: romanticism.

To Laghouat

39

'The more light the desert receives, the darker it seems to become,' writes Eugène Fromentin.

Desert romanticism exists in that kind of paradox. Otherwise one must ask what a romantic is doing in the desert at all. The desert has no leafy groves, fragrant meadows, deep-soughing forests, or anything else which usually evokes in the romantic the right emotions. Desert romanticism already appears incomprehensible at a distance. Up close, it becomes absurd. What is romantic about an endless gravel pit?

Eugène Fromentin can tell you what. He wrote the classic desert book *A Summer in the Sahara* (1857). He is the first of a long line of writers and artists to experience the desert with an aesthetic eye.

Fromentin loves the desert because it has no appeal, because it is never lovely. He loves the expansiveness of its lines, the

Eugène Fromentin, *Arab Horseman*. (*Musée des Beaux-Arts de La Rochelle*)

Eugène Fromentin, *Interior of Arab tailor's workshop.*
(*Private collection, descendants of Eugène Fromentin*)

emptiness of its space, the barrenness of its ground. At last a sea which does not swell, but consists of a firm, immovable body. At last a silence which is never broken in a desolate country where no one comes and no one goes.

Strangely, that same silence seems so threatening in the town, lying there dark and mute under the sun.

The people appear to have lost their power of speech. They surround him with an immeasurable gravity, as mute and scorched as the landscape they inhabit.

Why this silence? Is it the sun? The heat makes the air vibrate with a faint but entirely audible note. The ground itself seems to gasp. Day and night change places. The midday sun annihilates and kills, the midnight darkness revives and gives life.

Fromentin sets off on nightly wanderings in town. But the inhabitants are just as hostile in the dark hours. They do not greet him. They pretend not to see him.

So that is what the Arab is – a man unwilling to show you his house, unwilling to say his name or say what he is doing or tell you where he is going. 'All curiosity is unwelcome to him.'

It must be the sun which has made the Arab like that. Fromentin feels himself being influenced. The sun persecutes him right into the night. 'I dream light,' he complains.

He stands all day out in the desert, painting, bathing in the sun. In the evening he is feverish from all the light his body has absorbed. Even when he closes his eyes he sees sparks, flames and circles of light in the darkness. 'I have no night, so to speak.'

People of the desert have lived under that sun since they were children. The terrible desert sun has marked them with its lack of emotion 'which has fallen from the sky onto objects and from objects has transferred to their faces'.

Hence the silence.

40

I've come from Algiers. I have rented a small Renault 4, buckled at all four corners and with the driver's seat sagging so much that it hits the floor. They did not want to let any other car go out into the desert. 'A single sandstorm takes off the paintwork in a few hours,' they said. So I put a couple of books and a rolled-up towel behind me and steered the little wreck out into the traffic of Algiers.

Algiers is a climbing town, all the streets on their way upwards or downwards, the traffic heavy and eternally at a standstill, until it suddenly hurtles forward with the roar of a tiger. I have seldom come across such a constant need to demonstrate the potency of your automobile and your driver's daring as I have here.

In a R4, there is nothing to do but calmly allow yourself to be passed on both sides, often so closely that your crumpled shirt gets a pressing into the bargain. So I cope with the latest passer's stinking exhaust fumes, perhaps muttering something about the fact that he is driving on camel shit to honour his mother.

Arabic oaths are often descriptions of the sexual behaviour with camels of the mother of the person concerned. Anyone who manages to combine the anal insult with the sexual gains extra points.

The road slices up the mountainside in sharp turns like a fretsaw. The R4 has no strength to fall back on – the trick is to accelerate between gears, as in the old days of double-declutching, and keep the engine running. Then the tough little car manages the Atlas mountains, and when I finally reach level ground, we get up to 60 mph, even 70 in successful moments.

It rumbles and it sways, but I can't help liking the R4 for the wind whistling through the coachwork and the sewing-machine buzz of the engine as it patiently carries me towards Laghouat.

Algeria is in the middle class of the world's countries. That is clear from the road, which is not dominated by shepherds and flocks of sheep but by heavy transporters – steel girders, pipes, cement. Roadworks occupy more machines than people – though the unemployed, currently 17%, would fight to be allowed to shovel macadam.

In the villages I try to buy some food for lunch, but there is only bread. There is always bread, subsidized by billions, very cheap to buy and sold in great quantities. Fresh morning bread has already been thrown away at midday to be replaced by even fresher afternoon bread. Even far out in the countryside, these bread habits have been adopted from the French and are considered sacred – Algeria literally throws away her oil income in the form of dry bread. A country which on liberation in 1962 was a great exporter of food now produces only 35% of what its people eat or throw away.

'*C'est la crise, c'est normale*,' they say in the shops as an explanation for there being no tea, no coffee, no sugar, no eggs – well, more or less nothing but detergents and powdered milk.

But there are schools. Everywhere I see children on their way to or from school. The first shift begins at dawn, the last is on its way home as the sun sets. Caring for the children and giving them an education despite 3.2% annual growth in population is the heroic feat of the schoolteachers – minor intellectuals who for twenty-five years have accepted these triple shifts, these remote posts in the countryside and these low salaries, to cope with the great task of teaching the people to read. But who feel themselves more and more deceived and abandoned as the years go by and others enrich themselves.

What did their sacrifices give them? When will things get better? In twenty years, when the oil runs out?

I stay with a teacher's family in Laghouat. My friend Ali, whom I got to know in the rue Valetin gym in Algiers. His brother Ahmed is leader of the big band 'Desert Brothers'. Like most young Algerians, they are enraged by the corrupt misrule.

'Before independence, we had five parties in the country. Now we're not considered mature enough to have more than one. What people lack is not maturity, but power!'

All evening we sit round the big couscous dish until the

meal is concluded with milk and dates. Then we all sleep together in the best room.

The moisture from our breathing glistens on the cold walls. Outside, the stars sparkle as brightly as only desert and darkness can make them. The silence is boundless, and the occasional distant barking of a dog makes it audible.

41

Early in the morning, I go up onto the roof. It is a beautiful day. White clouds have accumulated on the horizon like a further layer of sediment on dark mountains.

This is where Fromentin stood 130 years ago. The landscape we see is the same. The same sun, the same desert.

But not the same people. His Arabs were closed, menacing, hostile. Those I have met are open, lively, hospitable people.

Under the same sun.

Fromentin was wrong to think the merciless sun had marked the people of the desert for ever. Perhaps he actually knew that himself. In the 1980s, *A Summer in the Sahara* was published in new academic editions which also account for variations in the text. In them you find other explanations for the silence in Laghouat.

In the spring of 1830, Paris was already seething with the rebellion which was to find its outlet in the July revolution. De Polignac's militantly reactionary government was about to fall. As a final way of diverting dissatisfaction, it was decided to attack Algiers, on the pretext of an alleged insult to the French Consul.

In their proclamations to the people, the French said they had come to liberate the Arabs from Turkish oppression and make them 'lords in their own mansions'. But the supposed liberators committed the most hideous atrocities and retained power wherever they could seize it.

France under the July monarchy decided to keep just Algiers and its immediate surroundings; but the military was not to be deterred. Villages were burnt down in their hundreds, and thousands of refugees died of starvation. By the time the February revolution introduced the second empire, Algerian resistance had been broken all along the coast.

The mountains and the deserts remained. No political decision could stop the conquest that continued with military logic. On December 3, 1852, it was Laghouat's turn. The French seized the town after a two-day siege. Forty-five years later, the commanding officer described in his memoirs what happened next:

> The town had to endure all the horrors of war,
> experience all the atrocities that can be committed by
> soldiers when they are left for a moment to themselves,
> still feverish from the dreadful fighting, raging over the
> dangers they have undergone and the losses they have

suffered, excited by their hard-won victory. Terrible scenes were enacted.

Fromentin arrived in the early summer of 1853, scarcely six months after the massacre. 'I feel neither joy nor happiness here,' he writes. 'Difficult to explain why . . .'

43

Every morning, I go up onto the roof and sit there for a while, looking out over the brown slopes surrounding the town. They are covered with fresh green bushes and trees, although everywhere the actual ground is dry and infertile. The moisture has retreated from the sun and the winds, further down into the ground. That is where the roots seek it out.

Yesterday I drove through flowering nerium, a bush named after the Greek word for water, *nero*. It has a brilliant ability to find water at great depths and human water-diviners have always followed its roots.

The contrast between surface and depths, between what the eye sees up here and the real circumstances down there, are the fundamental experience of the desert.

From my viewpoint on the roof, I can follow the route of the victorious French into town. Fromentin did the same when the stench of corpses was still in the air. A French lieutenant who was present told him:

We literally waded in blood, and for two days it was impossible to get anywhere for the heaps of corpses.

Not only hundreds of men, shot or with bayonet
wounds all over them, but also – why not say it as it
is? – the bodies of huge numbers of women, children,
horses, donkeys, camels, yes, even dogs ... A terrible
book could be written about the episodes I heard tell
of the following morning alone, of what had been
enacted during the two or three hours the reprisals
lasted ...

Fromentin didn't write that book. He deleted the lieutenant's
story from his manuscript and contented himself with a summary: 'They waded in blood; there were corpses by the
hundred.'

In Fromentin's writing, too, there is a contrast between surface and depth, between what the eye sees up there and the
actual circumstances further down. In one place in the
manuscript he asks: 'A third of the population killed – with
what right, because of what crime or what threat and with
what doubtful results?'

But he at once stops himself: 'I have no right either to
describe or to judge a victory of this kind.'

Nor did he try. He deleted the passage. He blamed the
silence in Laghouat on the climate. It became romanticism.

44

The survivors of the massacre had fled south. Some returned
and were then directed to inferior neighbourhoods, all their
possessions confiscated, and the entire booty of mats, weapons,

jewellery and clothes removed. 'All the houses from the poorest to the wealthiest are empty,' Fromentin writes.

Under such circumstances, it was not easy to exercise the traditional Arab hospitality towards a travelling Frenchman. All the prerequisites were lacking.

Fromentin touches on the truth when he says that two societies confront each other in Laghouat: 'One has power and words. The other is a master of silence.'

Rhetorical phrasing. The lieutenant expresses himself more clearly:

It is impossible to know how long the desire for revenge will live on, *he says*. I could swear that when the day of reckoning eventually comes, it would give them great pleasure to fill my belly with small stones or flay me alive to make a drum out of my skin.

At night the silence is broken by the howls of dogs who had fled the massacre to a rock outside the town. It proved impossible either to get them to return or to drive them away. As long as they had plenty of food on the battlefield or in the burial places, all was calm. But then the dogs turned more and more wild and began to attack passers-by like wolves.

Today, in the chapel dedicated to Sidi el-Hadj Aissa, there are the following words: *Death is the door through which we all have to go*.

True. But those faced with imperialism often had to go through it somewhat in advance.

Fromentin in 1841. (*Daguerreotype by L.A. Bisson* fils. *Private collection, descendants of Eugène Fromentin*)

Eugène Fromentin, *Self-portrait*, early 1840s.
(*Private collection, descendants of Eugène Fromentin*)

After the conquest of Laghouat, the French threw corpses down the wells to punish the town.

They had never even considered remaining there themselves. No one had dreamt a garrison would be placed so far south.

But General Pelissier decided to keep Laghouat. The French became prisoners of the town.

They were to live there. They had to have water.

To clean the wells, well-workers were conscripted from other oases. They belonged to the lowest stratum of the desert's black proletariat. Only slave workers could be forced down into wells turned into graves.

Down there, the dead bodies had swollen with the gases of decay and were pressed against the well walls. The corpses were so firmly wedged in, they had to be levered apart.

Their flesh had begun to dissolve, the bodies disintegrating. The poisoned water became a mess of remains of corpses into which the well-divers were forced deeper and deeper.

The water-table in the northern part of the town was six metres below the surface, in the southern part twelve metres. The largest of the wells contained 256 corpses, not counting the bodies of animals.

This was something no one wanted made public. But nor did anyone try to hide it.

That year, in 1853, modern racism was born with de Gobineau's *Essay on the Inequality of Human Races*. Also in the bookshops was Herbert Spencer's *Social Statics* in which social Darwinism was launched, some years before Darwin produced biological Darwinism.

The French officers in North Africa could scarcely have

known about that. But they were children of their age. Some thought it, others did it.

And it was not the first time, far from it. The history of imperialism is a well full of corpses.

In Laghouat, the wells were confiscated and for the rest of the century remained under military administration. In the future, they would be cleaned out by the same black well-divers and their children, grandchildren and great-grandchildren.

To Ain Sefra

46

I drive westwards from Laghouat. The road follows the Atlas Mountains: empty grandstands facing the endless football pitches of the desert. Signposts indicate direction and give distances straight out into the gravel – but I see no other route apart from the one I am taking.

'Long hours of emptiness, nourished by silence,' in the words of Isabelle Eberhardt.

In Sweden, when trying to imagine the desert, I thought of sandy beaches which never reach the water. But it is fairly rare to see beaches in the desert, which is more like an endless schoolyard: a vast, hard-packed desolation extending without end towards the horizon.

Some rocks are left behind, alone on the bare ground. They were too heavy. The light ones have gone. Everything that can has fled.

Fromentin's success with *A Summer in the Sahara* tempted many writers to follow in his footsteps. Daudet, Gautier, Maupassant, even Flaubert, all travelled in Africa and had a relationship with the desert.

But the ultimate heir to Fromentin's romanticism is Pierre Loti.

Both came from the French Atlantic coast – Fromentin from La Rochelle, Loti from Rochefort. Between these two towns lies a water-logged marshy area sliced through by brim-full ditches and canals, the ebb-tide exposing muddy river banks. The oyster beds overflow like Chinese rice paddies, the farmland sticky, the water flourishing and stagnating in the pools.

A landscape completely opposite to the desert. In addition, Loti was a naval officer, the sea his profession. But he had the desert within him.

In Fromentin's life, the desert was more or less chance. In Laghouat, he accidentally found out things he never dared tell and shrouded them all in mystery, which attracted the general public. Success created a demand for his desert images, and they kept him busy, earning him a living for the rest of his life.

Loti's desert romance is no chance. It is part of a mendacity running far deeper, embracing his whole personality.

A small boy was once given a miniature landscape by his elder brother. All through his childhood he continued to add to this wonderful landscape, which extended into a whole little world where every stone and every butterfly was charged with fantasies.

When the boy left his childhood home, he locked up his museum and sealed the door, locking in his childhood. Time was not to be allowed.

By then disaster had already struck the family. First his beloved elder brother died. Then his father was charged with embezzlement, lost his job and crawled like a rat along the walls of the houses in Rochefort. The money for which the father had been responsible had to be repaid, the family sank into poverty, the childhood home was sold, the father died and the only son took on the debt.

This is how he became a writer. This is when he adopted the pseudonym of Pierre Loti.

Fifteen years later, when everything has been paid off, he asks his ship's watch to wake him *once an hour* to tell him he is free of debt.

When his success as an author has made him rich, he buys back the parental home and turns it into a museum of fantasy, into a world in miniature. The façade remains untouched, but he rebuilds the interior according to his exotic dreams. The old quarters are filled like a honeycomb with the different rooms of his writing: the Turkish room, the Gothic, the Renaissance salon, the Japanese room, the Chinese, the Egyptian . . .

One room alone is left untouched. It is the smallest of them all, squeezed between the Chamber of Mummies and the

Turkish room. It is bare, but not, like the bedroom, for calculated effect. It is simply an ordinary little French study with a black chair and a black desk.

This is where Loti worked. Here he wrote a great many of his forty books, at the same desk at which his father once did his accounts.

All around this sober little room was the scenery of his life. Few authors have had such a need to enter their dreams and inhabit them. To write a book set among Basque smugglers, he does not just live with them: he takes his Basque clothes and weapons home with him, has the back of the compound equipped as two Basque rooms and sends for an unknown Basque woman who bears him two Basque children. After work every day, he goes and plays with them for a little while.

But his existing wives, both the one at the front of the compound and the one at the back, mean less to him than the heroine in his first novel, *Aziyadé*. Every evening he retreats into his private mosque and spends several hours dreaming and weeping at her tombstone. The dead increasingly fill his existence – parents, relatives, favourite animals, all buried beneath the courtyard of his childhood home, incorporated into the museum of his life. His museum of death.

It started when he locked away his childhood. Then he locked away everything else bit by bit. He wanted to preserve, perpetuate, to prevent every change.

No wonder Loti loved the desert. In the desert all changes have already occurred. Nothing grows, nothing dies, nothing decays. Everything has gone. Only eternity remains.

The flatter the desert, the more you become imprisoned and locked in by the horizon. You welcome every movement that elevates you and provides a view. You welcome every interruption: hills with hard peaks like the neck of a broken bottle; great movable yellow boulders; or quite simply distant heights coloured milky white or pale blue by the distance.

This morning I saw a *marabout*, the sepulchre of a holy man, its distant white walls reflecting the light like a beacon.

It takes about an hour to climb up to the stillness and solitude. There is nothing there.

Nothing but a few lizard tracks in the sand.

Nothing but a few unglazed, cracked and crumbling jars, the tombstones of the poor.

Nothing but a few large split palm trunks, grey with age, their timber like pressed straw.

And then the *marabout* door glowing acid-green and sulphur-yellow in the morning sun.

Far down below, a man is hacking away in the dry riverbed and some dark men are spreading out their dark, moist dates to dry beyond a low mud wall.

I go down to them, where it is already hot in the sun. But when they greet you, the men's hands are still cool, almost cold – as if the night had remained behind in their bodies.

The only language we had in common was our hands.

Throughout his life, Pierre has himself photographed in ever more handsome costumes. He holds his head thrown back, thrusting out one leg in order to appear taller than he is.

That is when you see how small he is. And how that tormented him.

He walks on tiptoe in high-heeled shoes. His wives are made to measure, smaller than he is himself. To be on the safe side, his mistresses are of 'lower race'.

As a child, he read with thumping heart the letters from his admired older brother, Gustav, a ship's doctor who took a 'wife' in Tahiti. On his first trip abroad, Loti goes to Tahiti and looks up his dead brother's woman. The love of a brother, just as the little boy back home dreamt about, becomes the constantly recurring paradigm in his life and his art.

Again and again he writes the same novel. It is about a white man, often a naval officer, who has a romantic relationship with a woman of alien race or culture. She looks up to him as a higher being. Their love is estrangement, passion, departure. They part with pain, doomed to eternal longing for their lost paradise.

Once only does he fall in love with a Frenchwoman. He proposes and is turned down.

In the diary he kept with a bookkeeper's thoroughness all his life, these are the only pages missing.

That is when he becomes a bodybuilder. He can't change his height, but he can build up his muscles. He becomes an athlete and appears in a circus in close-fitting tricot.

Loti as a Turkish gentleman. (*House of Pierre Loti, Rochefort, France*)

Second floor. 17: Gustave's study. 18: Arabic room. 19: Turkish room. 20: museum of Loti's childhood. 21: gallery of the Gothic room. 22: second storey of the Gothic room. 23: Chamber of Mummies. 24: Mosque. 25: Loti's bedroom.

First floor. 11: terrace onto the garden. 12: Loti's childhood bedroom. 13: Room of Bees. 14: Gothic room. 15: gallery of the Renaissance room. 16: second storey of the Renaissance room.

Ground floor. 1: garden. 2: Red room. 3: Japanese pagoda. 4: court-yard. 5: cloister. 6: fountain. 7: Rural room. 8: Blue room. 9: Renaissance room. 10: Chinese room.

Areas in grey no longer exist.

1: Blue room. 2: Renaissance room. 3: entrance to the Gothic room. 4: Mosque. 5: Loti's bedroom.
(*Phillipe Oudin; House of Pierre Loti, Rochefort, France.*)

Loti as a circus performer. (*House of Pierre Loti, Rochefort, France*)

Loti as a naval officer. (*House of Pierre Loti, Rochefort, France*)

Loti as the goddess Osiris. (*House of Pierre Loti, Rochefort, France*)

With a certain satisfaction, I regard the body I have
created with my exercises. The muscles stand out in
relief in the close-fitting costume. An old juggler
elevates the effect by lightly shading in the contours of
my muscles with a pencil. This strange anatomical toilet
takes twenty minutes.

Even in his nakedness he has to disguise himself. He dyes his
moustache and rouges his cheeks; he sits in the French
Academy made up like an old whore – hoping no one will see
how small he is.

He loves his way through the world, conquering it in the
form of women. Asia, Africa, the South Seas and the Atlantic,
the deserts of Sahara, Sinai and Persia – he has been everywhere, he has skimmed the romanticism off existence and
taken it back with him into his art and home.

In his doll's house, the world at last is given its correct pro-
portions. Inside it, he is large.

51

A moon-pale and determined young woman has been given an
assignment by the French Academy to free Pierre Loti from
his enchanted house. The Academy Action Group arrives in a
helicopter and those most immortal climb down rope ladders
onto the roof of the mosque. They search through the house
without finding Loti. 'Search thoroughly,' says Isabelle. 'He's
always in disguise.' But they find nothing but a little dog
which she takes in her arms as she climbs up into the roaring

helicopter, its rotor blades making the roof tiles jump. The dog is a small black and white Scottie with a bristly moustache and yearning eyes. One of its hind legs is rather stiff from being almost constantly raised. It also carries its nose very high.

'You can see it's Pierre Loti's dog,' says Isabelle. Then the disguise suddenly falls away and little Loti is standing there with his nose in the air – without his dog-mask, but strangely dog-like all the same.

52

More people drown in the desert than in the sea. They drown from lack of imagination. They simply cannot imagine enough water to drown in.

An *oued* is a dried-out river channel. But it could be thousands of years since any river flowed there, so it is more correct to say that an *oued* is the track left by torrents that have passed by. The desert is full of tracks of that kind, and you can live a whole life without ever seeing them filled with water. It is like living by the main line south without ever seeing a single train. Gradually you begin to think none will come. And if the whole landscape is a shunting-yard full of similar railway lines where no trains run, either – well, then you finally feel absolutely safe.

When the express train comes thundering along one night in accordance with some unknown timetable, you are not prepared. The torrent suddenly roars through and drowns everything in its path.

It came to Ain Sefra on the night of October 21, 1904.

I admit that I cross the *oued* in Ain Sefra with some haste. I can see bits of skeleton in the sand on the other side. And further up, whole corpses of sheep, goats and cattle – swept down by a tidal wave? Or is it a kind of animal cemetery?

I come to a forest planted to bind the dunes. A shepherd is reading a book there.

'Sidi Bou Djema?' I say, in monosyllables.

He points to the faint outline of a wall on top of a dune and replies equally monosyllabically:

'Sidi Bou Djema!'

But when I get up there, it is just a wall enclosing a small garden where a lone man and his dog grow chickpeas and onions.

The man is very friendly and he speaks beautiful French. He knows exactly where the tomb is and is pleased to take me there.

It is his garden. He laid it out himself. He dug the well himself, eleven metres deep. He fired the clay bricks for the wall himself. It would have been ready by now if it hadn't rained the other day. His semi-fired bricks have run out into the ground – look at this! Now he has to start all over again. He is used to that. He was a guest-worker in France for eight years and has worked in Marseilles and Lyons. He has even been to Paris. Now he has come back, has a wife and six children, five of them boys, and he is looking forward to a secure old age when he no longer needs to do any work, other than potter around in his garden.

As he is telling me this, we have got as far as the burial ground of Sidi Bou Djema. It lies with dunes and mountains behind it and a view over the *oued* where it happened.

A few spindly stems of grass grow in the sand after the rain. But all the same, it is a very desolate place. The desolation seems to be concentrated on the absurd buckled aluminium saucepan hanging at the back of a tombstone. On the front it says in European letters:

ISABELLE EBERHARDT

54

The act of departure is the bravest and most beautiful
of all. A selfish happiness perhaps, but it is happiness –
for him who knows how to appreciate it. To be alone, to
have no needs, to be unknown, a stranger and at home
everywhere and to march, solitary and great, to the
conquest of the world . . .

That is what Isabelle Eberhardt writes in a piece sometimes called 'The Road', sometimes 'Notes in Pencil'.

Departure is a tradition in her family. Her surname comes from her German maternal grandmother, Fräulein Eberhardt, who left her country to live with a Russian Jew.

Her mother marries an old Russian general, but then leaves him to go to Geneva with the children's young tutor – a handsome, intellectual Armenian, Tolstoy's apprentice, Bakunin's friend. He has been a priest, is married and now leaves his wife and children to live with his beloved in exile.

He teaches Isabelle six languages: French, Russian, German, Latin, Greek and Arabic. But he never admits to her face that he is her father.

She grows up among exiled anarchists in a chaotic milieu in which catastrophe is the natural state.

When she is eight, her brother Nicholas joins the Foreign Legion.

When she is nine, her sister Olga runs away and marries against the will of her family.

When she is seventeen, her favourite brother Augustin joins the Foreign Legion.

When she is twenty, she goes with her mother to Algeria. They both convert to Islam. The mother dies and is buried in Annaba.

When she is twenty-one, her brother Vladimir commits suicide.

When she is twenty-two, she gives her father, who is dying of cancer, an overdose of a pain-killing drug which, intentionally or not, ends his life.

She is alone in the world. At the turn of the century in 1900 she writes in her diary that the only form of bliss, however bitter, destiny will ever grant her is to be a nomad in the great deserts of life.

55

In secret, my sister Isabelle winds wet cotton bandages round her chest. She wears these bandages under her clothes and with not the slightest sign betrays what is going on. Only I know about it and I cannot stop her. She winds the wet bandages tightly, tightly round her chest. When they dry and shrink, they slowly crush her chest and suffocate her heart. No one can save her.

'From where have I got this morbid craving for barren ground and desert wastes?' Isabelle Eberhardt asks.

In her teens, she was charmed by the melancholy escapism of Loti's first novel *Aziyadé*, and he became her favourite author. When his *The Desert* came out in 1895, she was eighteen years old. Two years later she set out into the desert on her own for the first time. Loti was the one she always took with her on her journeys, the only person she looked up to as a forerunner and example.

She thought she had found her soulmate. He had a beloved older brother who had gone to sea, she has a beloved older brother who became a legionnaire. Her life, like his, is shrouded in departure and loss. Both live in disguise. And both love the desert, where they see their emptiness and their longing for death take shape.

Eberhardt as a Bedouin.

Eberhardt as a spahi.

Michel Vieuchange set off into the desert disguised as a woman. Isabelle sets off into the desert disguised as a man.

To her it is not just a disguise. The French language mercilessly reveals whether the writer considers him- or herself to be a man or a woman. Even in her diary Isabelle uses the masculine to describe herself.

Pierre Loti disguised himself as an Arab, but also as a Chinese, a Turk and a Basque. In every harbour, in every book, he takes on a new disguise. He became a cut-out doll for ever in new costumes, a cultural chameleon melting into every environment and lacking authenticity wherever he went.

The disguise goes deeper in Isabelle. When she returns to Africa, she wants to free herself from her past and take on a new and Arab identity. She becomes the Tunisian author Si Mahmoud Essadi.

Dressed in the clothes of an Arab man, she sets off into the desert. She has been waiting for this moment all her life. She rides between the oases with a few native cavalrymen, with a group of legionnaires, with a *chaamba* caravan, with an African on his way home to his village to get a divorce. She writes:

> Now I am a nomad – with no other homeland than
> Islam, with no family, no one in whom to confide,
> alone, alone for ever in the proud and darkly sweet
> solitude of my own heart . . .

She soon finds a separate confidant in one of her Arab lovers. Slimene Ehni is a sergeant in the native cavalry. She meets him in El Oued and through him becomes a member of a Sufi community, which is secretly opposed to French rule.

Another Arab fraternity closer to the French tries to murder her. A stretched washing line softens the blow and saves her life.

The French army banish her from North Africa and she ends up in Marseilles, where she supports herself for a while by writing letters in Arabic for the guest-workers.

Slimene also goes there, and on October 17, 1901, they marry. By marrying an Arab in the service of France, she becomes a French citizen and can return to the desert.

With Slimene she rents a small house in Ain Sefra, which is the headquarters of the French troops during the 'pacification' of the border with Morocco.

Even as Madame Ehni, she wears men's clothes and continues her androgynous life beside camp fires and in soldiers' brothels. Only the male rôle provides her with the freedom to ride around reporting for the newspaper *l'Akbar* in the Sahara, which the French are just conquering. Only the male rôle gives her the freedom to make love with anyone, to drink anisette with the legionnaires and smoke kif in the cafés, where she shocks listeners with her expositions on the pleasures of brutality and the voluptuousness of subjection.

58

I push my way through a thick dark desert of trees which is called 'forest'. I am in a hurry and must not come too late. In the end the forest opens up into a clearing. I see a figure hanging by the feet from a branch and I rush over. It is Isabelle! Her normally moon-pale face is blue-black and contorted. I cut her down and carefully arrange the dead body on the ground.

59

The Globe, a sports arena in Stockholm, is transformed from a descending hot-air balloon into a diving bell. Isabelle and I are sluiced out into the water, spouting cascades of pearly bubbles from our oxygen masks. But very soon we are forced to go back as if into a womb. We have been born into an element that is not ours, in which we do not belong, in which we cannot live – except for short moments with the piece of bitumen between our teeth.

60

'The thought of death has long since been familiar to me,' wrote Isabelle towards the end of her life.

> Who knows? Perhaps I shall soon let myself slip into it, voluptuously and without the slightest worry. With time I have learnt not to look for anything in life but the ecstasy offered by oblivion.

Pierre Loti lived with his death-wish until he was seventy-three. Isabelle Eberhardt only lived to twenty-seven. By then she had

Eberhardt seated, cigarette in hand, about six months before her death, 1904.

no teeth, no breasts, no menstruation, was as thin as a well-diver, and almost always depressed. 'If this foray of mine into the darkness does not stop, what will be its terrifying outcome?'

Her life was an extended suicide. With increasing regularity she took refuge in drugs, alcohol and a brutal, self-destructive, indiscriminate sexuality. She suffered from innumerable illnesses, among them malaria, and probably syphilis.

At her own urgent request, she was discharged from the hospital in Ain Sefra on October 21 and returned to her house by the *oued*.

The torrent that drowned her came that night.

61

When Isabelle died, her first novel, *Vagabond*, was just being serialized in *l'Akbar*. Her sketches and short stories had often been included in Algerian newspapers. A large number of manuscripts was saved from the flood.

The editor-in-chief of *l'Akbar*, Victor Barrucand, published a selection in 1906. Quite well-meaningly, he had first prettied up her texts.

She wrote: 'Everyone laughed.' He added: 'People laughed at his rusticity; his gesture was that of a shepherd.'

She wrote: 'Freedom was the only happiness accessible to my nature.' That sounded too simple. He improved on it: 'Freedom was the only happiness that was necessary for my eager, impatient and yet proud nature.'

Despite the revisions, the book was a success and Barrucand continued to publish Isabelle's manuscripts in 1908, 1920 and

1922, by then with greater respect for the integrity of her writing. The diaries and other writings she left were published in 1923, 1925 and 1944 by R-L Doyon. Grasset began to publish her collected writings in 1988. Most of these editions also contain short biographies. More extensive biographies have been published in France, Algeria, England and in the USA in 1930, 1934, 1939, 1951, 1952, 1954, 1961, 1968, 1977, 1983, 1985 and 1988.

62

What is it about Isabelle Eberhardt that goes on fascinating generation after generation?

I have plenty of time to think about that as I drive on through the desert.

She did not write nearly so much as her master, Pierre Loti. As a rule, nor did she write so well. And yet she is the one to survive. Why?

'One must never look for happiness,' she writes. 'One meets it by the way – always going in the opposite direction.'

There is a great deal of sparkling use of words in her work. It is not the average that counts. It is the highlights.

It is not the quantity that counts, it is the totality. And that applies not only to her language, but also body language. The gesture of life.

Isabelle dressed in male clothes and dived into the wells of the Saharan Arab world. At the same time, Jack London was putting on working clothes and letting himself sink into *People of the Abyss* (1903).

Eberhardt on horseback. (*Painting in oils by G. Rossegrosse*)

He was conducting a social experiment. He wanted to experience with his own body what wretchedness means for the truly poor.

Isabelle was doing the same. But with no secret gold coin sewn into her waistband. She dived without any safety rope. She went undercover with no return.

The boundaries she crossed were not only social, but racial. A white woman in the American South openly preferring black men as lovers and marrying one of them without altering her unbridled life – considered in those terms, it is easier to understand what forces Isabelle was challenging.

The French Empire in North Africa rested ultimately on the myth of the superiority of the white race. Her whole way of life questioned that myth.

It also questioned the myth of male superiority. If a female transvestite could penetrate the world of men and acquire its freedoms, vices and privileges, then the gender rôles were made to waver. Unclear sexual identity aroused anxiety and aggression. Isabelle put herself outside all categories.

Even that might possibly have been forgiven, as her fate verified all prejudices, apparently confirming that anyone who defies the conventions sinks into the dregs. So far, so good. But throughout her deterioration, Isabelle had the insolence to maintain a sense of moral superiority. That was unforgivable.

In that respect she belongs to a totally different family from Loti. She belongs to a long line of French literature running from Villon via Baudelaire and Rimbaud to Céline and Genet. She may be the only woman in that company.

The Immoralist

63

André Gide's *Fruits of the Earth* was published in Swedish in 1947, when I was fifteen.

As soon as I opened the book I felt someone was speaking to me, not over my head to other adults, but directly to me. And so confidentially, almost whispering, as if it were late at night when everyone else was asleep.

The book gave me another name, Natanael, which drew me into the text so that we could be together there. I liked it very much.

Some writers hide themselves in Action, others conceal themselves in Facts. But the master in *Fruits of the Earth* despised such hiding places. He talked about himself. He had a message. It filled the whole book. It was already there in his voice, in his way of speaking to me.

I was looking for a Master. I heard his voice for the first time in *Fruits of the Earth*, and fortunately he was also looking for what I wanted to be: an apprentice.

That was dangerous and forbidden. I realized that at once. The Master defied all authority. He preached departure, departure from everything, even from himself. He said: 'When you've read my book, throw it away and go out! I would like it to have given you the desire to leave something, anything, your town, your family, your way of thinking. Don't take my book with you . . . Forget me.'

That voice made me happy. But it also frightened me, made me afraid of the demands it made, afraid of the great unknown awaiting me.

64

'Our actions consume us, but they give us our radiance.'

That could be an epitaph for Isabelle Eberhardt.

She went to North Africa in 1897, when *Fruits of the Earth* was on sale for the first time. She died in 1904 when *The Immoralist* had just been published. Her whole writing life was lived between these two of Gide's books.

She was obsessed by the same mystique of departure as Gide. She preached the same nomadism. As he did, she wanted to try every experience, even those that were bad, brutal or depraved. It is conceivable that the reason why she dressed as a boy was in order to become his favourite apprentice, Natanael.

But there is nothing to indicate that she read Gide, at that time still a little-known young writer. André and Isabelle were simply children of the same day.

And through *Fruits of the Earth*, that day also became mine.

65

I came to *Fruits of the Earth* from *Manual for Infantrymen*, which had long been my favourite book. I also came from the training guide *Physical Fitness and Strength*. I read Gide in the same way. I came from *Scouting for Boys*. In this last, the narrative and descriptive parts were interspersed with small comments in brackets: '(practise it!)'. I read parentheses of that kind into *Fruits of the Earth* as well.

When it said:

'Every creature is capable of authenticity, every feeling of fullness.'

Or:

'I lived in a state of almost uninterrupted, passionate surprise.'

Then I also read the invisible words 'Practise it!'

Passionate surprise . . . ?

I loved my father, but had he ever been passionate? Did he even know what the word meant?

Within me was a boundless need to be seized and elevated. Everything around me denied that need. Only in *Fruits of the Earth* was it understood: 'Never stop, Natanael. As soon as an environment has become like you, or you like your environment, it is no longer any use to you. Then you must leave it. Nothing is more dangerous to you than *your* family, *your* room, *your* past.'

Was I getting like my father? Would I become the Secretary of the Älvsjö branch of the Swedish Red Cross, as he was? Would I dilute my milk with water to spare my stomach? Would I live without travelling, without festivities, without thinking, without adventures?

'Families, I hate you!' says Menalces. Through a window, he sees a boy sitting reading beside his father. The next day Menalces meets the boy on his way back from school. The next day they talk to each other, and four days later 'he left everything to come with me'.

The biblical associations with the Apostles who left everything to follow the Master gave me the courage to abandon myself to such dreams: one day Someone would walk past in the November darkness out there on Långbrodal Road, Someone would see me though the window where I was bored to death doing my homework beside my father, and this Someone would call out to me and take me out into the great wide world outside Älvsjö.

We would wander in that fatal moonlight over the desert. We would walk barefoot on smooth blue rocks, our eyelids cooled by the night.

We would see the walls of desert cities turning red towards evening and glowing faintly on in the night – deep walls in which the midday light is stored. At night, they slowly repeat what the day has taught them.

We would see Bou Saada. We would see Biskra. 'Over the moonlit terraces in Biskra, Meriem comes to me through the tremendous silence of the night. She is entirely enveloped in a torn white haik which she laughingly lets fall as she stands there in the doorway . . .'

After every sentence of that kind, I read with racing heart a secret *Practise it! Live it!*

66

Bou Saada, 'the fortunate town', lies in a hollow between three mountains. Its fortune is that its wells are connected to an underground lake constantly supplied with fresh water from the three mountains. The old wells can be thirty metres deep and irrigate twenty-four thousand date palms.

Today the basis of the economy is not dates but oil. The powerful desert vehicles of the prospectors, covered in mud and sand, stand outside the Hotel Caida. The oil men swill beer in a bar like a swimming baths, their voices echoing between tiled walls. They gather noisily around the long tables in the dining room with their big laughs and big wallets. A small plate of soup and a mess of vegetables costs as much as a dinner at the luxurious Opera Cellar in Stockholm.

Exchange rates create the image of the Foreigner. If the Foreigner is to appear powerful, rich and generous, then there has to be an exchange rate which makes everything cost about half what the Foreigner pays back home. If the Foreigner is to appear powerless, poor, stingy and complaining, then there has to be an exchange rate such as there is in Algeria.

I am staying at the Hotel Transatlantic. When it opened in 1909, the Foreigner was rich and powerful. Then the water closets flushed, hot water rushed out of the taps from Jacob Delafont & Co in Paris, the piano was properly tuned, the lights in the chandeliers sparkled, the Ouled Nail girls danced and made love. Those were the days.

Fruits of the Earth speaks with rapture about these girls. Loti wrote a whole book about them. Maupassant praises them. He came across them at the Café Joie in the main

97

square and spread the rumour all over Europe that their wantonness was all part of the Ouled Nail tribal culture. According to ancient custom, the girls lived those happy days as prostitutes to save enough for their dowries.

Today, the Transatlantic in Bou Saada is the only surviving hotel of a chain that once stretched across the whole of North Africa. An infinitely old man shows me up the high stairs, as narrow and steep as a ladder. A yellow plastic bucket in the bath has to serve as both shower and WC. The beds are as cold and deep as graves.

67

I am lying on the ground in a strange town. A crowd of children dressed in white see me and come running over. They stand around me, chattering in French to each other, bending down and touching me, plucking at my clothes, touching my skin, lifting my hand. I am tremendously frightened. I expect them to say:

'He's dead.'

I don't know myself whether or not I'm alive .

68

In the morning, the infinitely old man has put on a once-white jacket and from the narrow spout of an enamel pot pours a bubbling, pale brown drink which could well be tea, may be coffee. His hands with their raised veins shake as he pours.

For five years after the death of my mother, I had my father's full confidence. Then he went behind my back and started seeing another woman.

The first time she visited us at home, as I was seventeen and was reading *Fruits of the Earth*, I suddenly felt terribly sorry for her.

Beside my old father, she seemed so young and lively, so unused. Did she really understand what she was letting herself in for? She didn't know what he was really like, as I did, from long experience.

After dinner, Father went out into the kitchen to fetch the coffee. Then I said: 'Surely you're not considering marrying someone who is already dead?'

She looked at me in horror.

'Ssh, he can hear what you're saying.'

I thought I had nothing to hide, and actually raised my voice as I went on. 'He hasn't read a book for fifteen years, or thought a new thought. Everything about him has solidified into clichés and routines. He's dead.'

As I was saying this, I saw from her expression that it was hopeless. I fell silent. Then my father, as old as I am now, came back into the room. He poured the coffee through the narrow spout of an enamel coffee pot. He didn't say anything. But I can still see before me his hands, with their raised veins, shaking as he pours.

Eventually, Someone really did walk past and see me. He was a British composer called John. I was pleased a grown man was interested in me and taking me seriously. In the summer of 1948, I went to London to stay for a few weeks with John in his flat.

It soon turned out that our expectations of this meeting were quite different.

'You're reading *Fruits of the Earth*,' John said. 'Do you see what your favourite book is about?'

He showed me one place after another, for example the bit in the sixth book about the dazzling light in the towns of the Orient. I had often read that. But clearly not thoroughly enough. I hadn't seen that among the white-clad Arabs were also children who appeared far too young, don't you think, to know anything about love? 'Some of them had lips hotter than newly hatched baby birds.'

'Practise it! Live it!' said John, and kissed me.

I was scared. I had no desire to be involved like that. As soon as I could, I escaped from the flat and ran through the streets of London to the Swedish Embassy, where, still gasping with the fear and effort, I rang the doorbell.

It was Sunday morning. A gigantic British butler gazed down at me blankly from the top stratum of society.

Haughtily, he saw me off.

It was pouring with rain. I had nowhere to go. I went back to John. When he found out where I had been, he was instantly transformed from attacker into victim.

'Are you crazy?' he said. 'Do you want me sent to prison?'

He told me about Oscar Wilde. Wilde was the prototype for Menalces in *Fruits of the Earth*.

I could hardly believe it.

'What had a poseur like Wilde to teach the master of honesty, André Gide?' I said.

'Wilde was world famous,' said John. 'The young André Gide had still not had anything published when they met in Paris in 1891. They were together every day for three weeks. Gide tore those three weeks out of his diary.

'The same year the master of honesty published *Fruits of the Earth*,' John went on, 'the master of poseurs left prison a broken man. That could happen to me, too, if you report me to the Embassy.'

Naturally, I didn't. John and I made a pact – he left me alone and I didn't go to the Embassy. But the message in *Fruits of the Earth* had suddenly shrivelled. I no longer called myself Natanael.

70

On the road between Bou Saada and Biskra is a small place called Zaatcha.

The name has never become as famous as Song My or Oradour-sur-Glane, but what it denotes is the same: massacre. The French razed the town to the ground after the rebellion of 1849 and the whole population was slaughtered, men, women and children.

Today the name denotes some dusty palm trees, a petrol station and a café rattling with dominoes. The morning bread has all gone and the evening bread has not yet arrived. There are three red plastic chairs and an iron one outside. I sit down to wait.

Out of old Swedish habit, I turn my face to the sun and roll up my sleeves to get a bit of tan on my arms.

People around me are surprised and upset. They look at me as if I were a flasher. In the Sahara, the sun is the Enemy just as much as it is the Friend with us. Sunbathing in the Sahara – it's something you simply do not do.

Not so long ago, the sun was suspect in Europe too. The first really immoral thing that happens in *The Immoralist* is that the main character takes all his clothes off in the sun. He sees some sunburnt workers and is himself tempted to undress. At first it feels cold and unpleasant. But the sun burns and after a while he is pleasantly roasted right through. 'My whole self lived in my skin,' he says.

Was he the very first modern sunbather? The sun, the liberator, teaches him not to be ashamed of his body, but to look upon it with delight. 'I felt harmonious and full of sensuality. I almost thought I was beautiful.'

Gide writes that when it was still regarded as more natural to burn down a village than to undress in public. Nakedness was characteristic of the inferior races, along with dark body colour. What was morally superior was white.

Sunbathing became a bold symbolic action, full of rebellion and hedonistic mystery:

It seemed to me, *Gide writes in* If It Die . . . , as if when lit through by the rays of the sun my body had undergone a chemical renewal. When I took off my clothes, it was as if all torments, restraints and worries ceased to exist. While my will melted utterly away, I let my body, now as porous as a honeycomb, secretively purify and prepare the honey flowing into the *Fruits of the Earth*.

Respectable people do not do such things. A respectable person burns down villages, but is careful not to let his will melt away.

The sun is scorching in Zaatcha. The evening bread has still not arrived. The houses are pale blue and honey-yellow. Some heavy long-distance trucks stop to fill up, surrounded by chattering mopeds. The children gather on the playground. The only thing that makes it a playground is the fence. No need for a sandpit. The wet salt desert smells of sea.

71

At the spa hotel in Biskra, I spend one night drinking with Wolfgang, a German desert fanatic crossing the Sahara on a motorcycle. *The Immoralist* is lying on the table in my room and Wolfgang says: 'The wife has a miscarriage, doesn't she? Otherwise she would have given birth to me.'

'You?'

'Yes, I grew up in exactly that kind of family. My friends thought I had the most wonderful father in the world. He thought so too. But he was interested in their opinion, not mine. True, he was full of charm and imagination. True, I admired him enormously. But he betrayed me over and over again – without even noticing. The book ought to be called *The Self-Absorbed*. In his world, the immoralist is the only person who really exists – that's what makes him immoral.'

It was one of those night-time hotel conversations which become absolutely honest only because both people are equally sure they will never have to meet again.

'Father was always very attentive towards my mother. But beneath the courtesies and tokens of love, the silence between them grew deeper and deeper, until finally it became explosive.

'They didn't dare separate. My father thought that without Mother, reality itself would cease to exist. Only she could nourish and sustain him. For her too, it was a matter of identity. There was nothing beyond their lifelong love, not even herself.'

'What happened?'

'One day when my mother was in the bath, he locked the bathroom door on the outside, went downstairs, poured petrol all over the living room and set fire to it. Then he went straight to the police and gave himself up. I almost think he expected praise. A respectable person does not separate from his wife, but one does have the right to burn down one's house, doesn't one? And it did indeed burn to the ground.'

'And your mother?'

'She was rescued at the last minute. I went to the Sahara. My father was a desert soldier in Rommel's army in the Second World War. He often told me about the desert when I was small. I had got it into my head that the solution to the mystery of him might be found here.'

72

I am staying in Beeskra and publishing the *Honey Bee Magazine* containing news from the beekeeper front seen entirely through the eye of the bee.

Even beesexual keepers get sharp criticism for what they

regard as beeneficial. But naturally I avoid exaggerated and unbeeleevable standpoints. Since the Bee Party came into power, the honey harvests have multiplied. That way the supply of sugar-water for the bees is assured. Continued co-operation with the beekeepers is naturally for the beeneefit of the bees.

The final 'libeeration', as we call it, is a central beetail that unfortunately has had to bee put off into the future.

73

From the main character's point of view, Gide's *The Immoralist* is a story of liberation.

Michel has recently lost his wife. Some of his friends travel to an oasis in the Sahara to meet him. Lying on his roof, they listen as he confides in them about his marriage.

He had married Marceline largely to please his father. During their honeymoon in North Africa, he finds out he is in the advanced stages of consumption. He has already given up and prepared himself for death when the sight of a small child suddenly gives him a strong desire to live.

His whole being begins to resist the disease. 'My health was my assignment. Everything that was wholesome was to be regarded as good, but I must reject and forget everything that did not heal.'

What arouses his will to live more than anything else is the company of children. When he sees them playing in Biskra gardens, semi-obliterated memories from his own childhood come into his mind. It amuses him to learn their games and arrange little parties for them with juice and cakes in his hotel room.

He begins to regain his strength. He experiences exactly the kind of jubilant re-entry into life described in *Fruits of the Earth*.

Soon he does not only want to regain his health, but to be strong and full-blooded. He seems to discover within himself a new creature which teachers, relatives, yes, even he himself had previously tried to suppress. He begins to see himself as something that can be perfected. 'Never has my will been more excited than in trying to achieve this unknown, still unclearly imagined perfection.'

He shaves off his beard and lets his hair grow. He sunbathes and exercises his body. But he doesn't dare, or doesn't want to share these experiences with Marceline. He wants to keep them to himself. He soon finds it both easy and amusing to lie to her and he also thinks these lies simply increase his love.

One day he rescues his wife from a drunken driver, and with his newly won strength thrashes the man. Then he makes love to her for the first time. She becomes pregnant, they return to France and settle on a country estate which had belonged to his mother.

Among intellectuals, Michel now feels himself a stranger. He thinks life, for him infinitely valuable, is nothing to them but an annoying hindrance to their writing. Instead he finds his way to a gang of semi-criminals and with them devotes himself to nightly thieving of his own possessions.

But Marceline falls ill and has a miscarriage. They leave the estate and travel south to find a place where she can regain her health.

'So once again I made an attempt to retain my love,' says Michel. But he no longer has any need of it. Happiness with Marceline is to him as superfluous as rest is to someone who is not tired.

He thinks he possesses within him untouched possibilities which are being suffocated beneath layers of culture and morality. Sins and crimes are acts of liberation. Evil is natural: 'In every living being the instinct for evil seems to me to be what is most immediate.' And everything which is natural should be affirmed: 'I feel nothing within me that is not noble.' So even what is evil is noble.

They leave the Swiss resort where Marceline has begun to regain her health. In the middle of winter, they travel south to seek sun and warmth. But Marceline simply gets worse. They finally arrive in Biskra. There he was saved. There she will also regain life!

The children in Biskra, who once gave him back the will to live and made him take the first step towards self-discovery, have become almost unrecognizable. 'Work, vice and indolence have left their mark on faces which two years ago radiated youth.' The boys have become dishwashers, road workers and butchers. 'How honest occupations brutalize!'

The only one to retain his beauty is a petty criminal, Moktir. Michel invites him to accompany him to Touggourt the next day. But Marceline is more ill than ever and, trembling, she presses up against Michel. He thinks:

'Shall I not stop? – I have sought and found my real worth: a kind of stubborn obduracy in wickedness (*le pir*). But how can I bring myself to tell Marceline that tomorrow we are going to Touggourt? . . .'

They take the mail carriage at dawn. Moktir is with them, happy as a king. The dismal road seems endless. Oases he thought would be smiling are wretched and he prefers the desert – 'the land of lifeless magnificence, of unbearable lustre.'

'You love what is inhuman,' says Marceline.

The scorching sand irritates her throat. The inhospitable landscape torments her. As soon as they arrive, she goes to bed. The rooms are terrible. She eats nothing. He makes tea for her, but the water is salty and tastes disgusting.

He leaves Marceline and disappears out into the night to Moktir's 'beloved' and makes love to her while her fiancé sits beside them playing with a rabbit. When he returns to the hotel, Marceline has her second lung haemorrhage. She dies that night.

He buries her in El Kantera, where he now lives a solitary and frugal life, making love sometimes with the beautiful dancer Meriem, sometimes with her little brother.

Have I done wrong? That is the question Michel asks his listeners on the roof terrace. In that case how did that wrong begin? Was it when I wanted to regain my health? Was it when I wanted to be strong? Was it when I wanted to be free? Why does this useless freedom I have gained now torment me?

We are not born human. We become that. We become that through solidarity with each other. We become that by taking responsibility.

That is the kind of person I wanted to be. I thought I was that kind of person.

Decisions are made in Paris. They are carried out in the Sahara. Then when the emotions that the name 'Smara' once inspired have vanished, the decision still remains.

I wanted to be Saint-Ex, the flyer who does not abandon a friend in distress in the desert.

I became Vieuchange, the desert wanderer who lies his way into continuing his journey, because he 'had wanted it, in Paris'.

The immorality in *The Immoralist* is not that Michel has changed. One has a right to be changed. The immorality is that he does not dare admit the change. He prefers to become a murderer rather than admit the new being within him.

Is it right then, as Eberhardt writes, that departure is the bravest and most beautiful of all actions?

It is far from always beautiful. But swallow your pride! Admit your defeat! If you have already secretly departed, then admit it – the sooner the better! Your most immoral actions are carried out in order to maintain the illusion of being moral.

The road between Biskra and Touggourt follows an underground flow of water called Oued Rhir. The wells that took their water from the *oued* were fifty to sixty metres deep.

The water carried with it sand and gravel which was removed by the well-divers, *ratassin*. They descended more than thirty metres below the surface of the water and worked there for between 90 and 160 seconds at a time. After completing their task, they were praised as heroes.

During his honeymoon, André Gide arrived in Touggourt on April 7, 1896. There he saw a man being let down to clean out a well sixty metres deep, lined with palm trunks.

'The effort required of these well-divers when they work under the water is incredible,' Gide writes. 'It is said that this man in particular was one of the bravest. He was rewarded with a medal. That evening he went insane.'

Anyone digging a fifty- to sixty-metre well must first get through the upper, unstable layer of sand. The shaft is lined with palm trunks and the space between the trunks filled with a mixture of clay and palm fibre to keep the loose sand out.

Often the well-digger must then get through several layers of polluted water before he reaches the sub-soil water. A watertight passage has to be made straight through the unclean water. Inside this passage, the well-digger works downwards through alternating firm and loose strata until he reaches the hard stone roof of the underground aquifer.

Then the foreman of the well-diggers, *mhallen*, descends to the bottom of the shaft and opens a hole through which the water spurts up and fills the well.

In his journal from Touggourt, Gide says nothing about his

wife's tears. But he describes the bitter taste of the water as it spurts up from the depths and fills the well.

Today, Touggourt receives me with high-tension cables, gasometers, construction cranes – the profile of the modern oasis. A small trickle of European desert maniacs gather at the Hotel Oasis.

Touggourt is the capital of the date world in the Sahara, the anchor in a chain of oases which produces one of the most famous quality dates in the world, 'Fingers of Light' – amber-coloured, almost translucent, with soft, moist and fragrant flesh.

But this is only one kind among thousands. There are date shops in which the vendors are swamped by dates of various kinds, various vintages, from various places, and as distinguished in taste as French cheeses. Having tried only one kind of date, the kind imported into Sweden, is like having eaten only processed cheese from a tube.

Date wholesalers with gigantic warehouses and international distributors have mountains of dates of every colour – brown, yellow, black and red. Most of them are not the sticky Christmas kind, but dry and shrunken everyday dates. The people of the desert eat them like bread. They are often ground into flour. They are not sweet until right inside, by the stone.

Date traders have small stands of poles and sacking alongside the wise old men who sell herbal remedies and plant juices.

I see the white juice of *Launaea spinosa*, supposed to relieve headaches, but also used to exterminate rats. And the small brown angular seeds of *Peganum harmala*, an emetic which causes dreams of paradise. And henbane which is so common in the markets of the Sahara – used to relieve cramps and to dull pain as well as for its narcotic effect, but in larger quantities a deadly poison.

Different, apparently contradictory functions are combined in these modest bland substances. A few grains is the difference between intoxication and insanity, death and healing.

I make tea. It is so strong it's undrinkable. I make some more. That also blackens immediately. Where does the black come from? The answer is there. It is already in the water.

Two small girls are sitting on the floor picking lice out of each other's hair. The reason why they have lice is their arrogance at being human.

I visit a fort nearby. As I get closer, the imposing cannons turn out to be enlargements of old engravings, stuck on cardboard.

I find a note in my pocket which says *Canossa*. It refers to my divorce. I am being punished for my ignorant moralism. I thought those who could no longer love each other were just lazy. But work alone is not enough. Without grace, there is no love.

Michel has concluded his story. His friends remain lying silently on the roof beneath the stars.

Then the silence is unexpectedly broken by Marceline who is with them on the roof, concealed by the dark night.

'Now let me tell you what really happened,' she says. 'I didn't die in Touggourt, as Michel maintains. I'd had enough. I left him.

'Michel had married me to please his father. His mother died when he was fifteen and since then he and his father had lived in a very close and confident relationship. To the extent that the son acquired an old-fashioned air about him.

'He once said he had within him forces "which have retained all their secretive youthfulness". That was laughable coming from a twenty-five-year-old – but as I was married to him, I was able to refrain from laughing.

'After the wedding we went straight to his apartment in Paris, where two separate bedrooms were ready for our wedding night. His father's funeral and the wedding had exhausted Michel, and the honeymoon simply increased his exhaustion. In Tunisia he spat blood, and he arrived in Biskra unconscious. I had hoped to become a mother and found instead I was about to become a widow.

'That was why I loved the children in Biskra. Michel was angry at first, then more and more interested. To me he said with the conventional rhetoric of love: "Marceline, my wife, my life." But he didn't see me, he was looking past me at the Arab boy I had with me, at his tongue which was "rosy pink like a cat's", he said as he leant over and touched his narrow shoulder.

'He never touched me. But it was wonderful to see his will to live come back. He started eating again, he slept by the open window, and he was soon going out for walks with the children.

'During his entire recovery, he was much occupied with his own body. He sunbathed, exercised, looked at himself in the mirror with pleasure. I often wondered what moved inside him, but it appeared to be something vulnerable he wanted to keep to himself. By respecting his secrets – and even his lies – I hoped I would eventually gain his confidence.

'Sexually, I was still taboo to him. He appeared to be impotent. But once when I was out riding in a carriage, the driver had drunk rather too much and the horses bolted. Michel was beside himself with rage and thrashed the man, tied him up and took him back to town. More violence than the situation demanded, I thought; but it had an excellent effect on Michel's manhood. That night I became, as they say, "his".

'Perhaps it was that night which Michel always tried to live over again in our life together, though its reflection grew weaker and weaker for every repetition.

'Nonetheless, I managed to get pregnant. We returned to France and settled on an estate that had belonged to Michel's mother. Then suddenly he began to react to me like a child to his mother. He didn't see me as a fellow human being, but as an authority he had to defy, a supervisor he had to escape from.

'He couldn't remember his childhood, had never had any youth, and now he was slipping out into the woods night after night to partake in a kind of boyish adventure which would have been criminal if it hadn't been directed at himself. I pretended not to notice. I was absorbed in the expectation of the child – until my pregnancy was terminated by a miscarriage .

'When I was nursing Michel during his illness, I already knew, of course, that I was risking infection. And yet it came as a shock to me when I realized that I also had consumption.

80

'Now the tables were turned. Michel nursed me – with a tenderness his sick conscience made hectic and frightening. The more I needed him, the less he needed me. In the middle of his most tender care, he could exclaim: "I loathe compassion. All kinds of infections are concealed inside it. One ought not to feel sympathy for anyone but the strong!"

'Why shouldn't "one"? Because all compassion is as false and exaggerated as what Michel was now showing me? Because an unforced natural sympathy can only be aroused by the strong?

'That certainly isn't true of every "one". My own sympathy is aroused to its most irresistible by the frail and the vulnerable.

'It was because of that I loved Michel, who even in his newly won strength was so frail. I loved precisely what was vulnerable about him, what made him admire strength.

'"Now I understand your faith," I said. "Maybe it is beautiful, but it subjugates the weak."

'"That's just as it should be," he replied swiftly and involuntarily.

'It was horrible to feel the way he observed not only with "anxiety" but also with "expectation" the way my strength was fading. Full of consideration, he was forever taking me to new places which would be better for my health. But those exhausting journeys only took me closer to death – which Michel secretly had begun to long for as part of his own liberation.

'He wanted to go to Biskra. But his return was a terrible disappointment to him.

'Michel was fifteen when his mother died. That seemed to be a boundary he never crossed. As long as Charles, the bailiff's son, was fifteen, he interested Michel, but a year later he suddenly seemed foolish, ugly and indifferent.

'The same with the children in Biskra. Three years ago they had been under fifteen and delightful. Now they were simply repugnant.

'I begged him to stay in Biskra. He wouldn't listen. During the journey to Touggourt, he had eyes only for that boy prostitute fawning for his attention. I was a burden he was about to throw off.

'When he left me in that filthy, fly-blown hotel room and slipped out into the night, with an expression so secretive that it concealed nothing, I had suddenly had enough. I gathered up all my instinct for survival and left him for ever.

'Was that wrong of me? Could I have saved our marriage?

'If so, what should I have done? Can you see any possibility I didn't see?'

81

No, Marceline, I see no possibility.

I think at best your marriage could have been a mutual

pregnancy. Two people becoming pregnant with each other and finally giving birth to each other.

Some pregnancies last longer than others – the elephant's and the whale's. There are marriages which last for decades. But the aim is not to extend the pregnancy at any cost. The aim is that out of inevitable birth pains, two people will rise, each one freer and happier than they could be together.

In your case, there were not two people pregnant, but one. You gave birth to Michel. He could not do the same for you.

82

'In Africa and particularly in the Sahara, there are practically no signs of the presence of oil,' said Gulf's senior geologist in 1949. Seven years later, oil was gushing from a depth of 3,329 metres in Hassi Messaoud. Since then, the poverty-stricken Sahara has supported Algeria.

The road to Hassi Messaoud is lined with bits of black rubber, the corpses of giant tyres that once bore steel pipes, enormous caterpillar track front-loaders, and bulldozers.

Nearer the oil fields, the road crosses a marshalling yard of black oil pipes half buried in the yellow sand. The actual production area can be made out at a great distance, from the light of vast torches and the smoke rising over the horizon – they are burning off the gas, the pressure of which forces the oil up to the surface.

It is a perverse sight; hot flames against an already over-heated sky, brilliant beneath a sun already providing more than enough light.

The town has a small square, with a few quick-growing trees and some concrete benches. The cool winter wind smells of sulphur.

Under a shared metal roof is a row of shop-huts, a small café where they sell a thin brown coffee-like drink and ochre-coloured lemonade, and a little post office where everyone ahead of me is surprised and embarrassed when I take my place at the end of the queue. They solve the problem by leaving. Soon I am at the head of the queue because I am the only one left.

The bookshop is advertising Rabia Ziana's new novel, *The Impossible Happiness* – an appropriate read for a night at the Hotel C.A.S.H. in Hassi Messaoud.

I crawl through the barbed-wire fence into a house which is at the same time half finished and an abandoned ruin. The barbs catch me. It's no use closing my eyes. It's no use covering my eyes. The light penetrates everywhere and so do the barbs.

Then a desert dune drifts in and covers the barbed wire. My lacerated eye sockets fill with flying soft warm sand. It is very pleasant. I was already blind. Now at last I can enjoy it.

André Gide went to North Africa for the first time in 1893. Twelve years earlier, the French had occupied Tunisia. Gide travels in Tunisia without mentioning the occupation. The conquest of Algerian Sahara is at its height. Gide does not mention it. In the occupied oases, military commanders rule like absolute monarchs and the Arab population is kept down with an iron hand. Gide sees nothing.

Others saw. Isabelle Eberhardt saw.

She was in North Africa while Gide was writing *The Immoralist*. She shows in her stories how France takes land from Arab small farmers, forcing them to work for the new French owners – who can't understand why their farm workers go around with such sly, sullen expressions.

She sees how those who object are taken away in chains to the prison in Tadmit. The guards force them to walk barefoot on the ridge of sharp stones formed between the wheeltracks on the road. 'With no verdict from the courts, punished by French administrators or local collaborators, with no chance of appeal, they are sent away to years of lonely suffering, with no hope of mercy.'

For Isabelle, like Gide, North Africa is primarily an erotic experience. When she falls in love with a young Tunisian, she leaves everything and goes with him, although he is a tax collector for the French. But her love affair does not stop her from seeing and reacting:

Everywhere among these poor, dark and recalcitrant tribes, we are given a hostile reception, *she writes*. Si Larb's good heart bleeds for them, and what we are

Gide at Biskra, 1893. (*Collection Roger-Viollet, Paris*)

doing – he out of duty, I out of curiosity – makes us ashamed as if we had committed an outrage.

There is no feeling in Gide that the conquest is an outrage. That doesn't come until the Congo books in the late 1920s. By then Joseph Conrad had taught him to see it.

Conrad and Gide were both in Africa in the early 1890s. Conrad was writing *Heart of Darkness* while Gide was writing *The Immoralist*. They were contemporaries – but it took Gide another thirty years to acquire Conrad's insight.

In *The Immoralist*, the moral conflict is enacted entirely between the husband Michel and the wife Marceline. The novel trembles with her unspoken reproaches and with his pride and shame when he discovers himself. Gide sees no other conflict.

85

'Nietzsche's small change' says the *Encyclopédie Universalis* contemptuously of *The Immoralist*.

Gide read Nietzsche, mad with jealousy at finding in him 'all his most secret thoughts'. An enormous Nietzsche moustache grew on Menalces' face, which had previously looked like Oscar Wilde's. It becomes a 'pirate face' and is given the famous Nietzschean gaze: 'a cold flame indicating more courage and determination than goodness.'

Gide, Saint-Exupéry, Vieuchange and Eberhardt – they have all looked into that gaze. All of them dive in after Nietzsche's small change.

The contempt, however, is unwarranted. Not until the vast wealth of high-flown rhetoric has been cashed into the ordinary small change of a household do we see what it really entails – for me, for you, for all of us.

86

So what was it actually all about?

Over the moonlit terraces, Meriem comes through the tremendous silence of the night, enveloped in a torn white haik.

'I am the "beautiful dancer" Michel lives with,' she says. 'Though, of course, this is a prettified circumlocution. My little brother Ali and I are prostitutes.

'Michel asks you: "Have I done wrong? How in that case did the wrong begin?"

'I reply: the wrong Michel does is naturally not that he wants to be healthy or strong or free. Nor is it that he is homosexual – we North Africans have always taken a more humane view of love between people of the same sex than you in Europe.

'What is shameful isn't there – but in the occupation, which makes love into prostitution and shrouds its crimes in myth.

'Maupassant saw my mother dancing in the Café Joie in Bou Saada. He was one of the first in Europe to spread the rumour about the wonderful wantonness of the Ouled Nail girls: they saved up their dowries by living life's happy days in the brothels.

'Similar legends are spread about the prostitutes in

Bangkok, for the same reason. Customers are given a moral alibi. The legends give an illusion of mutual desire to the exploitation of someone else's poverty.

'Isabelle Eberhardt was not deceived. In fortunate Bou Saada she wrote: "Never before have I been so well aware as here of the weight that hangs over all the occupied areas."

'Bou Saada had quite simply had the misfortune to be the first of the Saharan oases to be conquered by the French. After the conquest, the Ouled Nail tribe continued their resistance for another twenty years. When at last it ceased, the tribe was impoverished and their social network torn apart. War and occupation had led to social anarchy. With the misery also came prostitution, first around the garrisons, then around the tourist hotels.

'When the same thing occurred later in other oases, the legend had already made "Ouled Nail" into a brand name, used by all prostitutes regardless of which tribe they really came from. Many were children, who themselves had been led to believe the myth with which some of the greatest of Europe's writers marketed them.

'Michel's liberation presumes children "far too young, don't you think, to know anything about love?" It presumes child prostitution. That is the fundamental moral problem which is never put into words in *The Immoralist*.

'When my income is insufficient to support the family, my little brother Ali will have to let foreign gentlemen fuck his backside for money. That's what it is about. The rest is romanticism.'

'The journey is a door through which one goes out of the known reality and steps into another, unexplored reality, resembling a dream,' Maupassant writes in his travel accounts from Algeria.

Yes: the reality of the colonies functioned like a dream.

No one had asked the French officers to conquer Laghouat or Zaatcha. Far less had anyone asked the soldiers to massacre the population. No one forced them to do it. It was enough that no one stopped them. They were simply given an opportunity which they were unable to resist.

They took it – in the same way as Saint-Ex, Vieuchange, Loti, Eberhardt and Gide took the opportunity to step into their far more innocent dreams.

For them, the colonies were an arena in which they were able to *live out* everything not socially accepted in their own countries.

It is doubtful whether the colonies ever produced either the power or the income their supporters hoped for and advocated them in expectation of. But in the spiritual life of Europe, the colonies had an important function – as a safety vent, as an escape, a place to misbehave.

Like the dream, the colonies offered a refuge away from the demands of their own society, an outlet for the cruelty and self-importance not tolerated in Europe. Not yet tolerated.

In the colonies, while one represented the highpoint of civilization, it was possible to escape much of civilization's unpleasantness: the banality of the bourgeoisie, the *tristesse* of marriage, the inhibiting control of impulse – and become party to mass murder, child abuse, sexual orgies and other expressions of urges which at home largely found their outlets in dreams.

Maupassant alludes to it. Gide's *The Immoralist* is an indication of it. But apart from Conrad, of course, which of the writers of the epoch expressed it in art? Who is prepared even today to dive into this dark well and clean it out?

The Well-divers

88

Timimoun is the only oasis in the Sahara where I could imagine myself living.

I like the narrow winding alleys constantly changing direction to avoid the pursuing rays of the sun. The houses form bridges across the narrow shafts of streets, the streets becoming tunnels, the courtyards as deep as wells down which the sun cannot penetrate. The windows are narrow apertures, so deep the sun cannot shoot in through them. Over the centuries, innovations have built on the basic principle of desert architecture: defence against the sun.

I love the shimmering blue dragonflies hovering above the green flowering water of irrigation pools, a promising murmuring, rippling, gurgling everywhere. The water runs through a complicated system of gullies criss-crossing each other, branching out or merging. Black men plant cabbages in the soft silt.

I love the salt-white plains round Timimoun and the hour-glass fine sand. I love the mountains with their long red roots of sand. I love the new-moon dunes, shaped like sickles with sharp, wind-polished edges.

The car's shadow with its high wobbling wheels seems cut out of a comic strip as I return to Timimoun at sunset through a sea of dunes.

I would like to come back here always. I would like to spend the winters at the El Gourara hotel with my word processor and a small disc library of the classics of modern egoism from Hobbes to Huysmans. And soon all the other works 'on line' from all the national libraries and databases of Europe. Plus a discarded, bound and thumbed old desert novel by Pierre Loti.

That is my desert romanticism.

I would live here undisturbed by human complications, without love but also without pain.

Live off bread and dates, watching the wheatear and the desert crow, listening to the palm doves as they grumble, tut-tutting in the date grove. Sitting in the sunrise looking out over the salt marshes and enjoying the monotony and silence of the desert.

89

I have a bell. A copper sheep-bell. All round me in the great expanses of landscape I can hear the loud clanging of many different sheep-bells, some far off in the distance, others quite near.

Only my bell doesn't clang.

I feel inside it with my fingers and find a soft rag wound round the clapper.

It's a mangled, threadbare old towel, initials embroidered on it in blue, my mother's initials, which are also mine. I recognize the towel easily; as a boy, when I longed for love, I used to wrap it round my member and liberate myself into it.

90

A Swedish officer called Thorsten Orre wrote *Sketches from the Desert*, the first ever Swedish desert book, and he lived here in Timimoun.

I read Orre in the days when you could borrow two books 'for pleasure', but as many non-fiction, 'fact books', as you liked.

With this rationing system, Swedish libraries laid in my contemporaries the foundations of the often lifelong conviction that non-fiction was not 'for pleasure', that reality as an experience was always inferior to fiction.

Orre was one writer to help me out of that dogma. No fantasies ever matched his facts.

In a small village south of Timimoun, Orre met a man by the name of Abdelkader Ben Mohammed Omar, his professional title *rtass* – a thin, wretched thirty-year-old who looked fifty. He was also as good as deaf: both eardrums had been perforated. He was the last surviving well-diver.

Abdelkader undressed and tied a cloth around his hips, then greased his body with butter, stuffed tallowed camel wool into his ears and recited his prayer.

A well-diver at work.

The well to be cleaned was only eight metres deep. Orre measured the rope which fastened the basket. A heavy stone was put into the basket and lowered to the bottom. Abdelkader went over to the well and placed himself astride it, then thrusting his feet against the inside of the wall, he climbed down to water level.

There he took a deep breath, clapped his feet together and let himself sink.

The others stayed around the well, silent and grave. The work of the *rtass* is full of danger. He wears his life out in advance. Although a slave, or almost a slave, he is regarded as holy.

Orre stands with a watch in his hand. After twenty seconds of breathless silence, the rope begins to jerk as if someone were climbing up it. A cloud of bubbles rises to the surface and then Abdelkader's head appears.

He gets out of the well, wraps his *burnus* round him and watches in silence as the others hoist up the basket, now full to the brim with sludge from the bottom of the well.

He dives five times in a row that morning. In the afternoon, he again descends into the well and continues working. After his last dive, he goes to one side, dries himself thoroughly and sits down in the blazing sun with his back against a palm tree. His whole body is still shuddering.

91

I also shuddered.

I was afraid of wells. At Sunday School, I could hardly bear to listen when the brothers threw Joseph into the well. I looked down into the dark depths. I tasted the icy water. I sensed the absolute loneliness down there. I – who didn't even dare dive head first from the edge of the swimming pool – how could I read about the wells of the desert without becoming that diver myself?

It was always me, emaciated, marked by death, my eardrums already perforated from the tremendous pressure, who dived down to the bottom of the well to clean it out.

92

Götgat Hill has been transformed by the bulldozers into a deep shaft. I start climbing outside the milk bar at the foot of the hill. I am small but quite strong. I hold firmly onto the edge of the pavement and find good support for my feet from the stones and protruding iron girders. The situation looks hopeful.

But the pavement gets narrower, and by about halfway I am climbing directly on foundations of houses, like a façade climber, while at the same time the chasm below me grows deeper and deeper.

When the house foundations come to an end at Urväder Alley, I have nothing but loose gravel ahead of me and I can't go any further. Nor can I go back.

I am left suspended like the victorious Renaissance man in Leonardo's drawing, but am actually quite helpless, incapable of moving either hand or foot from their fragile holds.

The only thing that can save me now is a new ESCARP-MENT – the word itself comes as a great relief and subdues my panic. *If only* the entire universe would tilt like a motorbike on a corner, the centre of gravity would no longer pull me down into death, but would keep me there so that I could slowly crawl up the wall of the house.

Why not? I think. A great many hopes presumed to be the basis of our salvation are less reasonable than that.

93

I drive east towards El Golea. So little happens on this road that each well is marked by its name and depth on the map.

Because each individual moment in the desert is monotonous, it is assumed that it will always go on being monotonous in the same way. That is a mistake. There are a thousand different ways of being monotonous and the desert knows them all.

The emptiness draws you to it like a vacuum. I suddenly remember the smell of wood stacks, and the smell of trains in the days when compartment windows were shut with a leather strap hanging in a dark-brown perforated tongue below the window. And the delicate sound of my father's razor as he stropped the blade . . .

The damp cold in the earth cellar when you enter it to take the muslin covers off the bowls of soured milk. From the musty air in there, I suddenly step out into the warm summer smell of flowers. I close both doors behind me and replace the hasp, which is made of wood. The nettles on both sides of the narrow path are high and menacing. Holding the bowl of soured milk out in front, I hunch up my shoulders and walk between the nettles straight out into summer . . .

In a cloud of memories, I stopped the car at the last of the named wells, *Inhal*, the water in which is said to be '*bonne, abondante, à 12 m*'. Deep down there in the darkness of the well, the surface gleamed, covered in a film of dead insects.

There was neither rope nor chain at the well-head. You are supposed to take your own rope with you. Otherwise you die of thirst by a well of that kind. If you fall in you are lost.

If you fall in . . .

Suddenly I remember the ball, the pail, the rough walls, Edgar and Valter's faces as they disappeared above . . .

Suddenly I remember it all.

94

In my childhood, open wells were common in the Swedish countryside. The water was hauled up in a pail fastened by a rope or a chain to a balancing lever.

All parents warned their children about the well. That was just about as realistic as warning them about the traffic today. When the lid of the well was off, it was strictly forbidden to play by the well. But as soon as we played ball, the ball was drawn in that direction by some mysterious force and often vanished down into the hole. Many a time have I seen the ball floating on the dark gleaming water down there and stood fishing for it with the pail.

When we failed to retrieve it in that way, one of us had to sit on the pail and be lowered down. Edgar was eldest, so went first. Valter was youngest and went down next. The third time, I could hardly refuse.

I sat on the pail, clutching onto the chain. With a jerk, I shot up in the air when Edgar seized the other end of the lever. Valter grabbed the chain and swung it round towards the well. I hung there slowly twirling above the well opening. My expression must have shown that I was about to burst into tears, had changed my mind and no longer wanted to do this. They stopped for a moment, waiting for me to say something. But I said nothing. Then they began slowly lowering me down the shaft. The longer the chain became between me and Valter, the more the pail spun around, first in one direction, then the other, so that I bounced against the sharp flintstone walls of the well. My hands shook. It was only six or seven metres down to the water, but I daren't look down. Nor did I dare look at the white hole up there growing smaller and smaller and further and further away. Supposing I let go? Supposing I let go! Who would save me down here? It was already too cramped for one person, let alone two. And Valter would never be able to lift both Edgar and me. Now I was down there! My feet and the seat of my trousers were already in the icy water. Now I had to let go with one hand to try and reach the ball. The cramped space suddenly seemed enormous, the ball constantly dancing away. The boys up there tried to move the chain so that I could get nearer the ball. The result was that I swung like a pendulum between the well walls and had to grab the chain with both hands again. I suddenly slipped down half a metre and was seized with panic. I thought I was lost, but they had only ducked me. I still had my head above water. The ball came floating towards me and when I pressed my arms together, it caught in my grip.

'I've got it!' I cried, and they started pulling me up. I sat curled up with the ball against my stomach and chest, twirling around, bouncing through the shaft.

In the Sahara there were wells ten times as deep. In the Sahara it is a profession, the *rtass*'s, descending into wells of that kind and continuing, diving below the surface of the water to clean them out.

There is a book of life which can be read in two directions. I read it from the beginning. Then my lips begin to twitch. Quite out of my control, my lips keep trembling against each other. The unpleasant feeling of the actual trembling is made almost unbearable by the sensitive surfaces of my lips rubbing against each other. To relieve it, I try to tremble with my mouth open, but at once it dries up and starts cracking.

Not until I turn the book over and start reading it from the back do my lips grow still and the twitching stops just as suddenly as it had begun.

In the low light of the morning sun, I drive between sabre dunes and star dunes on towards Ouargla. The sand trickles and murmurs across the road, like the film of water trickling down the butcher's shop window when I was small.

The entire landscape is based on that contrast: the heavy, firm, dark gravel lying there, sweating desert varnish and being baked together into the rigid base on which the light, bright, mobile sand appears, as fine as pollen and soft as velvet.

Here and there a few sparse twigs of broom are scattered in the sand, sometimes gathered into bushes resembling punk hair styles.

Ouargla has been a town since the sixteenth century. For a long time it was the southernmost post in the French Empire, the starting point for the great Saharan expeditions.

Today, Ouargla is the administrative centre for the oil-rich area of the south. But there are also half a million date palms in the oases and almost as many in the suburbs.

The old houses in Ouargla are built in the characteristic style which in the Sahara goes by the name 'Sudanese'. The material resembles clay, the shapes are soft and organic, the houses apparently growing like fungi or rising like dough. The windows are diagonal slices in the thick fabric of the walls. 'As if the rays of the sun had sliced their way through the walls,' I think – but the cuts are naturally placed counter-clockwise in order to let in as little sun as possible.

At the El Mehri hotel, the starter consists of spaghetti with bread, the main course rice and potatoes. But they play Beethoven's Fifth during the meal and my table napkin is so heavy and moist that when I put it on my lap I can feel the chill right through my clothes.

This dampness is not because the weather in the Sahara isn't good for drying – it is the desert's re-ordering of all values. Damp is the very best. The Sahara has taught me to love the weight and coolness of a really wet table napkin to the sound of Beethoven's Fifth.

After dinner, I go down to the hotel yard as usual for a last check on the car locks and lights. The car park guard has made a small fire of yellow seed-cases and date palm leaves. We start talking.

He was born a *ghattasin*, as the well-divers are called in Ouargla.

'They say we are descendants of prisoners who were sentenced to death. The Turks let them choose between being executed immediately or becoming well-divers in the Sahara. When they came here, they were forced down the wells. But their children and grandchildren were the first to become truly skilled, we who were trained from an early age for this difficult work.

'During the war of liberation, the French tortured their prisoners by holding their heads under water until they almost suffocated. Perhaps you've heard about it? Well, that's also a way of training a child to become a well-diver.

'Many died, so many that the shortage of well-divers threatened to leave the oases deserted.

'"Our children aren't tough enough," the old men said, those who had survived. "May He-who-makes-all-miracles have mercy on us, otherwise the pitiable performance of our children will bury the entire oasis in sand."

'It was the French who saved us from slavery in the wells by their deep drilling. That's also a side of the French Empire that oughtn't to be forgotten.

'The deep bore was first tried in Ghardaia in the late 1890s. They drilled down to 320 metres without finding water.

'The first kilometre-deep borehole was made in Touggourt in 1927, with no result.

'Here in Ouargla, they drilled down just as deeply, again in vain.

'The first successful borehole was made in Zelfana near Ouargla in 1946.

'Like most *ghattasin*, I was trained as a digger as well as a diver. The most dangerous part of digging was the geyser-like eruptions of water which arose when we broke through the sandstone roof at great depths. Here in Ouargla, the water-bearing stratum is under enormous pressure and many *ghattasin* died in accidents of that kind. But in 1946, they stopped digging wells with those risky old methods.

'What remained was the task of cleaning the existing wells. We used tallow to plug our ears and nostrils, and descended to great depths. It was dangerous and painful work with low social status, even lower than the status of the Haratin outcasts. Before we had been praised as the heroes of the oases, but in the days of well-borers, we were no longer as important.

'When the oil began to flow in Hassi Messaoud, many of the *ghattasin* changed identity and became oil workers. It's a less risky and better-paid profession, with high status.

'I myself became a truck driver. I learnt French from the French. I drove the Hassi Messaoud to Constantine route. But I've also driven to places as far away as Insalah and Tammanrasset, and once went to Zinder. I've seen the desert.

'I've had two wives. I have five sons, all employed by the oil company. Now I'm the car park guard here at the hotel. It's a good job for an old man. I look back on an eventful life (*une vie substantielle*). I am glad I survived the horrors of childhood. I'm glad I didn't have to torment my children in the same way.'

The Sahara's water problems appear to have been solved once and for all. Today they bore down to four thousand metres, extracting water which is fifty degrees Celsius. Ouargla is supplied with fifteen thousand litres a minute.

But there is a difference between water and water.

'The water in the wells we used to dig and clean came from self-renewing sources. The fifteen-thousand-litres-a-minute the oases use today are non-renewable. They say it has come trickling through the base rock of the Atlas mountains, two hundred miles north. It has been on its way for thirty-five thousand years.

'So every litre used takes thirty-five thousand years to replace with a new litre of water.

'That worries me. Sometimes I wonder whether the real future profession in the Sahara will be oil-drilling or well-diving.'

That is what he said. Now I know. But what I was looking for – where is that?

I haven't dared talk about myself. I am still hiding. I am evading death, the door of childhood and dreams is open only a crack. Almost everything remains.

I am small. My hand has five fingers. With them, I hold life in a firm grip.

I grow and my fingers fire shoots. They branch out like cacti. Every branch seems to provide new possibilities. I reach out more, grasp more.

But soon my hand is so full of fingers that they are completely occupied coping with each other. Whatever they are gripping glides away and disappears in the crush.

I realize what is happening and set about thinning out my fingers like carrots in the vegetable garden.

It takes longer than I had calculated. It turns out to be a labour without end.

Then suddenly I am small again. Once more my hand has five fingers.

With them, I take a firm grip on empty air. What I am trying to grasp has come to an end.

Notes

To Tarfaya:
Chet Raymo, *The Crust of our Earth*, Englewood Cliffs, 1983.
Curtis Cate, *Antoine de Saint-Exupéry, His Life and Times*,
    London, 1970.
Antoine de Saint Exupéry, *Oeuvres*, Bibliothèque de la Pléiade,
    1959.
John Mercer, *Spanish Sahara*, London, 1976.
Tony Hodges, *Western Sahara*, Westport USA, 1983

To Smara:
Michel Vieuchange, *Smara the Forbidden City*, London, 1933.

To Laghouat:
Eugène Fromentin, *Un été dans le Sahara*, with introduction
    and notes by Anne-Marie Christin, Paris, 1982.
    Oeuvres complètes, Bibliothèque de la Pléiade, 1984.
James Thompson and Barbara Wright, *La vie et l'oeuvre
    d'Eugène Fromentin*, Paris, 1987.

To Ain Sefra:

Christian Genet, *Pierre Loti – l'enchanteur*, Poitiers, 1988.

Alain Quella-Villéger, *Pierre Loti, l'incompris*, Paris, 1986.

Lesley Blanch, *Pierre Loti, Portrait of an Escapist*, London, 1983.

Isabelle Eberhardt, *Oeuvres complètes* I, Paris, 1988.

Edmonde Charles-Roux, *Un désir d'Orient, la jeunesse d'Isabelle Eberhardt*, Paris, 1988.

Isabelle Eberhardt, *The Passionate Nomad*, London, 1987.
Vagabond, London, 1988.
The Oblivion Seekers, San Francisco, 1982.

Cecily Mackworth, *The Destiny of Isabelle Eberhardt*, New York, 1975, 1986.

Annette Kobak, *Isabelle*, London, 1988.

Lesley Blanch, *The Wilder Shores of Love*, London, 1954, 1984.

The Immoralist:

André Gide, *Romans, Journal 1, Journal 2*, Bibliothèque de la Pléiade.

Pierre de Boisdeffre, *Vie d'André Gide*, Paris, 1970.

Claude Martin, *La maturité d'André Gide*, Paris, 1977.

Yousset Nacib, *Cultures oasiennes, Bou-saada – essai d'histoire sociale*, Algiers, 1986.

'Exterminate
All the Brutes'

To Olof Lagercrantz
who traveled with *Heart of Darkness*
and Etienne Glaser
who was Adolf in *Hitler's Childhood*

'All Jews and Negroes ought really to be exterminated. We shall be victorious. The other races will disappear and die out.'

WHITE ARYAN RESISTANCE, SWEDEN, 1991

'You may wipe us out, but the children of the stars can never be dogs.'

SOMABULANO, RHODESIA, 1896

Contents

PREFACE

THIS IS a story, not a contribution to historical research. It is the story of a man traveling by bus through the Saharan desert and, at the same time, traveling by computer through the history of the concept of extermination. In small, sand-ridden desert hotels, his study closes in on one sentence in Joseph Conrad's *Heart of Darkness*: "Exterminate all the brutes."

Why did Kurtz end his report on the civilizing task of the white man in Africa with these words? What did they mean to Conrad and his contemporaries? Why did Conrad make them stand out as a summary of all the high-flown rhetoric on Europe's responsibilities to the peoples of other continents?

I thought I had the answer to these questions when in 1949, at the age of seventeen, I first read *Heart of Darkness*. Behind the "black shadows of disease and starvation" in the Grove of Death I saw in my mind's eye the emaciated survivors of the German death camps, which had been liberated only a few years earlier. I read Conrad as a prophetic author who had foreseen all the horrors that were to come.

Hannah Arendt knew better. She saw that Conrad was writing about the genocides of his own time. In her first book, *The Origins of Totalitarianism* (1951), she showed how imperialism necessitated racism as the only possible excuse for its deeds. "Lying under anybody's nose were many of the elements which gathered together could create a totalitarian government on the basis of racism."

Her thesis that Nazism and Communism were of the same stock has been well remembered. However, many forget that she also held the "terrible massacres" and "wild murdering" of European imperialists responsible for "the triumphant introduction of such means of pacification into ordinary, respectable foreign policies," thereby fathering totalitarianism and its genocides.

In the first volume of *The Holocaust in Historical Context* (1994), Steven T. Katz has begun a demonstration of the "phenomenological uniqueness" of the Holocaust. On some of his seven hundred pages, he speaks with contempt for those who have instead emphasized the similarities. Sometimes, though, he is more tolerant and says, "Their approach might be called, nonpejoratively, a paradigm of similarity; mine, in contrast, is a paradigm of distinctiveness."

The two approaches seem to me equally valid and complementary. My desert traveler, employing a paradigm of similarity, finds that Europe's destruction of the "inferior races" of four continents prepared the ground for Hitler's destruction of six million Jews in Europe.

Each of these genocides had, of course, its own unique characteristics. However, two events need not be identical for one of them to facilitate the other. European world expansion, accompanied as it was by a shameless defense of extermination, created habits of thought and political precedents that made way for new outrages, finally culminating in the most horrendous of them all: the Holocaust.

PART I

1

You already know enough. So do I. It is not knowledge we lack. What is missing is the courage to understand what we know and to draw conclusions.

2

Tademait, "desert of deserts," is the deadest area of the Sahara. No sign of vegetation. Life all but extinct. The ground is covered with that black, shiny desert varnish the heat has pressed out of the stone.

The night bus, the only one between El Goléa and In Salah, with a little luck, takes seven hours. You fight your way to a seat in competition with a dozen or so soldiers in crude army boots who have learned their queuing technique in the close-combat school of the Algerian army in Sidi-bel-Abbès. Anyone carrying under one arm the core of European thought stored on an old-fashioned computer is obviously handicapped.

At the turnoff toward Timmimoun, hot potato soup and bread are served through a hole in the wall. Then the shattered asphalt comes to an end and the bus continues through roadless desert.

It is pure rodeo. The bus behaves like a young bronco. With windows rattling and springs screeching, it rocks, stamps, and leaps forward, and every jolt is transmitted to the hard disk I have on my lap as well as to the stack of swaying building blocks that are my spinal disks. When it is no longer possible to sit, I hang on to the roof rack or squat down.

This is what I had feared. This is what I have longed for.

The night is fantastic beneath the moon. Hour after hour, the white desert pours past: stone and sand, stone and gravel, gravel and sand—all gleaming like snow. Hour after hour. Nothing happens until a signal suddenly flares up in the darkness as a sign for one of the passengers to stop the bus, get off, and start walking, straight out into the desert.

The sound of his footsteps disappears into the sand. He himself disappears. We also disappear into the white darkness.

3

The core of European thought? Yes, there is one sentence, a short simple sentence, only a few words, summing up the history of our continent, our humanity, our biosphere, from Holocene[1] to Holocaust.

It says nothing about Europe as the original home on earth of humanism, democracy, and welfare. It says nothing about everything we are quite rightly proud of. It simply tells the truth we prefer to forget.

I have studied that sentence for several years. I have collected quantities of material that I never have time to go through. I would like to disappear into this desert, where no one can reach me, where I have all the time in the world, to disappear and not return until I have understood what I already know.

4

I get off in In Salah.

The moon is no longer shining. The bus takes its light with it and vanishes. The darkness all round me is compact.

It was outside In Salah that the Scottish explorer Alexander Gordon Laing was attacked and robbed. He had five saber cuts on the crown of his head and three on the left temple. One on his left cheekbone fractured his jaw bone and divided his ear. A dreadful gash in his neck scratched his windpipe, a bullet in his hip grazed his spine, five saber cuts on his right arm and hand, three fingers broken, the wrist bones cut through, and so on.[2]

Somewhere far away in the darkness is a glimpse of a fire. I start lugging my heavy word processor and my even heavier suitcase in the direction of the light.

Banks of red wind-driven sand cross the road, the loose sand gathering into drifts on the slope. I take ten steps, then ten more. The light does not come any nearer.

Laing was attacked in January 1825. But fear is timeless. In the seventeenth century, Thomas Hobbes was just as frightened of solitude, of the night and death, as I am. "Some men are of so cruel a nature," he said to his friend Aubrey, "as to take a delight in killing men more than you should to kill a bird."[3]

The fire still seems just as distant. Shall I dump the computer and suitcase in order to be able to move on more easily? No, I sit down in the dust to await the dawn.

Down there, close to the ground, a breeze suddenly brings the fragrance of burning wood.

Do desert scents seem so strong because they are so rare? Is the desert firewood more concentrated, so it burns more fragrantly? What is sure is that the fire that seems so distant to the eye suddenly reaches my nose.

I get up and struggle on.

When I finally reach the men crouching around the fire, it is with a great feeling of victory.

Greet them. Ask them. And am told that I am going completely the wrong way. There is nothing to do but turn back, they say.

I follow my tracks back to the place where I got off the bus. Then I go south in the same darkness.

"Fear always remains," says Conrad. "A man may destroy every-thing within himself, love and hate and belief, and even doubt, but as long as he clings to life, he cannot destroy fear."[4]

Hobbes would have agreed. In that they shake hands across the centuries.

Why do I travel so much when I am so terribly frightened of traveling?

Perhaps in fear we seek an increased perception of life, a more potent form of existence? I am frightened, therefore I exist. The more frightened I am, the more I exist?

6

There is only one hotel in In Salah, the large and expensive state-owned Tidikelt Hotel, which, when I finally find it, has nothing to offer except a small, dark, icy cold room in which the heating devices have long since ceased functioning.

Things are just as usual in the Sahara: the smell of strong disin-fectant, the screech of the door's unoiled hinge, the blind half torn down. I recognize so well the rickety table, its fourth leg too short, and the film of sand on the surface of the table, on the pillow and the wash bowl. I recognize the tap that slowly starts dripping when you turn it full on, until after filling half a glass it gives up with a weary sigh. I recognize the bed made up with such mili-tary firmness that it never allows for feet, anyhow not at an angle from legs, and anchors half the bedclothes under the bed so that the blanket only reaches your navel all to preserve the bed linen's virginity.

OK, perhaps one has to travel. But why exactly here?

7

The sound of heavy blows from a club, falling on the larynx. A crackling sound like eggshells, and then a gurgling when they desperately try to get some air.

Toward morning I wake at last, still in my outdoor clothes. The bed is red with the sand I have brought with me from the bus. Each blow still crushes a larynx. The last one will crush mine.

8

The hotel is embedded in drifting sand, alone by a deserted road across a deserted plain. I plod out into the deep sand. The sun hammers down relentlessly. The light is as blinding as darkness. The air against my face is like thin ice crackling.

It takes half an hour to walk to the post office, which is equally far from the bank and the market. The old town huddles together, inaccessible to sun and sandstorms, but the new town is spread out thinly, with modern town planning, doing its best to maximize the desolation of the Sahara.

The reddish brown clay facades of the center of town are enlivened by white pillars and portals, white pinnacles and copings. The style is called Sudanese, black, after *"Bled es sudan,"* the country of the blacks. In actual fact, it is an imaginary style, created by the French for the 1900 Great Exhibition in Paris, then planted out here in the Sahara. The modern town is gray international-style concrete.

The wind is blowing from the east. I have it stinging in my face as I return to the hotel, where long-distance truck drivers and foreigners dominate, all on their way "upward" or "downward," as if on a staircase. All of them inquire of the others about the road, about gas, about equipment, all of them occupied with the thought of moving on as quickly as possible.

I tape the map up on the wall and consider the distances. It is 170 miles to the nearest oasis in the west, Reggane. It is 240 miles of desert road to the nearest oasis in the north, El Goléa, from which I have just come. It is 250 miles as the crow flies to the nearest oasis in the east, Bordj Omar Driss. It is 400 miles to the nearest oasis in the south, Tamanrasset. It is 600 miles as the crow flies to the nearest sea, the Mediterranean, and 800 miles as the crow flies to the nearest river, the Niger. It is 900 miles to the sea in the west. Eastward the sea is so far away, it doesn't matter.

Every time I see the distances surrounding me, every time I realize that here, at the zero point of the desert, is where I am, a stab of delight goes through my body. That is why I stay.

9

If I could only get the computer to work! The question is whether it has survived the jolting and the dust. The disks are no larger than postcards. I have a hundred of them, in airtight packs, a whole library that together weighs no more than a single book.

At any time I can go anywhere in history, from the dawn of paleontology, when Thomas Jefferson still found it unfathomable that one single species could disappear out of the economy of nature, to today's realization that 99.99 percent of all species have died out, most of them in a few mass exterminations that came close to wiping out all life.[5]

The disk weighs five grams. I put it in the slot and switch on. The screen flares up and the sentence I have been investigating for so long glows up at me in the darkness of the room.

The word Europe comes from a Semitic word that simply means "darkness."[6] The sentence glowing there on the screen is truly European. The thought was long on its way before finally being put into words at the turn of the century (1898–1899) by a Polish writer who often thought in French but wrote in English: Joseph Conrad.

Kurtz, the main character in Conrad's *Heart of Darkness*, completes his essay on the civilizing task of the white man among the savages of Africa with a postscript summarizing the true content of his high-flown rhetoric.

It is this sentence radiating toward me now on the screen: "Exterminate all the brutes."

10

The Latin *extermino* means "drive over the border," *terminus*, "exile, banish, exclude." Hence the English *exterminate*, which means "drive over the border to death, banish from life."

Swedish has no direct equivalent. Swedes have to say *utrota*, although that is really quite a different word, "root out," which in English is *extirpate*, from the Latin *stirps*, "root, tribe, family."

In both English and Swedish, the object of the action is seldom a single individual, but usually whole groups, such as quitchgrass, rats, or people. Brutes, of course, reduces the object to its mere animal status.

Africans have been called beasts ever since the very first contacts, when Europeans described them as "rude and beastlie," "like to brute beasts," and "more brutish than the beasts they hunt."[7]

11

Some years ago, I thought I had found the source of Conrad's phrase in the great liberal philosopher Herbert Spencer.

He writes in *Social Statics* (1850) that imperialism has served civilization by clearing the inferior races off the earth. "The forces which are working out the great scheme of perfect happiness, taking no account of incidental suffering, exterminate such sections of mankind as stand in their way. . . . Be he human or be he brute—the hindrance must be got rid of."[8]

Here were both the civilizing rhetoric of Kurtz and the two key words *exterminate* and *brute*, and the human being was expressly placed on an equal footing with the animal as an object for extermination.

I thought I had made a neat little scholarly discovery, worthy of being taken up one day as a footnote in the history of literature, Kurtz's sentence "explained" by Spencer's fantasies of annihilation. They in their turn, I thought, were personal eccentricities, perhaps explained by the fact that all Spencer's siblings had died when he was a child. A calm and comforting conclusion.

12

It soon turned out that Spencer was by no means alone in his interpretation. It was common and, during the second half of the nineteenth century, became even more common, so that the German philosopher Eduard von Hartmann was able to write the following in the second volume of his *Philosophy of the Unconscious*, which Conrad read in an English translation: "As little as a favor is done the dog whose tail is to be cut off, when one cuts it off gradually inch by inch, so little is their humanity in artificially prolonging the death struggles of savages who are on the verge of extinction. . . . The true philanthropist, if he has comprehended the natural law of anthropological evolution, cannot avoid desiring an acceleration of the last convulsion, and labor for that end."[9]

At the time, it was almost a platitude Hartmann had put into words. Neither he nor Spencer were personally inhuman. But their Europe was.

The idea of extermination lies no farther from the heart of humanism than Buchenwald lies from the Goethehaus in Weimar. That insight has been almost completely repressed, even by the Germans, who have been made sole scapegoats for ideas of extermination that are actually a common European heritage.

A battle over the living past is going on at present in Germany. This *Historikerstreit*, as they call it, concerns the question: Is the Nazi extermination of the Jews unique or not?

The German historian Ernst Nolte has called "the so-called extermination of the Jews by the Third Reich" "a reaction or a distorted copy and not an original action." The original was, according to Nolte, the extermination of the Kulaks in the Soviet Union and Stalin's purges in the 1930s. They were what Hitler copied.

The idea that the extermination of the Kulaks *caused* the extermination of the Jews seems to have been abandoned, and many people emphasize that all historical events are unique and not copies of each other. But they can be compared. Thus both likenesses and differences arise between the extermination of the Jews and other mass murders, from the massacre of the Armenians at the beginning of the 1900s to the more recent atrocities of Pol Pot.

But in this debate no one mentions the German extermination of the Herero people in southwest Africa during Hitler's childhood. No one mentions the corresponding genocide by the French, the British, or the Americans. No one points out that during Hitler's childhood, a major element in the European view of mankind was the conviction that "inferior races" were by nature condemned to extinction: the true compassion of the superior races consisted in helping them on the way.

All German historians participating in this debate seem to look in the same direction. None looks to the west. But Hitler did. What Hitler wished to create when he sought *Lebensraum* in the east was a continental equivalent of the British Empire. It was in the British and other western European peoples that he found the models, of which the extermination of the Jews is, in Nolte's words, "a distorted copy."[10]

AN OUTPOST OF PROGRESS

"Exterminating All the Niggers"

14

On June 22, 1897, the same year *Lebensraum* was born in Germany, British expansionist policy reached its peak.[11] The greatest empire in the history of the world celebrated itself with unequaled arrogance.

Representatives of all the peoples and territories subjugated by the British, almost a quarter of the earth and its inhabitants, gathered in London to pay tribute to Queen Victoria on the sixtieth anniversary of her ascension to the throne.[12]

At the time there was a journal called *Cosmopolis*, which was aimed at cultivated people all over Europe, with untranslated contributions in German, French, and English.

To this cultivated European audience, Queen Victoria was compared with Darius, Alexander the Great and Augustus, but none of these emperors of antiquity was able to demonstrate such expansion as Victoria had.

Her empire had grown by three and a half million square miles and a hundred and fifty million subjects. It had caught up with and surpassed China, which, with her four hundred millions had hitherto been considered the most populous realm in the world.

Perhaps the other great powers in Europe had not sufficiently understood the military strength of the British Empire, it was said. There was more fighting instinct and military spirit in the British than in any other nation. As far as the navy was concerned, the empire had not only superiority, but supremacy over the high seas.

The British had not let themselves be intoxicated by their successes, but maintained a humble recognition that these results — perhaps unparalleled in history — were due to the grace and favor of Almighty God.

Also, of course, to the person of the queen. The moral strength of her character could not perhaps be measured with scientific precision, but its influence was obviously enormous.

"Today's ceremony," said one commentator, "means more, they think, than any triumph that has ever been celebrated: more national vitality, more commerce, more reclamation of wilderness, more suppression of savagery, more peace, more liberty. This is not bombast, it is statistic. . . ."

"The British nation seemed deliberately to determine to regard its vast power, its colonising success, its vital unity, its world-wide territory, and to glory in them."

"We were never so strong, the shouts meant. Let all the world realise that we mean to be not less so in the future."

Cosmopolis's German and French contributors joined in the chorus of rejoicing. So the story introducing the journal's jubilee issue has an unprecedented shock effect.

15

The story is about two Europeans, Kayerts and Carlier, who have been dumped by a cynical company director at a small trading post by the great river.

Their reading matter is a yellowed newspaper that praises in high-flown language "our colonial expansion." As in the jubilee issue of *Cosmopolis*, the colonies are made out to be sacred work in the service of Civilization. The article extolled the merits of those bringing light, faith, and trade to "the dark places" of the earth.

At first the two companions believe these fine words. But gradually they discover that words are nothing but "sounds." The sounds lack content outside the society that created them. As long as there is a policeman on the street corner, as long as there is food to buy in the shops, as long as the general public sees you — only then do your sounds constitute morality. Conscience presumes society.

But soon Kayerts and Carlier are ready to do trade in slaves and mass murder. When supplies run out, they quarrel over a lump of sugar. Kayerts flees for his life in the belief that Carlier is after him with a gun. When they suddenly bump into each other, Kayerts shoots in self-defense and does not realize until later that in his panic he has killed an unarmed man.

But what does that matter? Concepts such as "virtue" and "crime" are nothing but sounds. People die every day by the thousands, Kayerts thinks, as he sits by the body of his companion, perhaps by hundreds of thousands—who knows? One more or less was of little importance—at least not to a thinking creature.

He, Kayerts, is a thinking creature. Hitherto, like the rest of mankind, he has gone around believing a lot of nonsense. Now for the first time he is really thinking. Now he knows and draws the conclusion from what he knows.

When morning comes, the mist is shattered by an inhuman, vibrating shriek. The company steamer, which both men have been waiting for for months, has returned.

The director of the great Civilization Company goes ashore and finds Kayerts hanging from the cross on his predecessor's grave. He is hanging, it seems, to attention, but even in death sticks out his tongue at his managing director.

16

Not only at the director. Kayerts is sticking out his swollen black tongue at the whole of the jubilee celebrations going on in the newspaper columns around the story, at all of the triumphant imperial ideology.

It was natural that Joseph Conrad's "An Outpost of Progress," at its first publication in *Cosmopolis*, should have been seen as a comment on the jubilee. But it had been written the year before, in July 1896, during Conrad's honeymoon in Brittany. It was one of Conrad's very first short stories.

The material was based on his own stay in the Congo. He had traveled upriver on one of the company's steamers himself, seeing the small trading posts and hearing his fellow passengers' stories. One of them happened to be called Keyaerts.[13]

Conrad had had this material for six years. Why did he write his story just at that moment? The Congo debate did not start seriously for another six years, in 1903. What happened in July 1896 that made Conrad interrupt both his honeymoon and the novel he was writing and instead write a story about the Congo?

17

I have moved. I now rent a cheap room in the closed Badjouda Hotel opposite the entrance to the market and I eat at Ben Hachem Moulay's Friends' Restaurant. At dusk I sit under the trees on the main street, drink coffee with milk, and watch people passing by.

A hundred years ago the market in In Salah was the liveliest meeting place in the Sahara. Slaves from the south were exchanged for grain, dates, and industrial goods from the north. The slaves did not even have to be kept in captivity: to flee from In Salah meant certain death in the desert. The few who nevertheless made the attempt were easily captured and punished. They had their testicles crushed, their Achilles tendons slashed, then were left behind.

In this once renowned market today, only a few imported vegetables are to be found, already drooping on arrival, and shoddy textiles clashing in angry, poisonous colors. The market's literary offerings feature part two of classical masterpieces such as *Don Quixote* and Mme. de Staël's book on Germany. Presumably, part one has been delivered to some other oasis, since it wouldn't be fair to allow the same oasis both parts of a sought-after book.

The only really interesting thing the market has to offer is fossilized wood, the remnants of gigantic trees that died out millions of years ago and were buried in the sand. Silicon acid has turned the wood into stone; then, as the sand moved on, the stone was uncovered and landed in the market.

It is prohibited to take fossilized-wood pieces larger than a clenched fist. But even in a clenched fist there is plenty of space for the Sahara's verdant forests. My piece is on the table here, misleadingly like living wood, charged with the fragrance of rain-wet leaves and the soughing of leafy treetops.

18

When Father came home from work when I was small, he would first of all go in to see Grandmother.

Mother did not like this and felt betrayed every time.

Was the love between mother and son stronger and more real than that uniting man and wife? Father was Grandmother's favorite son, the son she was carrying when her husband died, the son she bore as a lone parent. And my father, who had never seen his own father, had placed all his love in her.

Mother sensed this. So did I. I myself liked Grandmother best. In her powerlessness as an old woman, I recognized my own powerlessness as a child.

Grandmother smelled. A strong sweetish-sour odor came from her room and her body. Mother loathed that smell, particularly at table, and Grandmother knew it. She ate in the kitchen.

Now and again, Mother used to raid Grandmother's room to try to remove the actual source of the smell. She was doomed to failure, as the smell came from Grandmother herself. But every time, Mother cleared out "a whole lot of rubbish Grandmother's accumulated around her" and threw it away to get rid of the smell.

Father could not protect Grandmother from this. After all, it was true that she smelled. He could not deny the smell, nor that the smell meant dirt and that dirt had to go. The logic was irrefutable. Father could only delay and tone down the actions when Grandmother tearfully begged for mercy. The rest was up to me.

Grandmother was the seamstress of the house, and in a bundle under her bed she kept a whole library of patches and leftover pieces of cloth she called oddments. When I was very small I loved playing with these rags. I made a man out of a piece of Father's striped nightshirt, a woman out of Mother's pink silk blouse. Grandmother helped me. Together, we made animals as well as people.

So I understood perfectly how desperate Grandmother was when the "rubbish" was to go. Mother's attempts to keep the place clean was to me a loveless outrage, perfectly in keeping with those I myself was exposed to. So I rummaged in the bin for Grandmother's things and hid them among my own until the danger had passed.

In that way I also saved a yellowed book called *In the Shade of the Palms*.

19

In my childhood home, the books were arranged so that unbound books were kept to the left of the bookcase, clothbound books in the middle, and half-bound books furthest to the right.

The books were placed thus with company in mind. "Company" meant everyone who did not belong to the family. If company stopped in the doorway, they could see only a little bit of the bookcase and might then think that all the books were half-bound with gold lettering on the spines. If they came into the room, they might then think that all the books at least were bound. Only if the guests came right into the room could they see the unbound books furthest to the left.

Among the half-bound books was one called *Three Years in the Congo* (1887). In it, three Swedish officers related their experiences in the service of King Leopold.

An experienced traveler in Africa had advised Lieutenant Pagels to take the *chicotte* as his best friend, the whip made of raw hippopotamus hide, "which at every blow slashes bloody runes."

It may sound cruel to European ears, said Pagels, but he knew from experience that it was true. Particularly important was to seem coldly unmoved while administering a flogging: "If you have to order physical punishment to a savage, have this punishment carried out with not a muscle in your face betraying your feelings."

Lieutenant Gleerup relates in his report how he flogged his bearers until he passed out in an attack of fever, then how tenderly the recently flogged men cared for him, covering him with their white cloths and looking after him as if he were a child, and how he lay with his head in the lap of one of the men while another ran down into the steep valley to fetch water for him, so that he soon recovered and was once again able to wield the whip.

But only individual blacks behaved like this. The complete opposite was true of "the savage in general."

Pagels had tried in vain to find a single good side to the savage. "Should I be at death's door and a glass of water were enough to save my life, no savage would bring me that water if I could not pay him for his trouble."

Morality, love, friendship—all such things are lacking in the savage, said Pagels. The savage respects nothing but brute strength. He regards friendliness as stupidity. So one should never show a savage any friendship.

It was a gigantic task the young Congo state had taken on, if the great civilizing assignment were to be crowned with victory, says Pagels, who called down the blessings of the Lord on the noble, sacrificing friend of mankind, the high-minded prince, ruler of the Congo, His Majesty Leopold II, leader of these strivings.

On September 30, 1886, the reports of these three officers were laid before the Swedish Anthropological and Geographical Society in the banqueting hall of the Grand Hotel, in the presence of His Majesty the King, His Royal Highness the Crown Prince, and their Highnesses the Grand Dukes of Gotland, Vestergötland, and Nerike.

No one raised any objections. On the contrary. The chairman of the society, Professor Baron von Düben, stated: "It is with pride we hear that these gentlemen travelers in the Congo, throughout toil, battles, and privations in that inhospitable country, have always managed to hold high the prestige of the name of Sweden."

Such was the truth in the half-bound book foremost in the bookcase. But among the unbound books in the corner was another truth which smelled of Grandmother.

20

Right up to 1966, Swedish parents had the legal right to thrash their children. In many European countries, that right still applies. Even today in France it is possible to buy a special leather whip for the chastisement of wives and children, what the French call a *martinet* and the English the cat-o'-nine-tails.

In my parents' home, the birch was used. On exceptional occasions, my mother took me with her to the forest to cut osiers. Her face was then exactly as Pagels said it should be, not a muscle betraying her feelings.

I avoided all looks and gazed down at my black rubber boots. We went to the old sports ground, where willows grew on the edge of the forest. Mother cut one osier after another and tried them out by striking a few whistling blows in the air. Then she gave them to me. I carried them all the way home, filled with one single thought: Please don't let anyone see us.

The shame was the worst punishment.

And the waiting.

The whole day passed waiting for Father to come home. When he came, he knew nothing. I could see that on his face, which was just as usual. He was about to go in to Grandmother when Mother stopped him and told him about the terrible thing that had happened.

I was sent to bed. I lay there waiting, while they talked. I knew what they were saying about me.

Then they came into the room, both their faces cold, empty, and hostile. Mother held the cane. Father asked me if it was true. Had I really behaved so badly at the Christmas party? Had I used swear words? Had I blasphemed and taken God's name in vain?

"Yes," I breathed.

Inside me I could see the girls' terrified delight and feel the warm glow of my arrogance as I sat there at the party surrounded by admiring friends and saying all those forbidden words—which still went on resounding within me when Father took the cane and started beating. "Fucking pissgod, fucking shitgod, fucking damned cunt who sneaked . . . bloody, bloody, bloody . . ."

Unlike Mother, Father had not been working himself up all day. He had started from cold, and at first he gave an impression that it was only with extreme reluctance he was doling out this "physical punishment," as Pagels called it.

I could not see his face as he beat me, nor could he see mine. But I could hear from the way he was breathing that something happened to him as he crossed the threshold into violence.

I imagined he was ashamed of hurting me so, that the shame had gone over into rage that made him strike even harder than he had intended. But perhaps it was my own shame I wrongly read into his actions.

I did know for certain only that people are seized with a kind of madness when they take to violence. The violence carries them along, transforms them and makes them—even afterward, when it's all over—unrecognizable.

21

The book I saved from destruction, *In the Shade of the Palms* (1907), was written by a missionary, Edward Wilhelm Sjöblom. He arrived in the Congo on July 31, 1892. On August 20, he saw his first corpse.

In his diary, we see him on his travels by steamer up the Congo to choose a suitable place for his mission station. As early as his first day on board, he witnesses a flogging with the hippo-hide whip Lieutenant Pagels had so warmly recommended. All the white men on board are in agreement. "Only the whip can civilize the black."

At a Catholic mission, they have three hundred boys taken prisoner during the war between the state and the natives. They were now to be handed over to the state to be trained as soldiers.

The steamer is delayed while one of the boys is captured. He is bound to the steam engine where the heat is greatest. Sjöblom notes:

> The captain often showed the boy the *chicotte*, but made him wait all day before letting him taste it.
>
> However, the moment of suffering came. I tried to count the lashes and think they were about sixty, apart from the kicks to his head and back. The captain smiled with satisfaction when he saw the boy's thin garb soaked with blood. The boy lay there on deck in his torment, wriggling like a worm, and every time the captain or one of the trading agents passed him by, he was given a kick or several. . . . I had to witness all this in silence.
>
> At dinner, they talked of their exploits concerning the treatment of the blacks. They mentioned one of their equals who had flogged three of his men so mercilessly that they had died as a result. This was reckoned to be valor. One of them said: "The best of them is not too good to die like a pig."

22

Grandmother never got that book back. I kept it where it was, well hidden in the corner for unbound books.

How would Pagels have reacted had he gone back and been able to see what Sjöblom was now seeing?

Perhaps the diary of E. J. Glave provides the answer.[14] Here is no gentle missionary speaking. From the very start Glave is in agreement that the natives must be treated "with the utmost severity" and that their villages must be attacked "if they won't work in some way for the good of the land."

"It is no crime but a kindness to make them work. . . . The measures adopted are severe, but the native cannot be satisfactorily handled by coaxing; he must be governed by force."

That was Glave's starting point. He is an old Congo hand, one of the first to serve Stanley. But when in January 1895 he returns to the Congo, he comes across a brutality that revolts him. What finally shatters his loyalty are scenes of torture very similar to those Sjöblom had witnessed:

> The *chicotte* of raw hippo hide, especially a new one, trimmed like a corkscrew and with edges like knife blades, is a terrible weapon, and a few blows bring blood. Not more than twenty-five blows should be given unless the offense is very serious.
>
> Though we persuade ourselves that the African's skin is very tough, it needs an extraordinary constitution to withstand the terrible punishment of one hundred blows; generally the victim is in a state of insensibility after twenty-five or thirty blows. At the first blow, he yells abominably; then quiets down, and is a mere groaning, quivering body till the operation is over. . . .
>
> It is bad enough, the flogging of men, but far worse this punishment inflicted on women and children. Small boys of ten or twelve with excitable, hot-tempered masters, are often most harshly treated. . . . I

conscientiously believe that a man who receives one hundred blows is often nearly killed and has his spirit broken for life.

24

This was the turning point, for Glave as it was for Sjöblom. After that entry in his diary, he becomes more and more critical of the regime.

At the beginning of March 1895, Glave comes to Equator, the station where Sjöblom is a missionary, the station Glave himself had helped found.

"Formerly the natives were well treated," he writes,

> but now expeditions have been sent in every direction, forcing natives to make rubber and bring it into the stations. The state is perpetrating its fiendish policy in order to obtain profit.
>
> War has been waged all through the district of Equator, and thousands of people have been killed and homes destroyed. It was not necessary in the olden times, when white men had no force at all. This forced commerce is depopulating the country.

As Sjöblom had been, Glave was transported together with a boatload of small boys who had been captured to be brought up by the state:

> Left Equator at eleven o'clock this morning after taking on a cargo of one hundred small slaves, principally seven- or eight-year-old boys, with a few girls among the batch, all stolen from the natives.
>
> They talk of philanthropy and civilisation! Where it is I do not know.

Of the *libérés*, brought down the river, many die. They are badly cared for: no clothes to wear in the rainy season, sleep where there is no shelter, and no attention when sick. The one hundred youngsters on board are ill cared for by the state; most of them are quite naked, with no covering for the night. Their offence is that their fathers and brothers fought for a little independence.

But when Glave, having completed his journey, is back among Belgians and his own countrymen, he is influenced by group pressure and smooths over his criticisms. His final judgment is mild: "We must not condemn the young Congo Free State too hastily or too harshly. They have opened up the country, established a certain administration, and beaten the Arabs in the treatment of the natives. Their commercial transactions need remedying, it is true."

It is the same final judgment made on Kurtz in *Heart of Darkness*: his trading methods were unsound and had to be abandoned.

25

Through his work as a missionary, Sjöblom comes into much closer contact with the natives than Glave does. Day after day, he notes down new examples of arbitrary killing.

On February 1, 1895, his sermon is interrupted by a soldier seizing an old man and accusing him of not having collected enough rubber. Sjöblom asks the soldier to wait until the service is over. But the soldier simply drags the old man a few steps to one side, puts the muzzle of his rifle to the man's temple and fires. Sjöblom writes:

A small boy of about nine is ordered by the soldier to cut off the dead man's hand, which, with some other hands taken previously in a similar way, are then the following day handed over to the commissioner as signs of the victory of civilization.

Oh, if only the civilized world knew the way hundreds, even thousands are murdered, villages destroyed, and surviving natives have to drag their lives along in the worst slavery....

26

In 1887, the Scottish surgeon J. B. Dunlop hit upon the idea of equipping his small son's bicycle with an inflatable rubber tube. The bicycle tire was patented in 1888. During the years to follow, the demand for rubber multiplied. That was the explanation for the increasing brutalization of the regime in the Congo which is reflected in the diaries of Sjöblom and Glave.

Belgium's king, Leopold II, issued a decree on September 29, 1891, which gave his representatives in the Congo a monopoly on "trade" in rubber and ivory. By the same decree, natives were obliged to supply both rubber and labor, which in practice meant no trading was necessary.[5]

Leopold's representatives simply requisitioned labor, rubber, and ivory from the natives, without payment. Those who refused had their villages burned down, their children murdered, and their hands cut off.

These methods at first led to a dramatic increase in profitability. Profits were used, among other things, to build some of the hideous monuments still disfiguring Brussels: the Arcades du Cinquantenaire, the Palais de Laeken, the Château d'Ardennes. Few people today remember how many amputated hands these monuments cost.

In the mid-1890s, this murky secret of rubber was still unknown. Glave would have been able to tell it, but he died in Matadi in 1895. Only Sjöblom and some of his colleagues knew what was happening and opposed the terror. In vain did they report the outrages to higher authority. As a last resort, they decided to appeal to world opinion.

Sjöblom wrote strong, factual articles in *Weckoposten*, the Swedish Baptist newspaper. He also wrote reports in English and sent them to the Congo Balolo Mission in London.[16]

The result was a small, almost unnoticeable comment in the mission society's monthly magazine, *Regions Beyond*: "Very serious disturbance amongst the natives, on account of the imposed traffic in india-rubber, has led to wholesale slaughter in several districts .... Official inquiry is being made as to the allegations against Free State administration in Equatorville. We want more, however, than investigation; the crying need is for redress. But the question is how to obtain this without a public *exposé*?"[17]

27

Charles Dilke knew how to read between the lines. He was an ex-cabinet secretary and member of the committee of the Aborigines Protection Society. With explicit reference to that brief report in *Regions Beyond*, he took up the situation in the Congo and wrote a sharp article under the heading "Civilisation in Africa."[18]

The article was the first sign that responsible circles in Great Britain had taken note of the missionaries' reports. It was published to reach a European readership in the newly started journal *Cosmopolis*, in which it appeared in July 1896, the same month Conrad wrote "An Outpost of Progress" and submitted it to — *Cosmopolis*.

Ten years have gone by, writes Dilke, since the ratification of the Berlin treaty that created the State of Congo. High-flown declamations in Brussels and Berlin had manifest themselves in the form of "the ivory stealing, the village burning, the flogging and shooting that are going on in the heart of Africa now."

In Conrad's story it is the declamations in the yellowed newspaper that take the visible form of ivory stealing, slave trade, and murder.

The old forms of government, Dilke writes, have broken down and no new ones created. Spaces in Africa are so vast, the climate and solitude so intolerable to Europeans, nothing good can be expected of European rule.

In Conrad's story it is just the distances, the climate, and the solitude that break down the two Europeans. Most of all the solitude, for that entails also an inner abandonment, Conrad writes; they lost something that previously "had kept the wilderness from interfering with their hearts."

What? Yes, "the images of home, the memory of people like them, of men who thought and felt as they used to think and feel, receded into distances made indistinct by the glare of unclouded sunshine."

Solitude erased society from within them, and left behind fear, mistrust, and violence.

Taxation in Africa cannot pay for an administration of the same quality as in India, writes Dilke. Even democratic governments have occasionally to hand over responsibility to sheer adventurers. Even worse is when the Niger Company and the Congo state rule over vast populations in enormous territories utterly out of sight from public opinion.

Conrad's two rogues had acquired their ivory through the slave trade. "Who will talk, if we hold our tongues? There is nobody here." No, that was the root of the trouble, says the narrator. There was nobody there and being "left alone with their own weakness," men can get up to anything.

Dilke's article reminded readers of what man in situations of that kind could do. It refers to the extermination of Native Americans in the United States, of the Hottentots in South Africa, of the inhabitants of the South Sea Islands, and of the natives of Australia. A similar extermination was going on in the Congo.

This theme can also be found in Conrad's story. It is Carlier who speaks of the necessity of "exterminating all the niggers" in order finally to make the country habitable.

Dilke's article is a draft of Conrad's story, which in its turn is a draft of *Heart of Darkness* published two years later. And Carlier's *"exterminating all the niggers"* is the first draft of Kurtz's *"exterminate all the brutes."*

28

In May 1897, Sjöblom himself went to London and, although very ill, appeared at a meeting arranged by the Aborigines Protection Society. Dilke was chairman.

With his intense gravity and dry, detailed, rather pedantic way of speaking, Sjöblom made a great impression and his testimony on the mass murders in the Congo received widespread publicity.

The debate that broke out in the press forced King Leopold II to intervene personally. In June and July 1897, he went to London and Stockholm to convince Queen Victoria and King Oscar II that Sjöblom's accusations were unfounded.

As a result of King Leopold's visit, leading Swedish papers carried long, critical articles on the Congo. But Leopold had greater success in London, where the preparations for the imperial jubilee were well underway; Queen Victoria had other things to think about than a few baskets of amputated hands in the Congo.

The great powers had little desire to interfere with Leopold's genocide, for they themselves had similar skeletons in their cupboards. Great Britain did not intervene until ten years later, when an organized movement called the Congo Reform Movement made it politically impossible for the government to remain passive.

It made no difference when Glave's diary in all its hideousness was published by *The Century Magazine* in September 1897. Nor did it make any difference when Sjöblom took the matter up in new articles. The Congo debate of 1897 was forgotten. The jubilee had erased it.

In 1898, the Congo received almost entirely favorable publicity, most of all in connection with the opening of the railway between

Matadi and Leopoldville, which gave rise to widespread reports in illustrated magazines. Not a word was said on all the lives the railway had cost.

That is, not until the Royal Statistical Society held their annual meeting on December 13, 1898, when the society's chairman, Leonard Courtney, spoke on the theme "an experiment in commercial expansion."[19]

A private person, King Leopold II had been made by the great powers ruler over what was estimated at anywhere from eleven to twenty-eight million natives in an area as large as the whole of Europe—that was the experiment. Referring to a series of Belgian sources, Courtney described the way the administration and commercial exploitation in the Congo were interwoven. With the help of Glave's diary, he described the violence the system had created.

This is what Glave had written from Stanley Falls ("The Inner Station" in *Heart of Darkness*):

> The Arabs in the employ of the state are compelled to bring in ivory and rubber and are permitted to employ any measures considered necessary to obtain this result. They employ the same means as in the days gone by, when Tippu Tip was one of the masters of the situation. They raid villages, take slaves, and give them back for ivory. The state has not suppressed slavery, but established a monopoly by driving out the Arab and Wangwana competitors.
>
> The state soldiers are constantly stealing, and sometimes the natives are so persecuted, they resent this by killing and eating their tormentors. Recently the state post on the Lomani lost two men killed and eaten by the natives. Arabs were sent to punish the natives;

many women and children were taken and twenty-one heads were brought to the Falls and have been used by Captain Rom as a decoration around a flower bed in front of his house!

According to a report in the *Saturday Review*, this is how Courtney rendered Glave's account:

> The Belgians have replaced the slavery they found by a system of servitude at least as objectionable. Of what certain Belgians can do in the way of barbarity Englishmen are painfully aware. Mr. Courtney mentions an instance of a Captain Rom, who ornamented his flower beds with heads of twenty-one natives killed in a punitive expedition. This is the Belgian idea of the most effectual method of promoting the civilisation of the Congo.

Perhaps Conrad had read Glave's diary when it was published in September 1897. In that case, he was again reminded of it. Perhaps he came across the information in Glave's diary for the first time. We do not know. What is certain is that he was able to read in his favorite paper, the *Saturday Review*, on Saturday, December 17, 1898, how Captain Rom ornamented his garden.

On Sunday, December 18, he started writing *Heart of Darkness*, the story in which Marlow turns his binoculars on Kurtz's house and catches sight of those heads — black, dried, sunken, the eyes closed, the result of their owner's motto: *"Exterminate all the brutes."*

30

In Salah is really called *Ain Salah*, which means "the salty spring" or, literally, "the salty eye" (the spring is the eye of the desert).

Water taken today from great depths still tastes of salt and is clouded by an average of 2.5 grams of dry substance per liter, some liters scarcely transparent.

Rainfall is fourteen millimeters per annum, but in fact rain falls every fifth or every tenth year. On the other hand, sandstorms are common, particularly in the spring. On an average, there are fifty-five days of sandstorm each year.

The summers are hot. 133°F in the shade has been measured. Winters are primarily marked by the sharp difference between sun and shade. A stone in the shade is too cold to sit on, a stone in the sun, too hot.

The light cuts like a knife. I draw breath and hold my hand in front of my face as I go from one patch of shade to another.

The best moments are the hour before and after sunset. The sun at last stops stabbing at your eyes, but a pleasing warmth still remains in your body, in objects, in the air.

31

In Salah is one of the rare African examples of *foggara* culture.[20] The word *foggara* is said to derive from the Arabic words for "dig" and "poor." It signifies the same kind of underground aqueducts that are called *kanats* in Persian. According to Arab chroniclers, a certain Malik El Monsour brought the *foggara* into North Africa in the eleventh century. His descendants live in El Mansour in Touat and call themselves Barmaka. They are specialists in *foggara* construction.

The *foggara* of the Sahara are often between two and six miles long. Together, there have been over eighteen hundred miles of them in the Sahara. You could walk upright in the galleries, which were sometimes fifteen to twenty feet high. The wells could be 120 feet deep, and the work was always carried out by slaves. Every time slavery was abolished, it remained in the tunnels, under another name.

It is a kind of mining, though the vein of ore is a vein of water. Work is carried out with a small short-handled mining pickax. The shaft is three square feet at the surface of the ground, and when down to the sandstone layer, the hole is reduced to two feet, just large enough to maneuver the pickax.

The waste is hauled up by an assistant and spread around the hole, so on the surface of the ground *foggara* look like rows of molehills.

When the well gets down to the layers of water-bearing sandstone, the tunneling starts. In the darkness of these tunnels, the digger easily loses direction. This is where his art is tested.

On the surface it looks as if *foggara* were dead straight, but underground, they are winding. The tunneler has to dig so that his tunnel connects with the tunnel from another shaft. Sufficient incline is also necessary, enough to keep the water running without prematurely using up the difference in height which has to extend the whole way.

When the French conquered In Salah—on New Year's eve between the nineteenth and twentieth centuries—the *foggara* had already started running dry. They have gradually been replaced by deep wells, but irrigation is still carried out at night to avoid evaporation. Every consumer of water has his star; when that star appears in the sky, it is a sign that his turn to have water has come. Those who are waiting for their star spend the night by the well. They are called the children of the stars.

One of the four quarters of In Salah is called Ksar Marabtine. There is not much to see there—ground, houses, sky, all have the same dust color. Only the burial places with their mysterious whitewashed *marabouts* glow suggestively in all the monochrome color of dust. Death is the only festive thing in life.

Rows of children sit on stones with slates on their laps, chanting the Koran. A man walks past kicking an empty bowl. Another man has fallen asleep in the dust, sleeping with his arms outstretched as if for an embrace and does not even hear the rattling bowl as it rumbles past.

The gym consists of one great hall with a very high roof. In the far corner is a dark changing room and a spiral staircase up to the balcony, where you warm up with jump ropes or gymnastics while looking over the hall.

It is all familiar, but somewhat primitive. The mirrors are few and small. The benches are wooden and not adjustable. The weight-lifting machines use rope instead of steel wires, but in order to hold, the ropes have to be so thick that the friction on return leaves no work left for the muscles. Otherwise everything is as usual—the smell of sweaty bodies, the clank of metal, the cries and groans.

I go down into the hall and am at once lucky enough to inherit a barbell, a narrow black barbell with loose weights.

Three times ten behind my head, three times ten up to my chin, and three times ten on the biceps. Then I abandon the barbell for some dumbbells that have just come free. I stand waiting for a moment, a dumbbell in each hand, looking around for a bench. A man invites me to "wedge between" on his bench and we do three times ten butterfly swings, although his dumbbells are twice as heavy.

The stand's black-steel tubing forms a little basket above my face as I lie on the bench and lift. A ten-year-old is just loading weights onto a barbell. I help him, and then we alternate; he three times ten, me three times twenty. Then he is satisfied.

A tall Arab with a white scar on his left cheek suggests we double the weights. Now I'm the one doing three times ten and he three times twenty. Then he doubles again, but I am satisfied.

So it goes on. One of the weight machines has slightly thinner ropes, which really do offer resistance in both directions. I work it three times fifteen behind my head. There are no rowing machines. The leg machines look rickety and risky, so I refrain. There's still a great deal to do.

The dreams and visions that came to me when I first started training are rare nowadays. I dream in bed, not in the gym. But my thoughts clarify. Maybe that provides nothing new. But what I already know comes closer.

33

"Seven!"

Suitably exhausted, I am sitting on one of the low benches outside Chez Brahim sipping at a glass of tea brewed from fresh green mint.

The training loosens up the hard surface of the mind, opens the pores of self and afterward it is particularly pleasant to sit here watching passersby.

"Seven! Seven!"

In Salah has twenty-five thousand inhabitants, most of them black. I have seen many of them so often that we have begun nodding to each other. Nonetheless, I start with surprise when I realize that "Seven" must be me, Sven.

The name jerks me out of my anonymity, as if out of a dream. I look incredulously around—and catch sight of the happy Turiner I got to know in Algiers, the man who drives from Turin to Cameroon several times a year and regards the Sahara as nothing but an unfortunate traffic obstacle.

He has just greased the front of his Mercedes with vaseline and now wants me to help him put drops of a transparent fluid into his turned-up eye—both measures intended to protect sensitive surfaces from the wear and tear of the sand. He will sweep on south early the next morning, driving as long as the light lasts, then sleep in the car.

"Can I come with you?"

"No," he says. "Your word processor and suitcase are too heavy. If you're going to Tam by car you have to be light."

His reply really suits me quite well. At the moment, my *foggara* work on the computer disk seems more tempting than continuing my geographical journey.

Hitherto I have shown that "exterminate all the brutes" is connected with the interrupted Congo debate of 1896–97, with Dilke's and Glave's contributions in particular.

But the sentence also has another background in time. When, in 1898, Joseph Conrad was writing about the unemployed sea captain Marlow seeking a job as skipper in Africa, he was building on memories of the autumn of 1889, when he himself, the unemployed sea captain Jósef Konrad Korzeniowski, aged thirty-one, was applying for a post as skipper on the Congo river.

My hypothesis is that if you want to understand *Heart of Darkness*, you have to see the connection between December 1889 and December 1898.

So the next morning I am again sitting at my computer, a towel spread over the seat of my chair, wearing nothing but a thin Chinese undervest and a pair of short Chinese underpants, ready to go on.

PART II

34

The great world event of the autumn of 1889 was Stanley's return after a three-year expedition into the interior of Africa. Stanley had saved Emin Pasha from the Dervishes.[21]

"The Dervishes" was the nickname of an Islamic movement that successfully resisted the English in the Sudan. The Mahdists, as they were also called, took Khartoum in January 1885. Relief arrived two days too late to save General Gordon. It was the most humiliating defeat the British Empire suffered in Africa.

But at the end of 1886, a courier reached Zanzibar with the message that one of Gordon's provincial governors, Emin Pasha, was still holding out in the remote interior of Sudan and was requesting relief.

The government hesitated, but some large companies made Emin Pasha's situation an excuse to equip an expedition, the main aim of which was to turn Emin's province into a company-ruled British colony.

Stanley was asked to take command. The man who saved Livingstone was to crown his career by repeating the exploit. "Dr. Emin, I presume."

35

But like Huckleberry Finn when he saved Jim, Stanley thought it too simple just to go straight on up to Emin and give him the arms and ammunition he had requested.

Instead, he led the expedition from Zanzibar, rounding the

whole of Africa to the mouth of the Congo, past the steaming waterfalls, up to the navigable upper stretch of the river. There, with the help of King Leopold's boats and the slave hunter Tippu Tip's bearers, he hoped to be able to ship hundreds of tons of military material from the Congo to Sudan through Ituri, the much-feared "forest of death," where as yet no white man had set foot.

There were, of course, no boats. There were no bearers. Stanley had to leave most of the military material behind in the Congo and hurry on himself with an advance force.

Stanley was stocky, lower-class, as muscular as a garbageman and scarred by years and experience. As his deputy he chose an elegant young aristocrat, Major Bartellot, soft as silk, handsome as a lush tenor—but with no experience of Africa. Why?

Stanley detested the English upper class and measured himself by it. Perhaps he hoped to see such an upper-class creature broken by the jungle, see him lose his fine manner, lose his superior confidence, his self-control, thus throwing greater light on Stanley's own capacity as a man and leader.

Bartellot was indeed broken. Left behind as leader of the rear guard, he tried in vain to keep discipline with terrible daily floggings. His racism flourished, he became more and more isolated and hated, and was finally killed.

36

Meanwhile Stanley is struggling on in the suffocating heat, moisture dripping from the trees, sweat soaking clothing, hunger a torment, diarrhea, festering sores, and rats gnawing at sleeping men's feet.

The inhabitants of the forest are frightened. They refuse to trade or act as guides. Stanley has no time for anything else but violence. To acquire food for his expedition, he murders defenseless people on their way to market and shoots unarmed men in order to get their canoes.

Perhaps that was necessary to get there. But was it necessary to get there? Everyone had advised him against taking the route he did. Only his own aspirations required that he should do the impossible, which in its turn required murder—murder to acquire a goat or a few bunches of bananas.

Shackleton, explorer of the South Pole, was not so vain. Rather than sacrifice lives, he swallowed his pride and turned back. Stanley goes on leaving heaps of corpses in his wake.

One of the most horrific scenes: Stanley has a young bearer hanged for "desertion." The bearers had taken on the job of marching across East Africa's dry savanna. Stanley had taken them into this dripping primeval forest, where half of them had already died. He's only a boy, hungry and a long way from home, the others plead. But Stanley is unrelenting. He could not afford, he thought, to show the slightest sign of weakness now.

He was possibly right in that. But he had deliberately put himself in a situation in which killing was the only way out.

Ragged, starving, evil-smelling, tormented by fever and boils, stumbling at every step, the survivors finally reach the shores of Lake Albert.

Emin arrives with his steamer to receive them. He is wearing his dazzling white uniform. He is in good health, calm, rested. He brings with him cloth, blankets, soap, tobacco, and provisions for his rescuer. Just who is rescuing whom?

37

The Mahdists have left Emin's distant province in peace for five years. But rumors of Stanley's expedition challenge them to attack. Stanley returns to the Congo to fetch the rest of the expedition. The Mahdists immediately conquer the whole province except the capital, where Emin's men mutiny.

Soon the only hope is for Stanley to return and halt the disaster he himself has triggered off. Day after day, they all wait impatiently for Stanley to arrive with machine guns, rifles, and ammunition.

Instead, Stanley again comes stumbling in the lead of a bunch of skeletons shaking with fever. They have lost the arms and ammunition and are scarcely in a state to defend themselves, far less to overcome ten thousand screaming Dervishes.

Nevertheless, Emin wants to stay. He pleads with Stanley to let him return to his province and try to defend it. But Stanley cannot allow that. For in that way his own failure would have been far too obvious. He had not been able to provide anything Emin had requested, and he had simply made the situation worse.

But by taking Emin with him to the coast, even if by force, Stanley hoped to decide just what news was to be telegraphed all over the world. "Emin saved!" Emin was the trophy that was to turn Stanley's defeat into a media victory.

The coup succeeded. It was the only thing in the whole expedition that did succeed—getting the general public to rejoice.

In the moment of triumph, no one was interested in examining the details. Stanley had once again done what no one else had been able to do. That became an established fact in the minds of the public. So the victory was at least for the moment a reality—whatever it had cost, whatever it actually contained.

38

When the unemployed sea captain Korzeniowski, whom we know as Joseph Conrad, came to Brussels in November 1889, to be interviewed by Albert Thys, the director of Société Belge du Haut-Congo, the city was in the throes of Stanley-fever. It was known that Stanley was on his way to the coast, but he still had not arrived.

On December 4, when Stanley triumphantly brought Emin to Bagamoyo, Conrad was back in London. The press hummed for weeks with homage to the great hero of civilization.

In January 1890, Stanley arrived in Cairo, where he started writing his version of the story of the expedition. For the first time in

The noble Emin Pasha, as he looked while everyone was awaiting his rescue. Illustrated London News. *November 30, 1889.*

sixteen years, Conrad returned to Poland and spent two months in his childhood Kazimierowka.

Meanwhile Stanley had finished *In Darkest Africa* and returned to Europe.

On April 20, he went to Brussels, where he was met with ovationlike tributes. At King Leopold's welcoming banquet, all four corners of the hall were decorated with a pyramid of flowers from which hundreds of elephant tusks protruded. The festivities went on for five days.

Meanwhile Conrad was on his way back from Poland. He arrived in Brussels on the 29th, while the Stanley festivities were still on everyone's lips. He met Albert Thys and was appointed and ordered to leave at once for the Congo. Conrad went on to London, where he made preparations for his Congo trip while the Stanley celebrations were at a pitch.

Stanley had arrived in Dover on April 26. He was taken by special train to London, where a huge crowd was waiting. On May 3, he spoke in St. James's Hall to thousands of people, including the royal family. He was awarded honorary degrees by both Oxford and Cambridge. Then countrywide celebrations took place.

Conrad was not present for all of them. On May 6, when Stanley was received in audience by Queen Victoria, Conrad returned to Brussels, and on May 10 he boarded a ship for Africa.

39

Conrad was on his way to Stanley's Africa.

Stanley was sixteen years older than Conrad. Like Conrad, he had grown up motherless. Like Conrad, he had been adopted by a benevolent father figure. Conrad was fourteen when Stanley found Livingstone and became world famous. At fifteen, Conrad ran away to sea, just as Stanley had done. Like Stanley, Conrad changed his name, his home country and his identity.

Now with all the homage still echoing in his ears, he was on his way to Stanley's Congo—knowing nothing about the murky reality behind the Stanley legend.

40

On June 28, 1890 (the same day Conrad left Matadi at the mouth of the Congo to set off on foot to Stanleyville further upriver), Stanley's *In Darkest Africa* came out.

The book was an enormous success and sold 150,000 copies. But it did not attract only flattering attention. Bartellot's father published his son's diaries to defend him against Stanley. During the autumn, all the European participants in the expedition published their own versions of what had happened. In November and December 1890, while Conrad was seriously ill in an African village, the English newspapers almost daily printed articles for and against Stanley.

During his eight months in Africa, Conrad found that reality differed glaringly from the grandiose speeches he had heard before his departure. When he returned to London at the New Year, 1891, sick and disillusioned, even opinion at home had begun to shift.

The discussion continued all through 1891. The most careful and detailed criticism was made by Fox Bourne in *The Other Side of the Emin Pasha Expedition* (1891). When everything had been said, a great silence settled over Stanley and his expedition, most of all about Emin Pasha.

41

In Africa Stanley had already discovered to his alarm that the man for whom he had sacrificed so many lives was no noble pasha but a stubborn Jew from Silesia.

Stanley was able to make Emin go with him, but could not make him appear in public. Emin protested during the return journey by maintaining total silence. During the actual welcoming banquet in Bagamoyo, he disappeared unnoticed from the table and was found on the paving stones below the balcony with his skull cracked. He was taken to the hospital while Stanley continued on his triumphal procession.

When, in April 1890, Stanley was being honored in Brussels and London as Emin's savior, Emin lay forgotten in a hospital in Bagamoyo. One night, he slipped out and, half-blind and half-deaf, started walking back to "his" province.

By October 1892, the Stanley fever in Europe was definitely over. By then Emin had also managed to get back home. The Dervishes found him and cut his throat.

A few years previously, his "rescue" had aroused hysterical attention in Europe. Now his death went unnoticed.

42

Six years later, in October 1898, George Schweizer's *Emin Pasha, His life and work, compiled from his journals, letters, scientific notes and from official documents* was published in London. In it the story of Emin was told for the first time from his own point of view.

The book was advertised and reviewed exhaustively through October and November. In December, Conrad sat down to write *Heart of Darkness*.

Just as Stanley traveled up the Congo to rescue Emin, in Conrad's story Marlow travels up the river to rescue Kurtz. But Kurtz does not wish to be rescued. He disappears into the darkness and tries to creep back to "his" people. Emin had also done that.

Kurtz is no portrait of Emin. On the contrary, everything sympathetic in Emin can be found in Marlow, the rescuer in Conrad's story. The monster is Kurtz, the man to be saved, who resembles Stanley.

Stanley also had an "intended," Dolly, who was told the untruth she desired. Just as the whole of the white world was told the lies they desired.

When Marlow lies to Kurtz's "intended" at the end of Conrad's story, he not only does what Stanley himself did, but also what official Britain and the general public were doing while Conrad was writing the story. They were lying.

43

History loves repetition. In the autumn of 1898, Stanley returned for a second time, now under the name of Kitchener.[22]

General Horatio Herbert Kitchener, called "the Sirdar," had done what Stanley had not managed to do. He had defeated the Dervishes and "saved" Sudan.

On October 27, 1898, he arrived in Dover. Just as when Stanley returned, great crowds had gathered to honor him. Just like Stanley, he was taken in a special train to London and granted an audience with Queen Victoria. At the welcoming luncheon, he maintained that the victory over the Dervishes had opened the whole length of the Nile valley "to the civilizing influences of commercial enterprise."

That was precisely what Stanley had said about the Congo River.

The following five weeks became a whirl of celebrations. In Cambridge, where Stanley had received his honorary degree, Kitchener received his on November 24. Some academics who had opposed the award were thrown fully clothed into the river while fireworks were let off in honor of the Sirdar. He went on to Edinburgh, where he received an honorary degree on November 28. Then countrywide celebrations took place.

A more exact copy of Stanley's return could hardly have been achieved. In the same issue of the newspaper that advertized and reviewed the book on Emin Pasha's journals, the book that showed how hollow the delirium had been the previous time—in the same issue the rejoicing of the people again resounded, cheers

Above: "*The Dark Side of the Sudanese Campaign: The Liquidation of Wounded Dervishes.*" *Below:* "*The Reason.*" The Graphic, *October 1, 1898.*

ringing out and empty phrases echoing.

Few questioned the victory at Omdurman. Few wondered how it came about that eleven thousand Sudanese were killed while the British lost only forty-eight men. No one asked why few or none survived of the sixteen thousand wounded Sudanese.[23]

But at Pent Farm in Kent, a Polish writer in exile interrupted the novel he was writing and instead started writing the story about Kurtz.

44

I go out into the sun, and as I draw breath, the hot air rushes into my mouth just as food often did when I was small and in far too much of a hurry to wait until it had cooled. Where now is that glass of cold milk that every breath demands?

45

At the battle of Omdurman, the entire Sudanese army was annihilated without once having got their enemy within gunshot.

The art of killing from a distance became a European specialty very early on. The arms race between coastal states of Europe in the seventeenth century created fleets that were capable of achieving strategic goals far away from the home country. Their cannons could shatter hitherto impregnable fortresses and were even more effective against defenseless villages.

Preindustrial Europe had little that was in demand in the rest of the world. Our most important export was force. All over the rest of the world, we were regarded at the time as nomadic warriors in the style of the Mongols and the Tartars. They reigned supreme from the backs of horses, we from the decks of ships.[24]

Our cannons met little resistance among the peoples who were more advanced than we were. The Moguls in India had no ships able to withstand artillery fire or carry heavy guns. Instead of building up a fleet, the Moguls chose to purchase defense services from European states, which thus were soon in a position to take over the part of rulers in India.

The Chinese had discovered gunpowder in the tenth century and had cast the first cannon in the middle of the thirteenth. But they felt so safe in their part of the world that, from the middle of the sixteenth century onward, they refrained from participating in the naval arms race.

Thus the backward and poorly resourced Europe of the sixteenth century acquired a monopoly on ocean-going ships with guns capable of spreading death and destruction across huge distances. Europeans became the gods of cannons that killed long before the weapons of their opponents could reach them.

Three hundred years later, those gods had conquered a third of the world. Ultimately, their realm rested on the power of their ships' guns.

46

But most of the inhabited world at the beginning of the nineteenth century lay out of reach of naval artillery.

So it was a discovery of great military significance when Robert Fulton got the first steam-driven boat to head up the Hudson River. Soon hundreds of steamers were to be found on the rivers of Europe. In the middle of the nineteenth century, steamers started carrying European cannons deep into the interior of Asia and Africa. With that a new epoch in the history of imperialism was introduced.[25]

This became a new epoch in the history of racism. Too many Europeans interpreted military superiority as intellectual and even biological superiority.

Nemesis is the name of the Greek goddess of revenge, the punisher of pride and arrogance. With profound historical irony, that was the name of the first steamer in 1842 to tow British warships up the Yellow River and the Great Canal in the direction of Peking.

Soon steamers were no longer used as tugs of the fleet, but were equipped with artillery of their own. The "gunboat" became a symbol of imperialism on all the major African rivers — the Nile, the Niger, and the Congo — making it possible for Europeans to control huge, hitherto inaccessible areas by force of arms.

The steamer was portrayed as a bearer of light and righteousness. If the creator of the steam engine in his heaven is able to look down on the success of his discovery here on earth, wrote Macgregor Laird in *Narrative of an Expedition into the Interior of Africa by the River Niger* (1837), then hardly any application of it would give him greater satisfaction than to see hundreds of steamers "carrying the glad tidings of 'peace and goodwill toward men' to the dark places of the earth which are now filled with cruelty."

That was the official rhetoric. At Omdurman it was demonstrated that the gunboat also had the ability to annihilate its opponents from a safe distance.

47

Until the middle of the nineteenth century, small arms in the third world were able to measure up to those of Europe. The standard weapon was a muzzle-loaded, smooth-bored flintlock musket, which was also manufactured by village smiths in Africa.

The musket was a frightening weapon for those hearing it for the first time. But its range was only a hundred yards. It took at least a minute to load the gun between each shot. Even in dry weather, three shots out of ten failed, and in wet weather the muskets ceased functioning altogether.

A skilled archer still fired more quickly, more surely, and further. He was inferior only in his ability to shoot through armor.

So the colonial wars of the first half of the nineteenth century were lengthy and expensive. Although the French had an army of a hundred thousand men in Algeria, they advanced only very slowly, as the arms of the infantry on both sides were quite comparable.

But with the percussion cap came a musket that failed only five shots in a thousand, and then accuracy improved with grooved barrels.

In 1853, the British began replacing their old muskets with Enfield rifles, effective at a range of five hundred yards and firing more quickly because the bullet was enclosed in a paper cartridge. The French brought in a similar rifle. Both were used first in the colonies.

But these weapons were still slow and difficult to handle. They emitted puffs of smoke, which revealed where the marksman was, and the sensitive paper cartridges absorbed the damp. The soldier also had to stand up while reloading.

Prussia replaced its muzzle loaders with the breech-loaded Dreyse rifle. This was tested for the first time in 1866 in the Prusso-Austrian war over hegemony in Germany. During the battle of Sadowa, the Prussians lay on the ground and with their Dreyse rifles fired seven shots in the time it took the Austrians, standing up, to load and fire one shot. The outcome was obvious.

A race now began between European states to replace muskets with breech loaders. The British developed the paper cartridge into a brass cartridge, which protected the gunpowder during transport, kept in the smoke fumes when the shot was fired, and hurled the bullet three times as far as the Dreyse rifle did.

In 1869, the British abandoned the Enfield and went over to the Martini-Henry, the first really good weapon of the new generation: swift, accurate, insensitive to damp and jolts. The French came next with their Gras rifle, and the Prussians with the Mauser.

Thus Europeans were superior to every conceivable opponent from other continents. The gods of arms conquered another third of the world.

The new arms made it possible even for a lone European traveler in Africa to practice almost unlimited brutality and go unpunished. The founder of the German East Africa colony, Carl Peters, describes in *New Light on Dark Africa* (1891) how he forced the Vagogo people into submission.

The chieftain's son came to Peters's camp and placed himself "quite unembarrassed" in the entrance of Peters's tent. "At my order to remove himself, he only replied with a wide grin and, quite untroubled, remained where he was."

Peters then has him flogged with the hippo whip. At his screams, the Vagogo warriors come racing in to try to free him. Peters fires "into the heap" and kills one of them.

Half an hour later, the Sultan sends a messenger requesting peace. Peters's reply: "The Sultan shall have peace, but eternal peace. I shall show the Vagogo what the Germans are! Plunder the villages, throw fire into the houses, and smash everything that will not burn."

The houses turned out to be difficult to burn and had to be destroyed with axes. Meanwhile the Vagogo gather and try to defend their homes. Peters says to his men:

> "I shall show you what kind of mob we have here before us. Stay here, and alone I shall put the Vagogo to flight."
>
> With these words, I walked toward them shouting hurrah, and hundreds of them ran like a flock of sheep.
>
> I do not mention this in any way to make out our own circumstances as anything heroic, but only to show what kind of people these Africans in general are and what exaggerated ideas people in Europe have of their fighting abilities and the means required for their suppression.
>
> At about three, I marched further south toward the other villages. The same spectacle everywhere! After

brief resistance, the Vagogo took flight, torches were thrown into the houses, and axes worked to destroy all that the fire did not achieve. So by half past four twelve villages had been burned down. . . . My gun had become so hot from so much firing I could hardly hold it.

Before Peters leaves the villages, he has the Vagogo told that now they know him a little better. He intends to stay as long as any one of them is still alive, any village is still standing, and any ox remains to be taken away.

The Sultan then asks to hear the conditions for peace.

"Tell the Sultan I do not wish for any peace with him. The Vagogo are liars and must be eliminated from the earth. But if the Sultan wishes to be slave to the Germans, then he and his people may possibly be allowed to live."

At dawn, the Sultan sends thirty-six oxen and other gifts. "I then persuaded myself to grant him a treaty in which he was placed under German supremacy."

With the aid of these new weapons, colonial conquests became unprecedentedly cost-effective. In many cases, expenses were largely limited to the cartridges needed for the killings.

Carl Peters was appointed German commissioner over the areas he had conquered. In the spring of 1897, he was brought to court in Berlin. His trial caused a scandal and received a great deal of attention even in the British press. He was found guilty of the murder of a black mistress. What was actually being condemned was not the murder but the sexual relationship. The innumerable murders Peters had committed during the conquest of the German East Africa colony were considered quite natural and went unpunished.[26]

A new generation of weapons quickly followed: rifles with repeater mechanisms. In 1885, the Frenchman Paul Vieille discovered nitroglycerin, which exploded without smoke or ash, and this meant the soldiers could remain invisible as they fired. Other advantages were its greater explosive effect and relative insensitivity to damp. The musket's caliber, nineteen millimeters, could be reduced to eight millimeters, which dramatically increased the accuracy of the weapon.

The automatic rifle also came with the smokeless nitroglycerin. Hiram S. Maxim manufactured an automatic weapon that was light to carry and fired eleven bullets a second. The British supplied their colonial troops with automatic weapons early on. They were used against the Ashanti in 1874 and in Egypt in 1884.

At the same time, with the Bessemer method and other new processes, steel had become so cheap, it could be used for the manufacture of arms on a large scale. In Africa and Asia, on the other hand, local smiths could no longer make copies of the new weapons, as they had none of the necessary material, industrially manufactured steel.

At the end of the 1890s, the revolution of the rifle was complete. All European infantrymen could now fire lying down without being spotted, in all weathers, fifteen shots in as many seconds at targets up to a distance of a thousand yards.

The new cartridges were particularly good for use in tropical climates. But, on "savages," the bullet did not always have the desired effect, for they often continued their charges even after being hit four or five times. The answer became the dumdum bullet, named after the factory in Dum Dum outside Calcutta and patented in 1897. The lead core of the dumdum bullet explodes the casing causing large painful wounds that do not heal well.

The use of dumdum bullets between "civilized" states was prohibited. They were reserved for big-game hunting and colonial wars.

At Omdurman in 1898 the whole new European arsenal was

tested—gunboats, automatic weapons, repeater rifles, and dum-dum bullets—against a numerically superior and very determined enemy.

One of the most cheerful depicters of war, Winston Churchill, later winner of the Nobel Prize for Literature, was the war correspondent of *The Morning Post*. He has described the battle in *My Early Life* (1930), the first volume of his autobiography.

50

"Nothing like the battle of Omdurman will ever be seen again," Churchill writes. "It was the last link in the long chain of those spectacular conflicts whose vivid and majestic splendour has done so much to invest war with glamour."

Thanks to steamboats and a newly laid railway line, even out in the desert, Europeans were well supplied with provisions of every kind. Churchill observed

> many bottles of inviting appearance and large dishes of bully beef and mixed pickles. This grateful sight arising as if by enchantment in the wilderness on the verge of battle filled my heart with a degree of thankfulness far exceeding what one usually experiences when regular Grace is said.
>
> I attacked the bully beef and cool drink with concentrated attention. Everyone was in the highest spirits and the best of tempers. It was like a race luncheon before the Derby.
>
> "Is there really going to be a battle?" I asked.
>
> "In an hour or two," replied the General.

Churchill thought it a "good moment to live" and determinedly set about the meal. "Of course we should win. Of course we should mow them down."

But there was no encounter that day. Instead they all concentrated on the preparations for dinner. A gunboat approached and the officers, "spotlessly attired in white uniforms," flung ashore a large bottle of champagne. Churchill waded out into the water up to his knees and grabbed the precious gift, then bore it in triumph back to the mess.

> This kind of war was full of fascinating thrills. It was
> not like the Great War. Nobody expected to be killed
> .... To the great mass of those who took part in the lit-
> tle wars of Britain in those vanished light-hearted days,
> this was only a sporting element in a splendid game.

51

Unfortunately the British often missed out on their splendid game. Their opponents learned all too quickly that it was pointless to fight against modern weapons. They gave up before the British had the pleasure of wiping them out.

Lord Garnet Wolsley, commander of the British troops in the first Ashanti war in 1874–76, met resistance and really enjoyed himself. "It is only through experience of the sensation that we learn how intense, even in anticipation, is the rapture-giving delight which the attack upon an enemy affords. . . . All other sensations are but as the tinkling of a doorbell in comparison with the throbbing of Big Ben."[27]

The second Ashanti war in 1896 provided no opportunity for experiences of that kind. Two days' march away from the capital, Kumasi, Robert Baden-Powell, the commander of the advance troop, later to found the Boy Scouts, received an envoy offering unconditional surrender.

To his disappointment, Baden-Powell did not fire a single shot at the natives. To get hostilities going, the British planned extreme provocations. The king of Ashanti was arrested together with his

"*They crept up to him on all fours.*" *The Submission of King Prempeh.*
Illustrated London News. *February 26, 1896.*

The Submission of King Prempeh. The final humiliation. The Graphic.
February 29, 1896.

whole family. The king and his mother were forced to crawl on all fours up to the British officers sitting on crates of biscuit tins, receiving their subjugation.

In *Heart of Darkness*, Harlequin describes how the natives used to approach their idol, Kurtz, crawling on all fours. Marlow reacts violently. He starts back and shouts that he does not want to know anything about the ceremonies used when approaching Mr. Kurtz. The thought of the crawling chieftains seems to him even more unbearable than seeing the heads of murdered people drying on poles around Kurtz's house.

The reaction becomes comprehensible when you see the drawings of the ceremony in Kumasi two years earlier. These drawings were all over the illustrated press and are an expression of a racist arrogance that does not flinch from the extreme degradation of its opponents.

This time the British found no use for their weapons. They returned sadly to the coast. "I thoroughly enjoyed the outing," Baden-Powell writes to his mother, "except for the want of a fight, which I fear will preclude our getting any medals or decoration."[28]

52

Sometimes, however, provocation did succeed.[29]

British consuls at the mouth of the Benin River had for years suggested that the kingdom of Benin should be taken. Trade demanded it, and the expedition would pay for itself by plundering the king of Benin's store of ivory. But the Foreign Office nevertheless regarded it as too expensive.

In November 1896, the suggestion was made again by the temporary consul, Lieutenant Phillips. Provisions and ammunition were ready for the assault scheduled for February–March 1897. On January 7, 1897, the Foreign Office reply arrived. As usual, it was negative.

But to be on the safe side, on January 2, Lieutenant Phillips had

"Unspeakable rites." Golgotha, Benin. Illustrated London News.
March 27, 1897.

Crucified human sacrifice from Benin–The City of Blood *(1897)*
by R. H. Bacon.

already set off with nine other white men and two hundred African bearers on a courtesy visit to the king of Benin.

That first evening he was met by a messenger from Benin who asked him to postpone his visit for a month as the king was occupied with ceremonies before their annual religious festival.

Phillips went on.

The following evening more representatives from Benin came and pleaded with the white men to turn back. Phillips sent the king his stick, a deliberate insult, and went on.

The next day, January 4, eight white men—including Phillips—and their bearers were killed in an ambush. On January 11, the news of "the Benin Disaster" reached London. The press raged and demanded revenge. The attack on Benin that Lieutenant Phillips had planned in November, but had been turned down in January, was now put into action as a punitive expedition in revenge for his death.

Despite stiff resistance, the British captured Benin City on February 18. The town was plundered and burned to the ground.

How many Benin inhabitants were killed by the British troops was never investigated. Instead, the human sacrifices by the Benin king were sensationally exaggerated in the illustrated magazines. Skulls glowing like wood anemones on the ground were clearly evidence that no inhabitant of Benin ever died a natural death. In Captain R. H. Bacon's book, *Benin—The City of Blood* (1897), the crucified who hung with ripped-open bellies were the real reason for civilization conquering Benin.

What is certain is that, when the first readers of Joseph Conrad's *Heart of Darkness* read two years later that Kurtz had allowed himself to be worshipped as a god and participated in "unspeakable rites," it was the pictures from Benin that readers saw in their mind's eye; then they remembered descriptions of the stench of mass graves into which the dead and living were thrown together and of the idols covered with dried blood.

These "idols" are today reckoned to be outstanding masterpieces of world art. But the press accounts of Benin as the special hell of the dark races were so powerful, the British could not see the artistic value of the sculptures. They were sold in London as curios to pay for the cost of the punitive expedition. German museums bought them cheaply.

53

What did the king of Benin feel as he was hunted like a wild animal in the forests while his capital was going up in flames? What did the king of Ashanti feel as he crawled up to kiss the boots of his British overlords?

No one asked them. No one listened to those whom the weapons of the gods subjugated. Only very rarely do we hear them speak.

At the end of the 1880s, the British South Africa Company advanced from the south into Matabeleland in today's Zimbabwe. In 1894, the Matabelele people were conquered. The company shared their grazing lands out to white agents and adventurers, reduced their herds of cattle from two hundred thousand head to fourteen thousand and prohibited all arms. White death patrols ruled with martial law, labor was forcibly recruited, and anyone who protested was immediately shot.

The rebellion comes in 1896. The company calls in British troops. Baden-Powell is with them, pleased "to have a go" at last against an enemy "without much capacity to inflict damage on trained soldiers." In the very first battle, he and his troops kill two hundred "natives" at the cost of one dead European.[30]

It had become easy and amusing to kill, but in this case still too expensive. The army was there at the request of the company and received payment for their military services. After a few months of fighting, the company was on the verge of bankruptcy. In order to bring about peace, on August 21, Cecil Rhodes and other white leaders were for the first time forced to listen to the black Africans.

"I once visited Bulawayo," said Somabulano.

> I came to pay my respects to the Chief Magistrate. I
> brought my indunas with me, and my servants. I am a
> chief. I am expected to travel with attendants and advis-
> ers. I came to Bulawayo early in the morning, before the
> sun had dried the dew and I sat down before the Court
> House, sending messages to the Chief Magistrate that I
> waited to pay my respects to him. And so I sat until the
> evening shadows were long. And then . . . I sent again to
> the Chief Magistrate and told him that I did not wish to
> hurry him in any unmannerly way; I would wait his
> pleasure; but my people were hungry; and when white
> men came to see me it was my custom to kill that they
> might eat. The answer that came from the Chief Magis-
> trate . . . was that the town was full of stray dogs; dog to
> dog; we might kill those and eat if we could catch them.

Lord Grey's priest, Father Bihler, was convinced that the blacks
had to be exterminated. "He states that the only chance for the
future of the race is to exterminate the whole people, both male
and female over the age of fourteen," Grey writes to his wife on
January 23, 1897.

He himself did not wish to accept such a pessimistic conclusion.
But the idea of extermination was near to hand, produced again
and again in the white man's press.

African leaders were quite aware of the risk of their people being
exterminated. Somabulano himself took up the threat of extermination in his speech at the peace negotiations: "You came, you conquered. The strongest takes the land. We accepted your rule. We
lived under you. But not as dogs! If we are to be dogs it is better to
be dead. You can never make the Amandabele dogs. You may wipe
them out. But the Children of the Stars can never be dogs."[31]

At Omdurman, the strongest African military resistance was crushed. The battle can best be followed in the book Churchill wrote immediately after the experience, *The River War* (1899). The morning of September 2, 1898, the following occurred:

> The white flags were nearly over the crest. In another minute they would become visible to the batteries. Did they realise what would come to meet them? They were in a dense mass, 2,800 yards from the 32nd Field Battery and the gunboats. The ranges were known. It was a matter of machinery. . . .
>
> The mind was fascinated by the impending horror. I could see it coming. In a few seconds swift destruction would rush on these brave men. They topped the crest and drew out into full view of the whole army. Their white banners made them conspicuous above all. As they saw the camp of their enemies, they discharged their rifles with a great roar of musketry and quickened their pace. . . . For a moment the white flags advanced in regular order, and the whole division crossed the crest and were exposed.
>
> About twenty shells struck them in the first minute. Some burst high in the air, others exactly in their faces. Others, again, plunged into the sand, and, exploding, dashed clouds of red dust, splinters, and bullets amid the ranks. The white flags toppled over in all directions. Yet they rose again immediately, as other men pressed forward to die for the Mahdis' sacred cause and in defence of the successor of the True Prophet of the Only God. It was a terrible sight, for as yet they had not hurt us at all, and it seemed an unfair advantage to strike thus cruelly when they could not reply.

The Battle of Omdurman. "The maxims and infantry annihilated them. Whole battalions vanished under the withering fire."
The Graphic. *September 24, 1898.*

The outmoded character of this description is particularly evident in the last sentence. An old-fashioned concept of honor and fair play, an admiration for such pointless bravery, had still not been superseded by the modern understanding that technical superiority provides a natural right to annihilate the enemy even when he is defenseless.

56

Eight hundred yards away a ragged line of men was coming on desperately in the face of the pitiless fire, Churchill goes on. White banners tossing and collapsing, white figures subsiding in dozens . . .

The infantrymen fired steadily and stolidly, without hurry or excitement, for the enemy were far away . . . Besides, the soldiers were interested in the work and took great pains. But presently the mere physical act became tedious.

The rifles grew hot—so hot they had to be exchanged for those of the reserve companies. The Maxim guns exhausted all the water in their jackets. . . . The empty cartridge cases, tinkling to the ground, soon formed small but growing heaps round each man.

And all the time out on the plain on the other side the bullets were shearing through flesh, smashing and splintering bone; blood spouted from terrible wounds; valiant men were struggling on through a hell of whistling metal, exploding shells and spurting dust —suffering, despairing, dying.

Churchill's empathy with the opponents' situation was not concerned with an enemy in wild flight away from there. This concerned a still attacking enemy who, if not stopped, in a short while

The Battle of Omdurman. The picture portrays the battle as man-to-man combat—but no Sudanese got closer than three hundred yards from the British positions.

would have shown themselves to be superior. The Caliph had put fifteen thousand men into this frontal assault. Churchill finds the plan of attack wise and well thought-out except on one vital point; it was based on a fatal underestimation of the effectiveness of modern weapons.

> Meanwhile the great Dervish army, which had advanced at sunrise in hope and courage, fled in utter rout, pursued by the 21st Lancers, and leaving more than 9,000 warriors dead and even greater numbers of wounded behind them.
>
> Thus ended the battle of Omdurman—the most signal triumph ever gained by the arms of science over barbarians. Within the space of five hours, the strongest and best-armed savage army yet arrayed against a modern European Power had been destroyed and dispersed, with hardly any difficulty, comparatively small risk and insignificant loss to the victors.

57

For a few weeks in October, 1898, it looked as if the victory at Omdurman would lead to a major European war.[32] The French had dug in at the little outpost of Fashoda south of Omdurman and demanded a share of the booty Kitchener had gained. Day after day the patriotic press in both countries showed off their biggest guns, while Europe slid nearer and nearer to the precipice.

But finally, on November 4, at a major gala dinner in London at which Kitchener received the signia of victory (a gold sword in monstrous bad taste), the news came that the French had given way. The Fashoda crisis was over. Great Britain remained the undisputed superpower, and the great poet of imperialism, Rudyard Kipling, wrote

Take up the white man's burden
Send forth the best ye breed
Go bind your sons to exile
To serve your captives' need[33]

58

While Kipling was writing "The White Man's Burden," Joseph
Conrad was writing *Heart of Darkness*. That leading expression of
imperialist ideology appeared at the same time as its opposite pole
in the world of writing. Both works were created under the
influence of the battle of Omdurman.

Already in *An Outcast of the Islands* (1896), Conrad had described
what it felt like to be shot at by naval guns. Around Babalatchi, the
ground is slippery with blood, the houses in flames, women
screaming, children crying, the dying gasping for breath. They die
helpless, "stricken down before they could see their enemy." Their
courage is in vain against an invisible and unreachable opponent.

The invisibility of the attackers is remembered far later in the
novel by one of the survivors: "First they came, the invisible
whites, and dealt death from afar. . . ."

Few Western writers have described with greater empathy the
helpless rage when faced with superior forces killing without having to go ashore, victorious without even being present.

That novel had just been published when the battle of Omdurman was taking place. In *Heart of Darkness*, written during
the patriotic delirium after Kitchener's homecoming, Conrad
opens the imperial toolbox and one after another examines what
the historian Daniel R. Headrick calls "the tools of imperialism":
The ship's guns that fire on a continent. The railway that is to ease
the plundering of the continent. The river steamer that carries
Europeans and their arms into the heart of the continent. "Thun-
derbolts of Jupiter" carried in procession behind Kurtz' stretcher:
two shot-guns, a heavy rifle and a light revolver-carbine. Winches-

ter and Martini-Henry rifles spurting metal at the Africans on the shore.

"Say! We must have made a glorious slaughter of them in the bush. Eh? What d'you think? Say?" Marlow hears the whites saying.

"We approach them with the might as of a deity," Kurtz writes in his report to the International Society for the Suppression of Savage Customs. He means the weapons. They provided divine power.

In Kipling's verse, the imperial task is an ethical imperative. That is also how it is depicted by Kurtz, who surrounds himself in a cloud of Kiplingesque rhetoric. Only in a footnote to his torrent do we see what the task truly is, for Kurtz as well as for Kitchener, at the Inner Station as well as at Omdurman: "Exterminate all the brutes."

59

The buses that ply the four hundred miles between In Salah and Tamanrasset are rebuilt Mercedes trucks painted orange, to be visible in the swirl of sand. The passenger compartment on the back is like a diving bell with small peepholes instead of windows. It is hideously hot and cramped inside, and there is no question of anything like springs—you have to bring them with you in your own body.

I am frightened, as usual. But when departure finally cannot be postponed any longer, as I stand there at dawn with my heavy pack, crouching before the leap—then I am again elated at being where I am.

The Sahara lies spread out before me like a fireman's canvas sheet. All I have to do is to jump.

The day starts among white dunes, exquisite and conical like whipped cream. Sand-worn roadsigns with almost eradicated symbols. As the road changes direction, the sand also changes color— white dunes become ash gray, yellow, red, brown, even black when the light comes from another quarter.

Then the first mountains appear, coal black, purple, scorched. They are badly weathered, surrounded by masses of fallen rock resembling slag raked out of some immense forge. Occasional tamarisks, mostly withered and dead. The driver gets down and collects them for the fire that night.

The bus stops for the night in Arrak, where there is a small café calling itself a restaurant and hotel. You sleep two by two in straw huts on mattresses directly on the sand.

60

On the map it looks as if the road would improve after Arrak, but it is the same turgid grinding in first gear, second, or four-wheel drive. You drive straight into the desert within a track area about a kilometer wide, all the time searching for the most navigable in a tangle of tracks.

Now and again huge plumes of smoke from other vehicles appear on the horizon. Toward midday the smoke mixes with the clouds of sand the evening wind blows up. They surround the setting sun with a thick mist through which occasional mountains and tamarisks can be seen outlined.

The rocks are ancient, their shapes often like vertebrae fallen from the spine of a mountain. Nearer to Tam, inside the Ahaggar massif, the peaks are higher, the core of the mountains offering greater resistance—but even there the landscape testifies most of all to the terrible power of the forces of erosion.

You travel for miles through a desert of shards, searching for a reality that has been irretrievably shattered.

I start back when I catch sight of my face in the mirror. Even I have been exposed to eroding forces, sun and wind, heat and cold, those that make the mountains fall to pieces.

61

Tam is the focal point of southern Algeria, an international town in close contact with neighboring Niger and Mali owing to transit traffic, streams of refugees, and smuggled goods.

European desert expeditions and tourists—all come to Tam sooner or later; and all get lost in the corridors of Hotel Tahat.

Its architect had an exaggerated preference for symmetry. The hotel has sixteen precisely identical points at which precisely identical corridors radiate out to the four points of the compass.

When Reception shouts that they have La Suède on the phone,

225

I rush round in the labyrinth like an overstimulated lab rat until I finally come out at the right place, panting for breath; on the telephone I can hear my own gasps, vastly exaggerated, being thrown between relay stations in Ouargla, Algiers, and Paris. Wiped out by these huge reverberations, my daughter's voice disappears and grows fainter than a whisper. I finally have to give up, overpowered by my own echo.

One of the cleaners has a small child with her, and she puts it down on the stone floor in the broom cupboard, then goes to work. The child cries ceaselessly from eight in the morning until late afternoon, by which time it is so exhausted it can manage only a few pitiful whimpers.

If an adult lay crying so tortured as that, how long would it be before anyone reacted? But children—children cry, everyone knows that. Everyone seems to think it perfectly natural.

62

It is on your back you feel the loss.

Your front can keep up appearances. If nothing else, your face can face itself in the mirror. It's the nape of your neck that is lonely.

You can embrace your stomach and roll yourself round it. But your back remains, alone.

That is why sirens and djinns are portrayed with hollowed-out backs—no one ever presses a warm stomach from behind against them. The carving chisel of loneliness works there instead.

You don't meet loneliness. It comes from behind and catches up with us.

63

Conrad lost his mother when he was seven and his father when he was eleven. He emigrated from Poland to France, from

France to England. He served on sixteen different ships. Every time he changed country or ship, he had to find new friends or remain lonely.

Then he exchanged the loneliness of the seaman for that of the writer. His wife was his housekeeper. It was in his friends he sought sympathy and confirmation.

One of Conrad's oldest English friends was called Hope and lived in a small village called Stanford-le-Hope. After his marriage, Conrad moved with his wife to Stanford-le-Hope to be near his friend.

Marlow tells the story about Kurtz to a small circle of four friends. That kind of circle was just what Conrad longed for all his life. In 1898, he thought he had at last found it.

As he sat down to write *Heart of Darkness*, he had just left Stanford-le-Hope and moved to Pent Farm in Kent. With that, he also moved into a circle of writer friends who lived quite near to each other. They are all there as invisible listeners to Marlow's story.

64

I have rigged up a table to start work, but am having great problems with the dust invading the disks. Tamanrasset is as dry as an early spring day in Peking. Swirling dry and windy, the town is constantly shrouded in a cloud of its own dust.

Just as the Peking wind brings with it the Gobi, this wind brings with it the Sahara—the same desert that runs on through Libya and Egypt, through the Middle East and Iran, Baluchistan and Afghanistan up to Sinkiang and on from there to the Gobi. All those millions of square kilometers of dust show a definite inclination to make their way to Tamanrasset and collect right there on my disks.

Clusters of animals and people are incessantly on their way across the dried-out riverbed that is Tam's equivalent of Hyde Park. Weary camels lower their heads and blow at the dust to see if it conceals anything edible, and patient goats graze pieces of paper. Women come with their burdens, not on their hips as in In Salah, but on their heads. Groups of boys drift around, every step tearing up a cloud.

But Tam has a specialty. It has a road—indeed, a motorway—on which if necessary you would be able to make your way across the river bed with polished shoes. It is reserved for the army.

An officer comes across this bridge on his way to the post office, four men with him in white lace-up boots and white helmets, the chinstraps under their noses. Outside the post office they march on the spot while he walks past the queue, demands a stamp, and sticks it on. Then six steps forward and another spell in neutral as he mails the letter—at which they all march on with the same solemn expression of satisfaction.

65

The barber's in Tam has a poster of Elvis in its window and another of the Algerian national football team. I read Wells and listen to Algerian radio while I wait my turn.

Afterward, I slowly return to the hotel, zigzagging between the shadows. I think I know how I shall go on.

When Conrad was writing *Heart of Darkness*, he was not only influenced by the Congo debate, Kitchener's return, and other events of the day. He was also influenced by a literary world, a world of words, in which Kipling was the rival and the opposite pole, but several other writers meant more to him: Henry James, Stephen Crane, Ford Madox Ford, and, most of all H. G. Wells and R. B. Cunningham Graham.[34]

66

The time traveler in H. G. Wells's *The Time Machine* (1895) takes us with him into a future world in which the human family has divided itself into two species: the weak flower children of the upper world and the dark creatures of the underworld, the "morlocks."

It is as if Dr. Jekyll and Mr. Hyde had bred and created two different families, each of which populates the future. As if superego and alter-ego had been separated and each created a people of his own. As if the working classes of "darkest England" had been forced down below the earth and had created another race there. As if the inhabitants of "darkest Africa" had lived an underground life in the actual heart of the empire.

Of these potential interpretations, the last-mentioned is the one to carry the story on: the morlocks turn out to be cannibals, and they have the power. The beautiful people on the surface are simply fattened cattle the cannibals capture, slaughter, and eat.

Hatred and fear seize the traveler. He longs to kill morlocks. He wants to go straight into the darkness, "killing the brutes."

This killing in Wells is both horrific and voluptuous. The time traveler falls asleep as he sits there in the darkness, and when he wakes the morlocks are onto him, soft and repugnant. He shakes "the human rats" off him and starts striking out. He enjoys the feeling of a swishing iron pipe smashing into juicy flesh and crushing bones . . .

The leading philosopher of the day was Herbert Spencer. As a child, he had been very strictly brought up. The principle of this upbringing became for Spencer the innermost secret of life. All living things are forced to progress through punishment. Nature appears to be an immense reformatory in which ignorance and incompetence are punished with poverty, illness, and death.

The time machine is an experiment with Spencer's theory of evolution. The novel shows how mankind, as the time traveler puts it, "commits suicide" by minimizing the pain that is the mother of intelligence and evolution.

Wells's next book, which we know Conrad also read, was called *The Island of Dr. Moreau* (1896). In this, the opposite possibility is investigated: maximizing the pain and thereby hastening evolution.

Dr. Moreau uses his surgical skill to create a kind of human being out of animals. He tortures the animals so that pain will increase the pace of their evolutionary progress: "Each time I dip a living creature into the bath of burning pain, I say, this time I will burn out all the animal, this time I will make a rational creature of my own. After all, what is ten years? Man has been a hundred thousand in the making."

Dr. Moreau has created one hundred and twenty creatures, of which half are dead, but he has not succeeded in creating a real human being. As soon as the doctor takes his hand off the creatures, they revert to bestiality. The animal in them is strongest at night, in the dark. One night, the puma tears itself free and kills its torturer. The monsters rebel and take over power on the island. The narrator sees, day by day, the way they become hairier, their foreheads lower, and they growl instead of speaking.

When he has saved himself and returned back to civilization, he sees the same there. Human beings seem to him to be tormented; animals soon to revert to all fours. He chooses solitude beneath the stars. "It is out there in the starry sky that whatever is more than animal within us must find its solace and its hope. And so, in hope and solitude, my story ends."

The Island of Dr Moreau can be read as a story of colonialism. Just as the colonizer civilizes the lower, more animal races with the whip, Dr. Moreau civilizes the animals with torture. Just as the colonizer tries to create a new kind of creature, the civilized savage, Dr. Moreau tries to create the humanized animal. In both cases the means is terror. Just like Kurtz, he teaches his created creatures to worship him as a god.

68

In *An Outcast of the Islands*, which Wells reviewed in May 1896, Conrad assembles the criticisms of the colonialists in the image of "the invisible whites," who kill without even being present. Perhaps it was Conrad who inspired Wells to write another story of colonialism, *The Invisible Man* (1897).

This is the story of Kemp, a man who, owing to a much too successful scientific experiment, has made himself invisible and does not know how to get his visibility back again. At first he is desperate about his position, but he soon realizes it can be exploited. As no one can see him, he can commit any outrage he likes without being punished. No one can stop him from killing anyone who resists his reign of terror. Invisibility has made him inhuman.

"He is mad," said Kemp. "Inhuman. He is pure selfishness."

"Pure selfishness" were also the words Conrad chose when he described to his publisher the main theme of *Heart of Darkness*.

The men representing civilization out in the colonies were "invisible" not only in the sense that their guns killed at a distance, but also in that no one at home really knew what they were doing. Cut off from their native country by enormous distances, poor communications and impenetrable jungles, they exercised imperial power without any control from home.

Charles Dilke had taken up these questions in "Civilisation in

Africa" in the summer of 1896. They were discussed in 1897 in connection with some articles in *The Times* by Benjamin Kidd and again in 1898 when the articles came out in book form under the title *Control of the Tropics*. Wells was topical as usual.

Conrad had already taken up this theme when he found it in Dilke and wrote "An Outpost of Progress," about the two rogues who become more and more inhuman when no one can see them. On November 17, 1898, he asked Wells if he would send him *The Invisible Man* because he had mislaid his own copy. On December 4, he praised it enthusiastically in a letter to Wells, and, at Christmas, Conrad wrote to his young relative Aniela Zagórska and urged her to read it. *The Invisible Man* was one of the books Conrad had just read when he was writing the story of Kurtz.

69

The letter to Zagórska also recommends Wells's most recent book, *The War of the Worlds* (1898). Criticism of colonialism in this book is even more pronounced, perhaps because it was written in the 1897 jubilee year, during the orgy of self-satisfaction the British Empire was indulging in at the time.

In Wells's novel, London is attacked by an extraterrestrial master race. The Martians have lived in perpetual cold, which has sharpened their brains and enabled them to invent spaceships and death rays. They envelop London bit by bit in a cloud of black gas, an impenetrable, irresistible killing darkness.

The story seethes with words that also have a signaling function in *Heart of Darkness*: "darkness," "blackness," "extermination," "brutes," "horror."

The Martians' weapons kill "like an invisible hand." They are as superior to those of the British as the British's are superior to those of the colored peoples. And just as the British consider themselves to have the right to conquer the lands of the lower races, the Martians think they have the right to conquer the Earth, taking it from people they regard as a lower species of animal. As Wells wrote:

> [B]efore we judge of them too harshly, we must remember what ruthless and utter destruction our own species has wrought, not only upon animals, such as the vanished bison and the dodo, but upon its own inferior races.
>
> The Tasmanians, in spite of their human likeness, were entirely swept out of existence in a war waged by European immigrants, in the space of fifty years. Are we such apostles of mercy as to complain if the Martians warred in the same spirit?

In the London area, humanity is soon exterminated, down to about a few stragglers. The narrator meets one of them on Putney Hill. He suggests future life and resistance in the sewers. The risk is that the humans "will go savage," degenerate into a kind of large wild rat. The extremes of the situation are motives for extreme solutions: "We can't have any weak and silly. Life is real again, and the useless, the cumbersome and mischievous have to die. They ought to die. They ought to be willing to die. It's a sort of disloyalty after all, to live and taint the race."

When that was written, Adolf Hitler was just eight years old.

The riddle of malaria was solved in 1897, when Wells wrote his novel. Just as malaria had long been the natives' best protection against the white conquerors, the bacteria in the novel become man's protection against the Martians. It is the bacteria that save humanity. The Martians have conquered the whole earth only to fall victim to its smallest and most insignificant inhabitants.

Just because we have been successful at one time, we should not think the future belongs to us, Wells warns. "In the case of every other predominant animal the world has ever seen, I repeat, the hour of its complete ascendancy has been the eve of its complete overthrow."

Wells had studied biology and paleontology under Thomas Huxley, and his popular science articles demonstrate a special interest in extinction. "On Extinction" (1893), for example, deals with the "saddest chapter" in biological science, describing the slow and inexorable extinction of struggling life.[35]

In the long galleries of the geological museum are the records of judgments that have been engraved on the rocks. Example: *Atlantosaurus*. Whether it was through some change of climate, some subtle disease, or some subtle enemy, these titanic reptiles dwindled in numbers and faded at last altogether. Save for the riddle of their scattered bones, it is as if they had never been.

The long roll of paleontology is half-filled with the records of extermination; whole orders, families, groups, and classes have passed away and left no mark and no tradition upon the living fauna of the world. Many fossils of the older rocks are labeled "of doubtful affinity." Nothing living has any part like them. They hint merely at shadowy dead subkingdoms, of which the form eludes the zoologist. They are index fingers, pointing into unfathomable darkness and saying only one thing clearly, the word *extinction*.

Even in the world today, the forces of extinction are at work. In the last hundred years, human beings have swarmed all over the globe and shoved one species of animal after another over the edge of the precipice. Not just the dodo, but hundreds of families and species.

The annihilation of the bison was swift and complete. Seals, Greenland whales, and many other animals are faced with the same cruel destiny. Their situation is almost beyond our ability to comprehend, Wells writes. Our earth is still warm from human beings, our future apparently full of human life. The most terrible thing we can imagine is a desolated earth in which the last human being, utterly alone, stares extinction in the face.

The air in the big department store is dry, and I find it more and more difficult to breath. They take me to the inhalation room, where the air is as moist as in a greenhouse, soft and pleasant to the lungs. After a minute or so in there, I feel quite recovered. But as soon as I come out into the dry air of the store, I am again breathless and hurry back into the inhalation room. In a few moments, it has been totally changed. It is empty. There is not a human being there, no equipment, nothing.

"I want the inhalation room," I say.

"You've gone astray," replies an invisible loudspeaker. "This is the annihilation room."

"I don't understand."

"There's a great difference," the matter-of-fact voice explains. "You're annihilated here."

"And that means?"

"This is the destruction chamber. All life ceases here. It ends."

The words explode in slow motion within me, their meaning unfolding like parachutes and slowly sinking down through the mind to the sudden realization: I don't exist any longer. The end has come.

In April 1897, while Wells was writing *The War of the Worlds*, the English newspaper *Social-Democrat* published a story marked with the same biting irony, the same rebellious pessimism. The piece was called "Bloody Niggers."

Why did God create man? Was it out of carelessness or ill will? We don't know. But in all events, man exists, black, white, red, and yellow.

Far back in history, Assyrians, Babylonians, and Egyptians lived and fought, but God was aiming all the time at something different and better. He let Greeks and Romans appear out of the darkness of barbarity to prepare the way for the race that from the start was chosen to rule over mankind, namely the British race—"limited islanders, baptised with mist, narrowed by insularity, swollen with good fortune and wealth."

Lower races live in Africa, Australia, and America and on all the thousands of islands in the South Seas. They perhaps have different names and petty differences between them, but all of them are essentially "niggers," "bloody niggers." Nor are Finns or Basques or whatever they are called anything to be reckoned with. They are just a kind of European nigger, "destined to disappear."

Niggers remain niggers whatever color they are, but the archetype is found in Africa. Oh, Africa! God must have been in a bad mood when He created that continent. Why otherwise fill it with people who are doomed to be replaced by other races coming from outside? Would it not have been better to make the niggers white, so that in all good time they could become Englishmen, instead of giving us all the trouble of exterminating them?

Niggers have no guns, so no rights. Their land is ours. Their cattle and fields, their wretched household utensils and all they possess is ours—just as their women are ours to have as concubines, to thrash or exchange, ours to infect with syphilis, leave with child, outrage, torment, and make by contact with "the vilest of our vile, more vile than beasts."

Our bishops scream to high heaven when the Armenians are violated by Turks, but say nothing about the much worse crimes committed by their own countrymen. The hypocritical British heart beats for all except those their own empire drowns in blood. The God who has created people like us—must not he have been a fool?

73

The author of this scream was the Scottish aristocrat and socialist R. B. Cunningham Graham. After an adventurous life in South America, he had returned to his native country and begun a new career as politician and writer.

A few months after "Bloody Niggers" was printed, Graham read "An Outpost of Progress" and recognized a soulmate in the criticism of imperialism and hatred of hypocrisy. He wrote to Conrad, and with that begins a correspondence remarkable in its seriousness, intimacy, and intensity. Graham became Conrad's closest friend.

The two friends always loyally praise each other's stories and articles, but in one case Conrad's reaction is much stronger than usual. That is when in June 1898 he read "Bloody Niggers," by then over a year old.

It is good, he writes. Very good, but . . .(here he switches into French) but, my dear friend, you spread yourself too thin, your thoughts drift around like wandering knights when they ought to be kept gathered together in firm and penetrating battle array.

"And why preach to the already converted?" Conrad continues. "I am being stupid. Honour, justice, compassion and freedom are ideas that have no converts. There are only people, without knowing, understanding or feeling, who intoxicate themselves with words, repeat words, shout them out, imagining they believe them without believing in anything else but profit, personal advantage and their own satisfaction."

The criticism of language Conrad made in the summer of 1896 — great words are nothing but sounds — is repeated here, sharpened to extreme despair: "Words fly away — and nothing remains, do you see? Absolutely nothing, you man of good faith! Nothing at all. One moment, and nothing remains — except a lump of dirt, a cold, dead lump of dirt thrown out into black space, spinning round an extinguished sun. Nothing. Neither thought, sound nor soul. Nothing."

74

Conrad calls Graham an *"homme de foi,"* a man of good faith.

Conrad neither wanted nor was able to have anything to do with Graham's socialism (or with politics in general). He was his father's son and knew what politics led to. Politics had killed his mother, broken his father, made him an orphan, and driven him into exile.

Graham, with his secure national identity, could perhaps afford politics. Conrad, writer in exile, could not. He could love and admire his father's politics in Graham, but he also hated them and could never forgive what they had done to his father.

Who today could be called an *homme de foi*? The species seems to have died out. Graham's problems, however, remain, utterly recognizable, his despair as well. It is only his faith and his hope that have been taken away from us.

75

On December 1, 1898, Conrad read Graham's newly published travel book *Mogreb-el-Acksa*. He wrote to Graham's mother on December 4: "It is *the* book of travel of the century. Nothing approaching it has appeared since Burton's *Mecca*."

And on December 9, Conrad wrote to Graham himself: "The individuality of the work imposes itself on the reader—from the first. And then come other things: skill, pathos, humour, wit, indignation. . . . This should work for material success. Yet who knows! No doubt it is too good."

Graham's book was one of the most recent Conrad had read when on December 18 he started writing *Heart of Darkness*.

The narrator in *Mogreb-el-Acksa* turns to a small circle of men lying around the evening fire, their pipes lit and staying their tin mugs on the way to their mouths when they hear the horses sneezing. He is a mounted equivalent of the seaman Marlow in his circle of sailors.

He tells, he says, only of what he has seen, with no flag waving, no pretence of fulfilling some great moral mission. He has no theories on empires, the destiny of the Anglo-Saxon race, the spread of Christian faith, or the expansion of trade. He is as guarded and distanced as Marlow.

He is on his way to Taroudant. At first, like Marlow, he is taken by boat along the coast of Africa. He thinks about "the Orient," "the East," a concept which at that time covered almost the whole of the non-European world.

"As I see the matter, Europeans are a curse throughout the East. What do they bring worth bringing, as a general rule? Guns, gin, powder, and shoddy cloths, dishonest dealing only too frequently, and flimsy manufactures which displace the fabrics woven by the women, new wants, new ways and discontent with what they know . . . these are the blessings Europeans take to Eastern lands."

The ruling classes in Morocco "understand entirely the protestations about better government, progress, morality and all the usual 'boniment' which Christian powers address to weaker nations when they can contemplate the annexation of their territory." Some areas are already in foreign hands, and "the Moroccans like the fact as much as we should like the Russians in the Isle of Wight," Graham writes.[36]

Even these modest attempts to see Europe from the point of view of the threatened were in the 1890s so rare and challenging that they gave Graham a profile as a writer entirely his own. It is the same narrative attitude Conrad had taken in "An Outpost of Progress" and that he again lets Marlow take at the beginning of *Heart of Darkness*.

When Conrad read Graham's story of a westerner traveling farther and farther into an unknown and dangerous Africa, he read not only what was in the book. Alongside or behind his friend's experiences, he saw his own. Behind his friend's words, he saw his own words, the story he himself would be able to write on the same theme, in the same spirit, with his friend as a secret addressee.

76

Earlier in the autumn, Graham had worded his criticism of European influence in "the Orient" even more sharply in his story "Higginson's Dream," which Conrad proofread for his friend, in September 1898.

"It is super-excellent," wrote Conrad to Graham's mother on October 16. "It is much too good to remind me of any of my work, but I am immensely flattered to learn you discern some points of similitude. Of course I am in complete sympathy with the point of view."

During the final battles over Tenerife, it says in "Higginson's Dream," the Guanches were afflicted by a strange disease which killed more than those who fell in battle. The whole country was covered with the dead, and Alfonso de Lugo met a woman who said: "Where are you going, Christian? Why do you hesitate to take the land? The Guanches are all dead."

The disease was called *modorra*. But in fact it only required the white man's presence—with his rifle and Bible, with his gin and cotton and his heart full of charity—to exterminate the people he wished to save from barbarism.

It is "apparently inevitable that our customs seem designed to carry death to all the so-called inferior races, whom at a bound we force to bridge a period it has taken us a thousand years to pass," writes Graham.[37]

It is worth noting that in contrast to most other intellectuals of the day, Graham writes "the so-called inferior races." According to him, the fact that colored peoples died out was not due to any biological inferiority but to what we today would call culture shock, the demand for immediate adaptation to a strange variant of Western culture (gin, Bible, and firearms).

77

In the autumn of 1898, Conrad was working on his novel *The Rescue*, about a noble and chivalrous imperialist who puts his whole existence at risk to help a Malayan friend who had once saved his life. The theme is the exact opposite of that in *Heart of Darkness*.

The novel caused Conrad endless torment and brought him several times to the brink of suicide.

It is also very bad. I have only one reason to concern myself with it, and that is a passage in which Mr. Travers "with some force" utters the following words: "And if the inferior race must perish, it is a gain, a step towards the perfecting of society which is the aim of progress."

These words appear in part three of the book, which means Conrad must have written them at about the time when he proof-read "Higginson's Dream." Both texts allude to the same widely known concept—that the "inferior" races must be sacrificed for "progress."

It is worth noting that the character in the novel pronouncing these words is Mr. Travers, and that his words immediately are associated with "the coming of utter darkness."

78

Things had gone well for Higginson. At this time he was already wealthy and lived in Nouméa, the group of islands he had "rescued from barbarism."

Higginson had spent his youth on the islands, loved their women, hunted with their youths, learned their language, lived their lives and considered it the best of lives. Tired of his wealth, he now often dreamed of returning to the little bay not far from Nouméa, where in his youth he had had a friend called Tean.

One day when the champagne seems flat and the demimonde particularly vulgar, he does return. The place is oddly changed. It seems deserted. He slashes his way through the undergrowth, finds a hut and a man digging yams. He asks:

"Where black man?"

The man leans on his hoe and replies, "All dead."

"Where Chief?"

"Chief, he dead."

Conrad read—not only read, but proofread—these words in his best friend's story a month or two before he himself wrote the words that would one day be the epigraph to T. S. Eliot's "The Hollow Men" (1925):

"Mistah Kurtz, he dead."

79

Inside the hut he finds Tean, the friend of his youth, dying. A strange conversation ensues in which Tean tries with metaphors—bird, mouse, rain—to explain what is happening within him, and Higginson replies as if the metaphors were an external reality in which the bird can be shot and the cat set on the mouse.

"It's no use," says Tean. "I die, John, black man all die, black women no catch baby, tribe only fifty 'stead of five hundred. We all go out, all same smoke, we vanish, go up somewhere into the clouds. Black men and white men, he no can live."

Having got that far in his story, Higginson starts blaspheming the gods, cursing progress, and railing at civilization (just as Graham had in "Bloody Niggers") in a torrent of half-French and half-English (just as Conrad had when he read "Bloody Niggers")—and then in confusion reminds himself that he made the roads, started up the mines, built the pier, that he and no one else had opened up the island to civilization. . .

Higginson is, as Kurtz is, a cosmopolitan, "half French, half English." In short, he is European. Just as Kurtz does, he represents a Progress that presupposes genocide.

PART III

80

How do I go on? The bus south from Tamanrasset stops at the Algerian border. The Niger State buses stop in Arlit, 170 miles from the border. You have to hitchhike those 170 miles, and if you don't want to find yourself stuck on the actual border, it is wise to start hitching as early as in Tam.

I purchase a place on a truck full of young Australians on their way to Nairobi. We start at dawn. The police let us through, but Customs refuses to.

At midday, the customs officials go for lunch without having let us through. The sun is oppressive, the strong light throbbing in your head. The queue of vehicles grows the longer the customs men's lunch lasts. Flies buzz and irritation increases. At half past two, the customs men come back, and suddenly, with no explanation, they let the whole queue through at once.

Ahead of us lies 240 roadless miles of desert. We cover seventy-two before darkness falls. The night is still and starlit, with no wind or moon.

81

When we crawl out of our sleeping bags in the dawn light, we find ourselves in a seldom used piste with no fresh wheel tracks. That can be an advantage, as the sand is not so churned up. But it can also be fatal if you have engine failure a long way from any other traffic.

Sure enough, we have trouble with the dynamo and have to continue on the batteries without recharging them.

Groups of white stones like bird droppings lie in the dark sand. That goes against the main rule of the desert: the brighter the lighter, the darker the heavier.

At about eleven, we meet a Tuareg in a Landrover who warns us not to continue. Ahead are dunes that are impassable for a heavy truck such as ours. We change direction and by lunchtime we are back on the "main road" in deeper and more churned up tracks.

We eat beneath some thin tamarisks before setting off into the ill-reputed Lion dunes.

There are plenty of wrecked vehicles in the desert, there forever, as there is no damp to rust them away. But the Lion dunes are the true cemetery for cars. For many people, it is a sport trying to get through the desert in ordinary sedans, and such attempts often end just here.

Wind and sand soon blast away all the paint, and in the end the actual metal would be worn away had the wandering dunes not buried the skeletons of the cars, just as they previously buried the bones of dead camels.

We drive through this landscape to the notes of Vivaldi's constantly interrupted *Four Seasons* on a tape on which they have superimposed recordings of third-rate cheap comedians—the kind who delight the audience by telling them of their poverty-stricken childhood and never having had a hot meal except when some rich bastard farted. Their anal comedy is oddly integrated with fear and contempt of women, and anti-intellectualism.

The dancers on board turn the music up as high as possible and add their own bouncing and swaying to the truck's movements in the sandy hollows. The photographers keep their cameras constantly at the ready and experience the desert only through the lens.

The afternoon is flat and eventless. We strike camp at Gra-Ekar, a collection of strange, probably volcanic rock formations that remind me of the stelae of Gotland. They are deeply furrowed, cracked and porous like sponges, but at the same time as hard as metal and clearly much more resistant than anything that had once existed around them.

82

The In Guezzam border station has a bad reputation. There are innumerable stories of the way police and customs men with dictatorial powers constantly manage to find new reasons for sending people back to Tam or preferably even Algiers. Others are said to have been made to stand waiting in the scorching sun from ten o'clock, when the policeman goes for his lunch, until half past four, when the same man comes back after his siesta.

So we are prepared for the worst. I put on a dark suit, clean white shirt, and tie, and as the only French speaker on the truck, I have been given the task of finding an appropriate topic of conversation.

So I say it couldn't be much fun sitting isolated out here down in In Guezzam, exposed to the heat, the dust, and the risk of infection from the refugee camps, for only a 31.5 percent bonus, when you know those who work in the comparatively centrally placed In Salah, 660 miles nearer to Algiers get a 35 percent bonus—just because they are at a greater distance from the provincial capital, Tam. The injustice of these wage differentials, I say, cry up to the skies.

After that, we had no difficulties with the customs or police. They worked overtime to clear us before lunch.

83

After journeying for an hour or two, great trees appear on the horizon. This is Assamaka.

You long for trees in the desert, not just for the shade they provide, but also because they stretch up toward space. When the ground is flat, the sky sinks. Trees raise the sky by being so big and yet having so much further to go. Trees create room.

The border policeman sits in a clay hut crammed like a junk dealer's shed with things left behind: tires worn smooth, broken radios, dusty rags, yellowing printed matter, cracked cups, half a lampshade, and a baton. In the middle of this confusion is a bed on which he sleeps, a table at which he works, and a transistor radio to which he listens.

His job consists of checking that those entering have either the equivalent of three thousand French francs or a valid air ticket for their return home. It is a delicate task to have to say to people that they are too poor to be allowed to travel in one of the poorest countries in the world. But he does this with good humor and good judgment, swiftly and in a friendly way, although he has no calculator and has to convert all currencies into francs in his head.

A stone's throw from there is a bar, the first since Tam. A Nigerian beer turns out to cost about half as much as an Algerian beer. The bottle is also twice the size and the supply of bottles apparently unlimited. Someone starts by ordering two beers each for the whole gang—then the party starts, communal singing, a babble of talk, great guffaws of laughter, tussles, drinking songs, and rhythmical hand clapping.

When the bar closes at midnight, eighteen whooping beery maniacs rush for the truck and set off with a bottle in each hand, yelling and laughing, straight out into the darkness, six miles, twelve miles, perhaps eighteen, then stop the truck somewhere in the sand and go on celebrating—chasing each other in the dark, rolling round, drinking, fighting, fucking, giggling, hiccoughing and spewing until the small hours, when they all fall asleep scattered about in the sand.

84

I am woken by the tent flapping like a whiplash. The wind has risen. It is four o'clock. Everything is covered with sand, my sleeping bag, my notebook, my suitcase, even my body. My eyelids are like sandpaper against my eyeballs. The air is too thick to breathe.

I am scared. I daren't stay lying there in my sleeping bag, frightened of being buried in sand if I fall asleep again. I crawl over and try to look out. The tent fills like a balloon and almost lifts off the ground. The truck is no longer visible. Everything has disappeared. The beam from my torch is useless against the flying sand.

I get dressed and wrap the sleeping bag around me like a quilt. The hours pass. The sand rustles over the tent canvas. Foolish strings of words run through my head. East, West, home's best. Be not afraid, young man. Hear the palm tree rustling, at your feet your date doth fall.

Sometimes I persuade myself the wind is dropping, sometimes that it is rising. Dawn makes no difference; the air is equally impenetrable. I am sitting as if walled inside it. Terror comes creeping up on me.

I rinse the sand out of my mouth with water from my flask and dip my fingers in so that I can wash out my nostrils and breathe a little more easily. I can consider myself lucky to have water. Don't you see the water is running low? What wouldn't I do for a glass of mineral water!

It is nine o'clock. I try to remember exactly where the vanished truck was. Anyone who has studied sandstorms will agree they are most dangerous close to the ground, where the heavy sand glides along like a flying carpet. Lighter grains of sand bounce on. Only the dust really lifts.

When this dust has blown away, the sand goes on moving over the ground like a thick, low-flying cloud with a clearly marked upper surface. You can often see people's heads and shoulders sticking up above the cloud of sand as if out of a bath, Bagnold says. When the ground consists of coarse gravel or stones, the cloud can be as high as six feet, but when the ground is loose sand as it is here, the cloud is usually considerably thinner.

So the high truck might be my salvation. If I remember rightly, it cannot be more than ten yards away. Or at the most twenty. Once up in the truck, I could perhaps get my head above the sand and be able to breathe again. The others are probably there already.

But what if I miss it? If I don't find my way back? All authorities say you should never move in a sandstorm, but stay where you are.

I stay. Suddenly, I realize this is my very last moment. That this is where I have come to die.

Dying of an overdose of heroin in a public convenience in Stockholm or of an overdose of desert romanticism in a sandstorm in the Sahara—the one is as stupid as the other.

85

"L'homme est entré sans bruit," says Teilhard de Chardin on the birth of history. Man entered with no fuss. Came unannounced. Arose with no commotion. Arrived soundlessly.

And how does he depart? Just as soundlessly?

86

Death was not included in my education. In twelve years of schooling and fifteen at various universities, I was never given any education in the art of dying. I don't even think death was ever mentioned.

Even now, afterward, after arriving in Arlit and having slept it all off and showered and filled my body's reservoirs with water— even now when terror has slackened its grip, I think it peculiar that death was never even mentioned.

The Norwegian philosopher Tönnesen said that to think about anything except death is evasion. Society, art, culture, the whole of human civilization is nothing but evasion, one great collective self-delusion, the intention of which is to make us forget that all the time we are falling through the air, at every moment getting closer to death.

Some of us get there in a few seconds, others in a few days, others in a few years—but that is a matter of indifference. The point in time is a matter of indifference; what is decisive is that the end awaits us all.

What should I do during my remaining time? Tönnesen would have answered, "Nothing." He believed that to be born is to jump off a skyscraper. But life is not like jumping off a skyscraper. It's not seven seconds you have, but seven decades. That is enough to experience and achieve a good deal.

The shortness of life should not paralyze us, but stop us from diluted, unconcentrated living. The task of death is to force man into essentials.

That was how I felt when I was still not yet thirty and had a long way to go down to the paving stones below. I did not even see them. Now I can see them rushing up toward me and feel myself falling headlong.

Then I realize something was missing in my education. Why have I never learned how to die?

CUVIER'S DISCOVERY

87

On January 27, 1796, the ambitious young Georges Cuvier, then aged twenty-six, had just arrived in Paris and held his first lecture at the newly opened Institut National de France.

Cuvier was a lively and captivating speaker. There and then, he had his great chance of making his name in the scientific world, and not least in Parisian society, which flocked to scientific lectures — if they were sufficiently sensational.

Cuvier was sensational. He spoke of the mammoth and the mastodon. Remnants of these huge elephantine animals had recently been found in Siberia and North America. Cuvier demonstrated that they did not belong to the same species as either the Indian or the African elephant, but constituted species of their own, now extinct.[38]

88

Now extinct — that was what horrified the listeners. In the eighteenth century, people still believed in a ready-made universe to which nothing could be added. Perhaps even more important to mankind's peace of mind, nothing could be subtracted from it. All the creatures God had once created still remained in his creation and could not disappear from it.

What then was the explanation for these gigantic bones and strange animal-like stones that had puzzled man since antiquity? For a long time scientists evaded the thought, so charged with anguish, that they could be the remnants of extinct animals. "If one link in Nature's chain be lost," wrote the vice president of the United States, Thomas Jefferson, in 1799, "another and another might be lost, till this whole system of things should vanish by piecemeal."[39]

89

The idea that there could be species that had died out gave rise to such resistance, it took over a hundred years to become accepted.

Fontenelle had begun cautiously in 1700 with an indication that there perhaps were species that had been "lost." As if Mother Nature had gone and dropped them. Half a century later, Buffon spoke in his *Theory of the Earth* of a "vanished" species. Perhaps it had gone astray and never found its way home again.[40]

Cuvier did not speak as if nature had been neglectful. He talked of a crime, a massacre. His dying species had not been lost nor had they vanished; they were creatures that had been destroyed, died, been killed, not one by one but en masse, by vast repeated catastrophes, which, what is more, Cuvier called "the earth's revolutions." This could not help but make an impression on an audience that had just experienced the French Revolution.

What Citizen Cuvier really showed that day was that the reign of terror of the French Revolution, which his audience had only just survived, while many other grand old families had been wiped out—this reign of terror had in the far distant past a geological equivalent that had eradicated forever some of the largest of the animal species extant at the time.

Not only that. Cuvier ended with the prediction that the new creatures that had taken the place of the extinct species would one day be annihilated themselves and replaced by others.

Cuvier advanced rapidly. He became the Napoleon of French science, but for a man of such power, he was unusually skeptical of hierarchies. To him, the belief in a "ladder" of creatures was the greatest of all scientific mistakes. In his lectures in comparative anatomy, he writes:

> The circumstance that we put one species or family before another does not entail that we consider it more perfect or superior to others in the system of nature. Only someone who thinks he can arrange all organisms into one long series can entertain such pretensions. The further I have progressed in the study of nature, the more convinced I have become that this is the most untruthful concept ever brought into natural history. It is necessary to regard every organism and every group of organisms separately. . . .

By selecting out a certain organ, one could indeed construct long series from simpler to more complicated, more perfect forms. But one acquired different hierarchies depending on which organ one selected. Instead of one single "ladder," Cuvier found a "network" of connections between creatures, all of which had a feature or some features in common. Only through arbitrary choice could a scientist set up an apparent hierarchical order in this network.

Cuvier knew that. And yet apparent hierarchical orders of that kind had an invisible power over his mind. When in his great sixteen-volume work *The Animal Kingdom* (1827–1835) he divided human beings into three races, he had forgotten that no hierarchies existed.

On the negroid races, he wrote that with their protruding jaws and thick lips, they approached the primates. "The hordes belonging to this variant of human being have always remained in a state of total barbarism."[41]

In the medieval hierarchy, the human being had been one and indivisible, created by God in His image and by Him placed on the top rung of the ladder of Creation.[42]

The first person to divide the abstract human being of medieval theology into several species, of which some were considered to be closer to animals, was William Petty. "There seem to be several species even of human beings," he wrote in *The Scale of Creatures* (1676). "I say that the Europeans do not only differ from the aforementioned Africans in colour . . . but also . . . in natural manners and in the internal qualities of their minds." Here human beings are divided up not only into nations or peoples, but also biologically separate species. This occurred in passing and aroused no particular attention.

At the beginning of the 1700s, the anatomist William Tyson set off on a search for the missing link in the hierarchy of creation. In his book *Orang-Outang*, or *The Anatomy of a Pygmie* (1708), Tyson demonstrated that in its build, this primate is more like humans than other animals and the pygmy more like primates than other people. Tyson classified the pygmy as an animal, "wholly a brute," but so close to humans that "in this chain of creation for an intermediate link between ape and man I would place our pygmy."

Nor did Tyson cause any commotion. Not until the end of the eighteenth century, when Europeans were well on their way to conquering the world, did the idea of a hierarchy of the races seriously strike root.

The same year as the publication of Cuvier's first lecture, 1799, a doctor from Manchester, Charles White, produced the first extensively motivated and illustrated hierarchy of race, entitled *An Account of the Regular Graduations in Man*. In it he "proves" that the European stands above all other races: "Where shall we find unless in the European that nobly arched head, containing such a quantity of brain . . . ? Where that perpendicular face, the prominent nose and round, projecting chin? Where that variety of features and fulness of expression . . . those rosy cheeks and coral lips?"[43]

White's illustrations to his thesis—a series of profiles with primate and native halfway between ostrich and European—had enormous power and were still common in my childhood. At the moment of publication, White's thesis seemed to have an almost irresistible authority that continued to increase throughout the nineteenth century, in pace with the development of European arms technology.

92

I am called up for military service. The orders are in soft pastel colors, delicious, as if illustrating a fish recipe from Wedholm's restaurant in Stockholm. The background is mildly sand-colored like a desert dune and decorated with dark mussel shells. The actual dish is bluish with a touch of lilac. I look more closely at it and see that it is a corpse. It is myself who is dead, hideously swollen and distorted.

93

According to Cuvier there is one, and only one, state that hinders chemical and physical forces in their constant striving for the dissolution of the human body. That state is called "life."

For Cuvier, the state called life ceased in 1832 in the first great cholera epidemic that afflicted Europe. All his children died before he did. The species Cuvier was extinct.

Balzac paid tribute to him in *La peau de chagrin* (1831). Have you ever let Cuvier's geological works throw you out into the infinity of space and time? Balzac asks. Is Cuvier not the greatest poet of our century? He calls forth destruction, death becomes alive; in a kind of retrospective apocalypse we experience the terrifying resurrection of dead worlds, "and the little scrap of life vouchsafed us in the nameless eternity of time can no longer inspire anything but compassion."

Thus Cuvier captured the imagination of his day. He performed a postmortem on death and showed that it is not only of a personal nature, but wipes out whole species. He took the Parisians to the limestone quarry, where they could see that their city was an immense mass grave of long-since annihilated creatures. As they had gone under, so would we ourselves, their descendants, go under. Our future destiny could be read in the ground we were treading on.

It was a major scientific contribution. Cuvier cannot be blamed for the fact that, after his death, it all became associated with the hierarchical thinking he had seen through and loathed, but nevertheless yielded to.

94

On February 23, 1829, the young British geologist, Charles Lyell, describes in a letter his visit to Cuvier. He is full of admiration for the perfect order in Cuvier's study. In actual fact, this mania for order was probably Cuvier's great weakness.

Cuvier had been very strictly brought up both at home and at school. The chaos of the years of revolution reinforced the need for order he brought from home. All his life, he studied in fossils the results of the annihilating catastrophes. All his life, he sought calm and stability. Nature, like society, must obey inexorable laws. Metamorphosis frightened him. It was in his very nature to prefer destruction to transformation.

The French Revolution was the decisive experience of Cuvier's youth, while Lyell was instead marked by the Industrial Revolution in England. He had seen society fundamentally changed, not through one single violent catastrophe, but through thousands of small changes, each one scarcely perceptible.

Lyell wrote the classic work of nineteenth-century British geology, *Principles of Geology* (1832). In it he transfers his image of society to the geological history of the earth. No catastrophes have ever happened. All geological phenomena can be explained as the result of the same slow processes we see around us today: erosion, decomposition, stratification, rising land, sinking land.

What about mass destructions, then?

Extinct species, according to Lyell, have gone under in the same way, through slow changes in conditions of life: floods and droughts, diminishing access to food, the spread of competing species. The empty places have been filled by the immigration of species better adapted to the changed circumstances.

The ultimate cause of extinction was lack of flexibility and ability to adapt when unfavorable changes occur. Lyell had seen that in the markets during the Industrial Revolution: he now saw it in nature as well.

95

In Arlit, where I am sitting in my hotel room writing this, I suddenly catch sight of a man carrying an empty picture frame.

I usually see quite different things through my window—the woman on the corner making small pancakes in green oil on a black metal plate with circular hollows, the tea vendor swinging his glowing metal basket to get the water to boil, some boys playing at being a band with wooden sticks and empty cans. The rhythm is clearly different in Arlit than in Tam: at the same time more indolent and more active, as it is less tense.

That is the kind of thing I usually see from my window. But then a white-cloaked black man suddenly comes along carrying a heavy gold frame.

It frames his own person as he carries it, only his head and feet outside it. It is strange to see the way the frame separates him, brings him out, yes, even elevates him. When he stops for a moment to move it from one shoulder to the other, he seems to step out of the frame. It looks as if that were the simplest thing in the world.

96

Even in the most authentic documentary there is always a fictional person—the person telling the story. I have never created a more fictional character than the researching "I" in my doctorate, a self that begins in pretended ignorance and then slowly arrives at knowledge, not at all in the fitful, chancy way I myself arrived at it, but step by step, proof by proof, according to the rules.

Cuvier, Lyell, Darwin—they are all, in their work, fictional characters. The story of how they made their discoveries is nothing but a story, as it says nothing about them themselves. The omission of all that is personal makes the scientific "self" into a fiction lacking any equivalent in reality.

The reality "I" experience in the desert is authentic, however condensed. I really am in Arlit. I can see the black man with the gold frame. But I can never, by the very nature of things, step out of the frame.

As a reader, as soon as I see the word I used (or avoided, for even avoidance is a way of using it) I know I have a fictional character in front of me.

97

Darwin took Lyell's *Principles* with him on his voyage on the *Beagle*.[45]

In the spring of 1834, he was in Patagonia and found the remains of gigantic animals that had lived in late geological periods. No great land risings or sinkings had occurred since then. What then had exterminated so many species, yes, even whole families?

"The mind at first is irresistibly hastened into the belief of some great catastrophe," Darwin writes, clearly alluding to Cuvier's disaster theory. "But thus to destroy animals from southern Patagonia up to the Behring's Straits, we must shake the entire framework of the globe."

A geological investigation shows no sign of such shakings.

Well, what about the temperature? Darwin replies with a counter question: What change of temperature would exterminate the animal world on both sides of the equator, in tropical, temperate, and arctic areas?

"Certainly, no fact in the long history of the world is so startling," Darwin observes, "as the wide and repeated extermination of its inhabitants."

But looked at from another direction, this extermination is less amazing, Darwin goes on. In cases in which man exterminates a certain species in a certain district, we know that the species at first becomes increasingly rare and then dies out. That a certain species in nature is already rare does not surprise us, nor that it gradually becomes rarer and rarer; why then should we be surprised that it finally dies out?

98

The study of fossils, Darwin says, will throw light not only on the destruction of living creatures but also on their origins.

He already knew enough. His problem was now to understand it and draw conclusions.

In Cuvier's world there is in the beginning an act of creation, when life occurs, and in the end an act of destruction, when it is wiped out. Lyell destroyed this happy symmetry by replacing the destructive disaster with a number of small causes working slowly.

But if it were admitted that old species slowly and naturally could die out, then why could not new species arise in the same way, for the same natural reasons that had destroyed their predecessors? If dying out did not require a catastrophe, why should genesis require a creation?[46]

This was the logic that led Darwin step by step to *The Origin of Species* (1859).

99

Cuvier fought all his life with his colleague Lamarck. The question was: Can species evolve? Lamarck believed in evolution without having discovered its mechanism, natural selection. Cuvier, on the other hand, faithful to his nature, maintained that species were unalterable.

To this standpoint he brought very powerful scientific reasoning: if animal species had evolved from each other, then somewhere one ought to have come across intermediate forms between the extinct and the present living animal species. As such intermediate forms were absent, the hypothesis of evolution was faulty, Cuvier says.[47]

Darwin took Cuvier's objection very seriously. If it could not be refuted, the whole theory of evolution would have to be rejected, he wrote.[48]

But Darwin thought he had an explanation. The intermediate forms had existed, but they had been forced out by new, better adapted species, so quickly that they had had no time to leave any traces behind them in the geological record before they had gone under in the struggle for existence.

Darwin considered the struggle hardest between the forms that most resemble each other. "Hence the improved and modified descendants of a species will generally cause the extinction of the parent-species."

So according to Darwin, the explanation for the lack of intermediate forms is a kind of biological patricide. Evolution does not eat its children as revolutions do: it is the parents evolution wipes out.

In a letter to Lyell in 1859, Darwin considers the idea that this process perhaps also occurs between the human races, "the less intellectual races being exterminated."[49]

In *The Descent of Man* (1871), Darwin made public his conviction. Today between the primates and civilized man are intermediate forms such as gorillas and savages, he says in chapter 6. But both these intermediate forms are dying out. "At some future period not very distant as measured in centuries, the civilised races of man will almost certainly exterminate and replace throughout the world the savage races."

Similarly, the gorillas will die out. An even larger gap than that now found between the gorilla and Australian aborigine will in the future widen between the lower apes and the coming, even more civilized man. Namely, the gap left behind by those who have been exterminated.

TO AGADEZ

"dashing out their brains"

101

At the bus station in Arlit I turn to the veiled man in the entrance and ask, "Is the office open?"

"Let us first say good-day to each other," replies the native, correcting me mildly. For a moment we devote ourselves to mutual and repeated "Ça va? Ça va bien. Ça va?" Then he tells me that unfortunately the office is closed. Better luck next time.

The next time I actually succeed in buying a ticket. Then I have to leave my luggage on the ground, go to the police at the other end of town to show the ticket, get my passport, go back to the station, where my luggage is now being stowed onto the roof of the minibus together with some oily barrels, several sacks of grain, and a whole market stall, including stands to support the roof, a counter to spread the goods out on, and a whole assortment of bundles. Plus a dried camel head with empty eye sockets.

Then the passengers are packed in. There are three benches, one for women, one for black men, and one for Tuaregs. I am placed among the Tuaregs. Thirty-two people are squeezed in. It is not cramped as long as you can lick your lips. The two conductors push the bus to start it, run alongside, then throw themselves inside, and slam the door shut behind them.

It is a good 150 miles to Agadez. The ground consists of great floes of stone. The desert is flaking off like the dry skin on an arm. Then the first thin, pale steppe grass appears, salt to the tongue, accumulated in the depressions, blond, straw white, glowing like the down on your arm.

I recognize it from the abandoned limestone quarries in Gotland. There is a light in this short white grass, which makes me intensely happy.

In the middle of all this desolation, we sit pressed close together, body to body, breath to breath. Slim Tuareg youths in copper-purple veils, with long, dark eyelashes, enveloped in inviolable silence, embraced by the people of great laughter and beaming smiles, with their swelling backsides and noisy, colorful women.

Are these the savages Darwin had thought we civilized white men should exterminate? That is hard to imagine when you are sitting in the same minibus.

102

Hotel de l'Air in Agadez was once the Sultan's palace. It is famous for its dining room with four thick pillars that two men can hardly embrace, and for its rooms perpetually sunk in darkness, each with its own way up to the evening cool on the roof terrace.

From up there I look out over the market square, where a brand-new Peugot 504 has just stopped. Two young men in shiny suits jump out and go up to an old man by a small metal-covered desk decorated with two crossed letters. They squat down on their heels in the dust and have their letter written by the old man.

Who is it who is condemned to go under? Those glossy young illiterates, or the literate old man?

He is leaning against the minaret, seventeen floors high with protruding beams splaying out like a prickly fruit. It contains a spiral staircase that, toward the end, is so narrow you can no longer turn round. Everyone has to go up before anyone can come down.

The sun sparkles in the small round pieces of mirror decorating the bedposts of the furniture dealer. Some salt-bitten tamarisks spread thin shade.

The first evening wind brings with it the sound of clunking charcoal and the clatter from the mill that has started grinding the wheat for the evening meal. Chez Nous down on the corner has

263

already thrown open its doors; Au Bon Coin and Bonjour Afrique will soon be open.

Cuvier filled his day with horror when he demonstrated that a biological species can go under. Seventy-five years later, few people even raised an eyebrow when Darwin confirmed that whole human races are condemned to extermination. What happened? What were the "Tasmanians" Wells talked about? Who were the "Guanches"?

The Guanches were an advanced, Berber-speaking Stone Age people, the first people to be destroyed by European expansion.[50] They were of African origin but had lived for a long time in "the fortunate isles," what are now the Canary Islands, and had lost contact with the mainland. Their numbers have been estimated at about eighty thousand—before the Europeans arrived.

In 1478, Ferdinand and Isabella sent an expedition with guns and horses to Grand Canary. The plains were quickly captured by the Spaniards, but in the mountains the Guanches continued a stubborn guerilla warfare. Finally, in 1483, six hundred warriors and one thousand five hundred women, children, and old people capitulated—all that remained of a once numerous population.

Las Palmas surrendered in 1494. Tenerife held out until 1496. Finally, one lone native woman signed to the Spaniards to come closer. "There was no one left to fight, no one to fear—all were dead."

Neither horses nor guns decided the outcome of the war. Bacteria were victorious. The natives called the unknown disease *modorra*. Of Tenerife's fifteen thousand inhabitants, only a handful survived.

The forest was cleared, the flora and fauna Europeanized, the Guanches lost their land and thus their living. The *modorra* returned several times, and dysentery, pneumonia, and venereal disease ravaged.

Those who survived the diseases instead died of actual sub-jugation—loss of relatives, friends, language, and lifestyle. When Girolamo Benzoni visited Las Palmas in 1541, there was one single Guanche left, eighty-one years old and permanently drunk. The Guanches had gone under.[55]

This group of islands in the eastern Atlantic was the kinder-garten for European imperialism. Beginners learned there that European people, plants, and animals manage very well even in areas where they did not exist by nature. They also learned that although the indigenous inhabitants are superior in numbers and put up bitter resistance, they are conquered, yes, exterminated—without anyone really knowing how it happened.

104

When Europeans went east as Crusaders in the twelfth and thirteenth centuries, they came across people who were superior to them in cul-ture, diplomatic cunning, technical knowledge, and not least in expe-rience of epidemics. Thousands of Crusaders died because of their inferior resistance to bacteria. When Europeans went west in the fifteenth century, they themselves were the bearers of those superior bacteria. People died everywhere the Europeans went.

In 1492, Columbus arrived in America. The extent of the so-called "demographic catastrophe" that followed has been esti-mated differently by different scholars. Certainly it was without equivalent in world history.[51]

Many scholars today believe that there were roughly equal numbers of people in America as in Europe—over seventy million. During the following three hundred years, the population of the world increased by 250 percent. Europe increased fastest, by between 400 percent and 500 percent. The original population of America on the other hand *fell* by 90 or 95 percent.

Swiftest and most thorough was the demographic catastrophe in the heavily populated parts of Latin America that had first come into contact with Europeans: the West Indies, Mexico, Central America, and the Andes. In Mexico alone there may have been 25 million people when the Europeans arrived in 1519. Fifty years later, the number had fallen to 2.7 million. Fifty more years later there were 1.5 million Indians left. Over 90 percent of the original population had been wiped out in a hundred years.

The great majority of those people did not die in battle. They died quite peacefully of disease, hunger, and inhuman labor conditions. The social organization of the Indians had been wrecked by the white conquerors, and in the new society only a small fraction of the Indians was as yet usable, for, as a labor force for the whites, the Indians were of low quality. And there were many more Indians than the few whites could exploit with existing methods.

The direct cause of death was usually disease, but the underlying cause was this: the Indians were far too numerous to be of any economic value within the framework of the conquerors' society.

Was it defensible to continue a conquest with such disastrous results? That question became a major subject of discussion among Spanish intellectuals of the sixteenth century. This went so far that on April 16, 1550, Carlos V prohibited any further conquests pending a debate on their justification—"a measure with no equivalent in the annals of Western expansion," writes the historian Magnus Mörner.

The debate was held in Valladolid in August 1550 before a court of senior lawyers, who could not agree on any judgment.

And what purpose would that have served? No judgment in the world would have persuaded the Spanish conquerors to carry out what they considered Indian's work. No judgment had stopped them treating the Indians as inferior beings, making them submit to their natural masters. The fact that the Indians also died in the process was unfortunate, but apparently inevitable.

Adam Smith framed the law said to regulate the supply of labor: "The demand for men, like that of any other commodity, necessarily regulates the production of men: quickens it when it goes too slowly, and stops it when it advances too fast."[52]

That law also applies, of course, to Indians. They went on dying until there was a shortage of Indian labor in Latin America. Then they became valuable. A series of social reforms were carried out to safeguard the remaining Indians, binding them to economic units where they were needed and rationally exploiting their labor. During the seventeenth century the Indian population slowly began to rise.

By the middle of the nineteenth century, Latin America was affected by economic and technical renewal stemming from western Europe. This entailed increased demand for raw materials and foodstuffs from Latin America. The population increased even more quickly than before, and available labor was exploited even more.

The population continued to increase at a swift pace. At the same time, technical and economic renewal in Europe, which had for a while created an increased demand for labor in Latin America, during later decades, on the contrary, tended to reduce the demand. There can be no doubt that this tendency is continuing.

Industry keeps up with automation in order to be competitive in international markets. Large agricultural holdings are mechanized or go over to ranching. A growing share of the swiftly growing population becomes unsuitable or superfluous from the point of view of employers.

Does not Adam Smith's law still apply today? In the long run, will a society that is unable to maintain the right to work be able to maintain the right to live?

To me it seems clear that some of the decisive conditions for the sixteenth century demographic catastrophe exist again today in Latin America, as in several other parts of the world.

The pressure of the hungry and desperate billions has not yet become so great that world leaders see Kurtz' solution as the only humane, the only possible, the fundamentally sound one. But that day is not far off. I see it coming. That is why I read history.

107

I am in a tunnel or a cellar passage together with many other people. We move on at an excruciatingly slow pace in the darkness. They say we can get out somewhere far ahead, but only one by one up a narrow spiral staircase. The intake is far greater than the discharge and so it becomes insufferably cramped in the tunnel. Some have been standing there for several days and have moved only a few steps. Malthus himself has climbed up the pipes under the roof to get away from the crush on the floor. Irritation goes over into apathy and desperation. Beneath the surface, panic is already trembling.

108

About five million of the indigenous American population lived in what is now the United States. At the beginning of the nineteenth century, half a million still remained. In 1891, at the time of Wounded Knee—the last great massacre of Indians in the United States—the native population reached rock bottom: a quarter of a million, or 5 percent of the original number of Indians.

The fact that the Indians died out in the Spanish occupation was explained in the Anglo-Saxon world by the well-known cruelty and bloodthirstiness of the Spaniards. When the same phenomenon occurred as a result of Anglo-Saxon occupation of North America, other explanations were required. At first it was thought to be divine intervention. "Where the English come to settle, a Divine Hand makes way for them by removing or cutting off the Indians, either by Wars one with the other or by some raging, mortal Disease," Daniel Denton wrote in 1670.

During the nineteenth century, religious explanations were replaced by biological ones. The exterminated peoples were colored, the exterminators white. It seemed obvious that some racial natural law was at work and that the extermination of non-Europeans was simply a stage in the natural development of the world.[13]

The fact that natives died proved that they belonged to a lower race. Let them die as the laws of progress demand, some people said. Others thought that for humanitarian reasons the natives ought to be protected by moving them to some distant place—and then, as if by sheer coincidence, Europeans were able to take over their good arable lands and use them for their own purposes.

Thus, from the 1830s a number of tribes and peoples in North America, South America, Africa, and Australia were displaced, exterminated, or moved away. When Darwin wrote that certain human races are doomed to be exterminated, he built his prediction on generally known historical events. Occasionally, he had himself been an eyewitness.

109

In the backward southwestern parts of South America, the European conquests had not yet been completed when Darwin arrived in August 1832. The Argentine government had just decided to exterminate the Indians who still ruled the Pampas.

The assignment was given to General Rosas. Darwin met him and his troops by the Colorado River and thought he had never seen a more loathsome army of bandits.

In Bahía Blanca, he saw more forces, drunken and covered with blood, filth, and vomit. He interviewed a Spanish commander who told him how they had forced information out of captured Indians about where their kinfolk were. In this way, he and his soldiers had recently found 110 Indians who had all been captured or killed, "for the soldiers saber every man."

> The Indians are now so terrified that they offer no resistance in a body, but each flies, neglecting even his wife and children; but when overtaken, like wild animals they fight, against any number to the last moment. One dying Indian seized with his teeth the thumb of his adversary, and allowed his own eye to be forced out sooner than relinquish his hold.
>
> This is a dark picture, but how much more shocking is the undeniable fact that all the women who appear above twenty years old are massacred in cold blood! When I exclaimed that this appeared rather inhuman, he answered "Why, what can be done? They breed so!"
>
> Everyone here is fully convinced that this is the most just war, because it is against barbarians. Who would believe in this age such atrocities could be committed in a Christian civilised country.
>
> General Rosas' plan is to kill all stragglers and having driven the remainder to a common point, to attack them in a body in the summer, with the assistance of the Chilenos. The operation is to be repeated for three successive years.[4]

When Darwin published *The Descent of Man* in 1871, the hunting down of Indians was still going on in Argentina, financed by a bond loan. When the land was cleared of Indians, it was shared out among the bondholders, each bond giving a right to twenty-five hundred hectares.[5]

All night I search for flowers in a dark dirty city landscape. All round me is deserted, ruined, urinated. In a stinking tunnel, two men are coming toward me. Flowers? They don't understand what I am talking about. I sign "bouquet" by gripping the stalks in my hand. They take it as a sign for "knife" and understand exactly what I mean.

III

Darwin was disturbed by the brutality of the Argentinian hunt for human beings. His teacher, Charles Lyell, helped him to place what he had seen into a larger context. Man was a part of nature and in nature even destruction is natural.

We human beings, Lyell says in his *Principles of Geology* (the chapter headed "Extirpation of Species by Man"), have no reason to feel guilty because our progress exterminates animals and plants. In our defense, we can state that when we conquer the earth and defend our occupations by force, we are only doing what all species in nature do. Every species that has spread over a large area has in a similar way reduced or wholly eradicated other species and has to defend itself by fighting against intruding plants and animals. If "the most insignificant and diminutive species . . . have each slaughtered their thousands, why should not we, the lords of creation, do the same?"

The gentle Lyell had as little desire as the gentle Darwin to do the Indians any harm. But the right to eradicate other species that Lyell so thoughtlessly ascribed to man had already long been used even to exterminate humans.

112

The Tasmanians were the most well known of the exterminated peoples and were often held up as symbols for them all.[56]

Tasmania is an island the size of Ireland and lies southeast of the Australian continent. The first colonists—twenty-four prisoners, eight soldiers, and a dozen volunteers, of whom six were women—arrived in 1803. The following year, the first massacre of the natives occurred. The "bushrangers," escaped prisoners, had a free hand, killing kangaroos and natives. They took their women. They threw native bodies to the dogs or roasted them alive.

A man called Carrots became renowned for having murdered a Tasmanian; he then forced the man's wife to carry her dead husband's head hanging round her neck. The natives did not have to be treated like humans, they were "brutes" or "brute beasts."

In the 1820s, white immigration increased and with that the pressure on the livelihood of the natives. As they starved, they began to steal from the whites, who set traps for them and shot them from the treetops. The Tasmanians replied by attacking isolated settlers. The natives' leader was captured and executed for murder in 1825.

Van Diemens Land Company exterminated the kangaroos and brought in sheep on half a million acres. The white population doubled every fifth year. The local press demanded more and more loudly that the government should "move" the natives. If not, they should be "hunted down like wild beasts and destroyed."

That was what happened. In 1827, *The Times* (London) reported that sixty Tasmanians had been killed in revenge for the murder of a settler; on another occasion seventy Tasmanians lost their lives. The violence increased until the settlers also hauled women and children out of their caves, "dashing out their brains."

In 1829, the government decided to concentrate the natives in an area on the infertile west coast. Prisoners were sent out to hunt them down and were given five pounds for every native they brought with them to the assembly camp. It is estimated that nine Tasmanians died for every one to arrive alive. The "black war" went on.

In 1830, five thousand soldiers were mobilized for a search party to drive all the natives onto a small headland in the southeast. The operation cost thirty thousand pounds. For several weeks, the chain ran with forty-yard gaps right across the whole island. When it arrived, not a single native had been caught. There were, it turned out later, only three hundred left.

113

A Methodist mason by the name of G. A. Robinson wanted to save them. He went unarmed into the bush, was close to being killed, but was saved by a native woman called Truganina. Together with her, he succeeded in convincing two hundred Tasmanians to join them and go to the safety of Flinder's Island, where no one would hunt them down.

It was at this stage Darwin visited Tasmania. "I fear," he noted in his diary on February 2, 1836, "there is no doubt that this train of evil and its consequences, originated in the infamous conduct of some of our countrymen."

Robinson tried to civilize his protégés by bringing a market economy and Christianity to Flinder's Island. He was soon able to report exceptional progress. The Tasmanians had started working, had bought clothes, and were eating with knives and forks. Nightly orgies had been replaced by hymns. Knowledge of the commandments was progressing fast. There was only one snag: they were dying like flies.

Six months later half of them were dead. When that half in its turn was again halved, the remaining forty-five left the island and moved to a slum outside the capital, Hobart Town, where they quickly died out from alcoholism.

When Darwin's *The Origin of Species* came out in 1859, there were only nine Tasmanian women left, all too old to have children. The last Tasmanian man, William Ianney, died in 1869. His skull was stolen even before his funeral, and afterward the body was dug up from the grave and the remains of his skeleton were taken.

The last Tasmanian was Truganina, the woman who saved

Robinson's life. She died in 1876, a few years after Darwin's *The Descent of Man* came out. Her skeleton is in the Tasmanian Museum in Hobart.

114

Nineteenth-century scholars interpreted the fate of the Tasmanians in the light of Cuvier's discovery, now common knowledge. Among the thousands of already extinct species, the Tasmanians had survived owing to their geographical isolation. They were "living fossils," remains of a vanished prehistoric time, which had not coped with sudden contact with the other end of the time scale. The fact that they were exterminated meant only that they had returned to the long since dead world in which they belonged from the viewpoint of evolution.

Nineteenth-century scholars interpreted the fate of the Tasmanians in the light of Darwin's discovery. The "ladder" of creation the Middle Ages had believed in, the zoological hierarchy that William Petty, William Tyson, and Charles White had thought up, with Darwin became an historical process. The "lower" forms in the hierarchy were the predecessors in time of the "higher." And not only that. "Lower" and "higher" were bound together as cause and effect. The struggle between them created ever "higher" forms.

We Europeans were modified and improved descendants of the Tasmanians. So according to the logic of the Darwinian patricide, we were forced to exterminate our parent species. That included all the "savage races" of the world. They were doomed to share the fate of the Tasmanians.

PART IV

THE BIRTH OF RACISM

*"Race is everything: literature, science, art,
in a word, civilization, depend on it."*

115

At the beginning of the nineteenth century, eighteenth-century criticism of imperialism still lived on, and for many it was self-evident to take a stand against genocide.

In his great history of colonialism, *European colonies in various parts of the world viewed in their social, moral and physical condition* (1834), John Howison writes:

> The continent of America has already been nearly depopulated of its aborigines by the introduction of the blessings of civilisation. The West Indian archipelago, from the same cause, no longer contains a single family of its primitive inhabitants. South Africa will soon be in a similar condition, and the islanders of the Pacific Ocean are rapidly diminishing in numbers from the ravages of European diseases and the despotism of self-interested and fanatical missionaries. It is surely time that the work of destruction should cease; and since long and melancholy experience has proved us to be invariably unsuccessful in rendering happier, wiser, or better, the barbarians whom we have visited or conquered, we may now conscientiously let them alone and turn a correcting hand towards ourselves and seek to repress . . . our avarice, our selfishness, and our vices.

This was an attitude with roots in both Christian faith and Enlightenment ideas of equality. But during nineteenth-century European expansion, another attitude appeared. Genocide began to be regarded as the inevitable byproduct of progress.

To the great anthropologist, J. C. Prichard, it was obvious that "the savage races" could not be saved. What had to be aimed at instead, he said in his lecture "On the Extinction of Human Races" (1838), was to collect in the interests of science as much information as possible on their physical and moral characteristics.[57]

The threat of extermination provided motivation for anthropological research, which in exchange gave the exterminators an alibi by declaring extermination inevitable.

116

That same year, 1838, Herman Merivale gave a series of lectures at Oxford on "Colonization and Colonies." He noted Prichard's theory that "the white is destined to extirpate the savage" was becoming more and more usual. Extermination was not only due to war and epidemics, but had deeper and more secret causes: "the mere contact with Europeans is fatal to him in some unknown manner."

Merivale fiercely rejects this theory. There are no examples of inexplicable mortality. "The waste of human life" is enormous, we know that. But it has natural reasons. The main reason is that "civilization" out there in the wilderness is represented by "the trader, the backwoodsman, the pirate, the bushranger"; to put it briefly, by whites who can do anything they like with no risk of criticism or control.

"The history of European settlements in America, Africa and Australia, presents everywhere the same general features—a wide and sweeping destruction of native races by the uncontrolled violence of individuals, if not of colonial authorities, followed by tardy attempts on the part of governments to repair the acknowledged crime."

A British parliamentary commission set up in 1837 to investigate the causes of the misfortunes that had afflicted the Tasmanians and other native peoples came to the same conclusion. The commission found that Europeans unlawfully took over native territories, reduced their numbers, and undermined their way of life. "Gross cruelty and injustice" were the main causes of the natives dying out.[18]

As a direct consequence of the commission's work, The Aborigenes Protection Society was formed in 1838 with the aim of putting a stop to the extermination of native peoples. For the rest of the century, this organization continued its increasingly uphill battle against genocide.

117

Where am I? In a concentration camp? In the Third World? The naked bodies around me are emaciated and covered with sores. Christmas is approaching. Some well-fed men are putting up a net with coarse, strong meshing. On the other side of the net is the sculpture of a naked giantess painted in red and gold and decorated with an iron, a club and boots. The net stops us reaching this fat and happy woman.

The men putting up the net are working in a hail of crude jokes. They will soon set their dogs on us. They are already laughing themselves silly when they see us scrambling on the net. In vain we reach out for club and iron. We don't even reach the boots.

118

Prejudice against alien peoples has always existed. But in the middle of the nineteenth century, these prejudices were given organized form and apparent scientific motivation. In the Anglo-Saxon world, the pioneer was Robert Knox. His book, *The Races of Man: A fragment* (1850) reveals racism at the actual moment of birth, just as it takes the leap from popular prejudice via Knox's conceded ignorance to "scientific" conviction.

Knox had studied comparative anatomy with Cuvier in Paris. Cuvier's great feat was to prove that innumerable animal species had ceased to exist. But how they died out and why, he did not explain, Knox says.

We know equally little about why the dark races go under. "Did we know the law of their origin we should know the law of their extinction; but this we do not know. All is conjecture, uncertainty."

All we know is that since the beginning of history, the dark races have been the slaves of those lighter skinned. What is that due to? "I feel disposed to think that there must be a physical and consequently, a psychological inferiority in the dark races generally."

This is perhaps not due to lack of size in the brain but rather a lack of quality in it. "The texture of the brain is, I think, generally darker, and the white part more strongly fibrous; but I speak from extremely limited experience."

How limited this experience was is clear in another part of the book, where Knox says that he had done an autopsy on only *one* colored person. He maintains he found in this corpse a third fewer nerves in arms and legs than in a white man of corresponding size. The soul, instinct, and reason of both races must therefore, it is obvious, he maintains, be different to a corresponding degree.

From total ignorance, via this autopsy, Knox takes a giant stride directly to statements such as: "To me, race, or hereditary descent, is everything; it stamps the man," and "Race is everything: literature, science, art, in a word, civilization, depend on it."

There is something almost touching about the childish openness with which Knox exposes the lack of empirical basis for his statements. The sixth chapter of *The Races of Man*, which deals with the dark races, goes on like this: "But now, having considered the physical constitution thus briefly of some of these dark races, and shown you that we really know but little of them; that we have no data whereon to base a physical history of mankind; let me now consider . . ."

Consider what?

Well, on the basis of this established lack of facts, Knox unhesitatingly delivers categorical statements on the inferiority and inevitable destruction of the dark races.

119

Darwin spoke of "the savage races," without clearly stating which he meant. Wallace and several other authors wrote "the lower" or even "the lower and more depraved races," leaving the reader in profound uncertainty. Was it what we in our day call the Fourth World they were talking about? Or was it the entire Third World? Or even more?

Many people considered that *every* race was inferior and more depraved than the white race; and among the white "races," *all* were lower than the Anglo-Saxon race. Under such circumstances, how large a part of mankind was condemned to extinction?

Knox uses the expression "the dark races." Which are they exactly? That question is not easy to answer, says Knox. Are the Jews a dark race? The Gypsies? The Chinese? Dark they certainly are to some extent; and so are the Mongolians, American Indians, and Eskimos, the inhabitants of almost the whole of Africa, the Far East, and Australia. "What a field of extermination lies before the Saxon, Celtic, and Sarmatian races!"

He is indignant over one thing only: hypocrisy. The British in New Zealand have just (1850) carried out the most audacious annexation in the history of aggression. "The Aborigenes are to be protected!" the British say. Thank you very much! says Knox. They may not become British, when their land is taken from them; they are to be "protected"!

The Saxons do not protect the dark races, says Knox, do not mix with them, do not let them keep a single acre of the land in the occupied countries; at least that is the situation in Anglo-Saxon America, and the Saxon conquerors are moving south.

"The fate, then, of the Mexicans, Peruvians and Chileans, is in no shape doubtful. Extinction of the race—sure extinction—it is not even denied."

Can the dark races become civilized? "I should say not," says Knox. "Their future history, then, must resemble the past. The Saxon race will never tolerate them—never amalgamate—never be at peace . . . . The hottest actual war ever waged—the bloodiest of Napoleon's campaigns—is not equal to that now waging between our descendants in America and the dark races; it is a war of extermination—inscribed on each banner is a death's head and no surrender; one or other must fall."

"I blame them not," Knox goes on. "I pretend not even to censure: man acts from his impulses, his animal impulses, and he occasionally employs his pure reason to mystify and conceal his motives from others."

The Americans were presumably already on their way to extinction when the Europeans first arrived. "Now, the fate of all these nations must be the same; it results from the nature of their populations, and nothing can arrest it."

Look at South Africa. The Saxon spirit of progress there led to massacres of the natives. "Have we done with the Hottentots and Bosjeman race? I suppose so: they will soon form merely natural curiosities: already there is the skin of one stuffed in England; another in Paris if I mistake not. . . . In a word, they are fast disappearing from the face of the earth."

And Chinese, Mongolians, Tartars or whatever they are called, how will things go for them? Well, it is known what happened in Tasmania. The Anglo-Saxon swept the natives out of their own country. "No compunctious visitings about the 'fell swoop' which extinguished a race."

The Chinese can expect the same. China appears to be totally at a standstill with neither inventions nor discoveries. The famous

Robert Knox. Contemporary caricature from Knox, the Anatomist, *by Isobel Rae, Edinburgh, 1964.*

Chinese art must belong to another race from which the Chinese borrowed it without really understanding it.

No, the Chinese have probably seen their best days, have lived through their definitive track and period of time, now hastening toward the terminal where all that remains are remnants left by extinct creatures—like the mammals and birds in Cuvier's world of the past—that have long since ceased to exist.

121

Who was this man who with such delight wallowed in the destruction of human beings? He was a Scot, had served as an army doctor in South Africa, and had founded a school of anatomy in Edinburgh. As a young student, Darwin heard his controversial lectures.[59]

All anatomists at that time bought specimens from grave robbers, but Knox was suspected of having turned to professional assassins to ensure suitable corpses. That was the end of his scientific career.

He saw himself as a voice crying in the wilderness. He and he alone had discovered a great truth, the truth of race, which only numskulls and hypocrites could deny.

Origin of Species meant a turning point for Knox's ideas. Darwin neither confirmed nor denied them, but his theory of evolution was clearly useful for the racists.

Knox was restored to favor and shortly before his death he became a member of the Ethnographical Society, in which a new group of "racially conscious" anthropologists were now setting the tone.

In 1863, Knox's followers broke away and formed the Anthropological Society, which was more markedly racist. The first lecture—"On the Negro's Place in Nature"—emphasized the negro's close relationship to the ape. When a rebellion of rural blacks was ruthlessly crushed in Jamaica, the society held a public meeting. Captain Gordon Pim stated in his speech that it was a philanthropic principle to kill natives; there was, he said, "mercy in a massacre."

Time had begun to catch up with Robert Knox. Previously, race had been seen as one of several factors influencing human culture. After Darwin, race became the wholly decisive explanation in far wider circles. Racism was accepted and became a central element in British imperial ideology. [60]

122

I am in good company, simply following those in front of me and knowing others are following behind. We are on our way up a narrow staircase. The banister is a thick rope suggesting safety. The stairs go around and around inside a church tower; or perhaps it is a minaret? The whorls of the staircase grow narrower and narrower, but as there are so many people behind, there is no longer any possibility of turning around or even stopping. The pressure from behind forces me on. The staircase suddenly stops at a garbage chute in the wall. When I open the hatch and squeeze my way through the hole, I find myself on the outside of the tower. The rope has disappeared. It is totally dark. I cling on to the slippery, icy wall of the tower while vainly trying to find a foothold in the emptiness.

123

After Darwin, it became accepted to shrug your shoulders at genocide. If you were upset, you were just showing your lack of education. Only some old codgers who had not been able to keep up with progress in natural history protested. The Tasmanian became the paradigm, to which one part of the world after another yielded.

W. Winwood Reade, a member of both the Geographical Society and the Anthropological Society in London, and a correspondent member of the Geological Society in Paris, ends his book *Savage Africa* (1864) with a prediction on the future of the black race.

Africa will be shared between England and France, he prophesies. Under European rule, the Africans will dig the ditches and water the deserts. It will be hard work, and the Africans themselves will probably become extinct. "We must learn to look at this result with composure. It illustrates the beneficent law of nature, that the weak must be devoured by the strong."

A grateful posterity will honor the memory of the blacks. One day, young ladies will sit tearfully beneath the palm trees and read *The Last Negro*. And the Niger will be as romantic a river as the Rhine.[61]

124

On January 19, 1864, the Anthropological Society in London arranged a debate on the extinction of the lower races.[62]

In his introductory talk, "The Extinction of Races," Richard Lee reminded his listeners of the fate of the Tasmanians. The turn had now come of the Maori people of New Zealand, whose population had been halved in a few decades.

The reason for this could not yet be clearly given. Disease, insobriety and "the antagonism between the white and the coloured population" were important external factors. But they did not explain why the female population diminished more quickly than the male, nor did it explain the large number of infertile marriages.

Whatever the reasons, everywhere around us we could see the way one world leaves room for another more highly developed world. Within a few years the surface of the earth will be quite changed. We civilized people know better how to the use the land that for so long has been "the black man's" undisturbed home. A new era is dawning that will multiply the undertakings of man.

The tide of European civilization is rising over the earth.

Through its moral and intellectual superiority, the Anglo-Saxon race is sweeping away the earlier inhabitants. Light is consuming the darkness, said Richard Lee.

His opponent, T. Bendyshe, named the Philippines as one of the many examples of higher and lower races actually being able to live together without the lower being eradicated. So there was no question of any natural law.

The natives die out only where their land is taken from them and thus their means of earning a living. Although some Indian tribes of North America had been almost exterminated, there are sufficient numbers left to repopulate the continent—as long as they were given back their lands. For man reproduces himself regardless of race, according to Malthus's laws, said Bendyshe finally.

A. R. Wallace, the codiscoverer of the theory of evolution, maintained that the lower a race was the more land it needed to live off. When Europeans with their greater energy took over the land, the lower races could only be saved if they were swiftly civilized. But civilization could be acquired only slowly. So the disappearance of the lower races was only a question of time.

125

Later that same evening, in his lecture on "The Origin of Human Races," Wallace explained in greater detail how he looked on extermination. Quite simply, it was another name for natural selection. Contact with Europeans leads the lower, mentally underdeveloped peoples of other continents to inevitable destruction, says Wallace. The European's superior physical, moral and intellectual qualities meant that he reproduces himself at the expense of the savage, "just as the weeds of Europe overrun North America and Australia, extinguishing native productions by the inherent vigour of their organisation, and by their greater capacity for existence and multiplication."

When Darwin read that, he heavily underlined the word

"weeds" and added in the margin his own example: the rat. In *Descent of Man* he later wrote: "The New Zealander . . . compares his future fate with the native rat almost exterminated by the European rat."[63]

European animals and plants adapted without difficulty to the climate and soil of America and Australia, but only a few American and Australian plants, among them the potato, gained distribution in Europe.

These parallels from the worlds of plants and animals provided apparent confirmation of the belief in the biological superiority of Europeans and the inevitable decline of the other races.

But the parallels could also bring about doubts. Why did the weed spread more quickly and effectively in the colonies than any other European plants? Was it really through its moral and intellectual superiority that the European rat exterminated other rats?

126

We are having Christmas dinner with the Tideliuses across the street. I hardly reach the height of the table, which has been laid in the big salon with its black mirrored cupboard and formal high-backed oak chairs. The chandelier sparkles, the cutlery and porcelain, too. The tablecloth is of thick stiff white material, so it bulges a little at the creases and Mrs. Tidelius reaches forward to smooth out the bulge with her hand. A pitiful little squeak is heard, as when the mower exposes a mouse nest in the cornfield. In those days the fields stretched right up to the edges of our lawn. Uffe and I often hung around by the big barn of the manor house, where the rats were as natural as the barn cat. That is the direction our thoughts go as the rat squeaks and Mrs. Tidelius starts up with a shriek. Mr. Tidelius hurries to her rescue. He is twice as old as she is, an elegant, active old man, vigorous in his gait as every morning at six o'clock he takes a walk to the train to go to his ladies' tailoring business in Samuelsgatan. An excellent tailor, but no specialist in rats. He lifts the tablecloth to look underneath it—and whoops, the rat runs on along the crease, toward the center of the table, tipping over glasses on its way. A tremendous hullabaloo ensues as everyone tries to rescue glasses and plates, while they all lift the cloth, pull at the underlay, trying to trap the rat, now squealing with rage and terror and rushing hither and thither underneath the cloth, apparently growing each time it changes direction.

It is difficult to imagine my father doing what he now does. Later, in his old age, he became so mild and gentle. But when I was small, he was different. I still remember when that old rat, its fur quite gray, and as large as a small cat, coming leisurely gliding across our lawn. It was precisely the rat's untroubled way of moving as if it had a perfect right to that enraged my father. He threw open the terrace door, rushed down the slope, grabbing a piece of boarding in passing, caught up with the rat, which too late saw the danger, and killed it against the base of the fencing just as it was about to save itself. That is what he is like in his rage when he goes out into the kitchen for the big ax—we all still had wood-burning stoves in kitchens—raises it above his head and, to the joint squeals of bravo from the women, brings it down with all his strength straight through the bulge in the tablecloth. The cutting edge goes right through the damask and underlay and thuds into the dark oak table. It is sure also to have killed the rat, which is no longer rushing back and forth under the cloth, but is suddenly quite still. The shrieks stop. We all stand immobile, looking at the handle of the ax slanting up toward the ceiling and still trembling from the force of the blow. We can't continue Christmas dinner with the corpse of a rat on the table. The four parents clear the table. Finally they loosen the axe. Then they each go to a corner of the table and first lift the cloth, then the underlay. There is no sign of the rat. It has disappeared. But no one says anything. No one asks where it has gone. They all just stand there looking at the deep white bite the axe has made in the top of the table. "I'll cut a piece of oak," says my father, who is a woodwork master, "and stain it the same color. It'll hardly be noticed." His host and hostess thank him effusively.

But dinner is eaten in an oppressive atmosphere and we do not stay late.

Even those who remained in the Ethnographical Society realized that the lower races were doomed to destruction.

On March 27, 1866, Frederick Farrar gave a lecture on "Aptitude of the Races." He divided the races into three groups: savage, semicivilized and civilized. Only two races, the Aryan and the Semitic, were civilized. The Chinese belonged to the semicivilized, as they had once been brilliant but suffered from "arrested development." The savage races had always lived in the same ignorance and wretchedness. Farrar argued that:

> They are without a past and without a future, doomed, as races infinitely nobler have been before them, to a rapid, an entire, and, perhaps for the highest destinies of mankind, an inevitable extinction.
>
> . . . nor out of all their teeming myriads have they produced one single man whose name is of the slightest importance to the history of our race. Were they all to be merged tomorrow in some great deluge, they would leave behind no other traces of their existence than their actual physical remains.
>
> And I call them *irreclaimable* savages . . . [because] so far as being influenced by civilization, they disappear from before the face of it as surely and as perceptibly as the snow retreats before the advancing line of sunbeams.[64]

The Indians are an example. Or take a specimen from the hundred millions of Africa, not one of the most degenerate such as the Hottentots, but a real, pure-blooded Negro. What hope was there that he could be civilized? The great majority of Negroes will go under in a decline from which only a few can be saved.

Many races have already disappeared. These races—"the lowest types of humanity, and presenting its most hideous features of moral and intellectual degradation"—were doomed to go under. "Because darkness, sloth, and brutal ignorance cannot co-exist with the advance of knowledge, industry, and light."

128

What actually did happen when knowledge, industry, and light exterminated the inferior races?

Darwin knew. He had seen General Rosas's men butchering Indians, smothered in blood and vomit. He knew how eyes were gouged out when an Indian had sunk his teeth into a thumb and refused to let go, how women were killed and prisoners made to talk. He had a name for it. He called it the "struggle for life."

Darwin knew what the struggle for life was like. And yet he believed it developed and ennobled the species of man. Wallace shared his belief. The eradication of the lower races was justified, for it would gradually reduce the differences between races until the world would again be inhabited by one single, almost homogenous race in which no one was inferior to the noblest example of the humanity of the day. That is what Wallace believed.

But the strange thing was, he went on, that the little progress made toward this goal did not at all appear to be due to natural selection. Clearly "the best" were not those who were victors in this struggle for existence. The intellectually and morally mediocre, not to say deficient, in short, the weeds, succeeded best in life and reproduced themselves most rapidly.

Wallace had put his finger on a tender spot. William Greg took up the problem in an article in *Frazer's* magazine (September 1868), which Darwin read and commented on.[65]

What worried Greg was primarily that the middle classes, "who form the energetic, reliable, improving element of the population" have far fewer children than the upper classes and the lower classes, as both, though for opposite reasons, lack any grounds for restraint.

"The righteous and salutary law of natural selection" has been eliminated, and so our societies threaten to become overcivilized, like the ancient Greeks and Romans once became.

But fortunately the laws of nature are still alive in relations between the races, Greg goes on. Here the most favored are still the most capable and stronger. They are the ones who win the competition and "exterminate, govern, supercede, fight, eat, or work the inferior tribes out of existence."

Greg sees the struggle between the races as the only way of keeping civilized societies vital and capable of progress. Only by exterminating others can we avoid the racial decay that will otherwise be the consequences of civilization eliminating natural selection.

I have been cooking food on the computer. I cook it on the screen in the door of the microwave oven where it heats the food.

On my way home with dinner on a disc, I am jumped on in the underground by a man in ethnic clothing and a colorful little knitted cap. He takes the disc away from me. I try to stop him and wake up from having kicked a chair beside my bed with great strength. It still hurts when I walk.

Darwin's cousin, Francis Galton, continued the discussion in his book *Hereditary Genius* (1869). The history of geological changes, according to Galton, demonstrates how animal species have constantly been forced to adapt to new conditions of life. Civilization is the kind of new condition human species have to learn to live with. Many have failed. A large number of human races have been totally eradicated under the pressure of the demands of civilization. Galton further observes that "probably in no former period of the world has the destruction of the races of any animal whatever, been affected over such wide areas and with such startling rapidity as in the case of the savage man."

This should be a lesson to us. For even we who have created civilization are succumbing to it. Statesmen and philosophers and equally craftsmen and workers are today faced with demands they cannot master, Galton writes.

The conclusion is clear: if we do not want to go the same way as extinct animals and humans, we must seek to improve hereditary factors and through that increase our ability to survive the conditions of life civilization has created.

Galton devoted the rest of the century to studying and suggesting various methods of achieving such an improvement of hereditary factors. He had many followers, not just in Germany. The State Institute for Racial Biology in Uppsala was still in existence in the 1950s.

That passage in Galton is taken up by Benjamin Kidd in his hugely successful *Social Evolution* (1894), in which he observes that the Anglo-Saxon has exterminated the less developed peoples even more effectively than other races have managed to. Driven by the inbuilt forces of his own civilization, the Anglo-Saxon goes to the foreign country to develop its natural resources—and the consequences seem to be inescapable.

This struggle between races, entailing that the inferior are driven to subjugation, even eradication, is nothing distant and past. It is what is still happening in front of our very eyes, under the protection of the Anglo-Saxon civilization we are so proud of and like to link with the most elevated ideals.

For the race that wishes to keep its place in the competition, the eradication of other races is one of the stern imperative conditions. We can humanize those conditions, but not change them fundamentally—they are far too deep-rooted in physiological grounds, the effects of which we cannot shirk, writes Kidd.

133

Common to Wallace, Greg, Galton, and Kidd was their unease over society's terrain not tallying with the map. The wrong people were reproducing themselves. The selection did not favor those who ought to be favored. Then it was a solace to look on the struggle of the races. There, at last, the theory seemed to tally with reality. For it was precisely that reality which had once given rise to the theory.

Common to them was also their unease over changes in society, already very different from what they had experienced as children. Had we created a society which one day would break us as it had already broken the savages? Did it threaten us from within with creeping racial decay? Had we moved too far away from nature?

Common to them all was also the desire to excuse and approve genocide. Extermination was inevitable, apparently vitalizing the exterminators, and it had profound secret causes. Nor was it certain that it was particularly unpleasant for the victims.

To be exterminated could not be called "misery," Galton maintains. It was more a question of listlessness and apathy. The sexes simply lost interest in each other after contact with civilization, and thus their descendants diminished. It was unfortunate, but could hardly be called "misery"...

But what caused the apathy? What were these profound physiological causes people talked about? At the beginning of the 1800s, in the days of Howison and Merivale, the answers to these questions seemed evident and clear.[66] In the 1890s they had vanished into a racist fog.

134

Put up to be shot from behind. Waiting for the shot, the pain, the end.

We are several. While we wait, we write. We stand writing before the shots are fired.

When our bodies are as cold as corpses, at last a postal order for two pounds arrives. "With thanks for your co-operation" it says on the counterfoil.

135

I believe I have demonstrated that one of the fundamental ideas of the nineteenth century was that there are races, peoples, nations, and tribes that are in the process of dying out. Or as the prime minister of England, Lord Salisbury, expressed it in his famous speech in the Albert Hall on May 4, 1898: "One can roughly divide the nations of the world into the living and the dying."[67]

It was an image that came frighteningly close to reality.

The weak nations become increasingly weaker and the strong stronger, Salisbury went on. It was in the nature of things that "the living nations will fraudulently encroach on the territory of the dying."

He spoke the truth. During the nineteenth century, Europeans had encroached on vast territories in northern Asia and North

America, in South America, Africa, and Australia. And the "dying nations" were dying just because their lands had been taken from them.

The word *genocide* had not yet been invented. But the matter existed.

I do not maintain that Joseph Conrad heard Lord Salisbury's speech. He had no need to. It was enough with what he had read of Dilke's in *Cosmopolis*, in Wells's *The Wars of the Worlds*, in Graham's *Higginson's Dream*. Conrad could no more avoid hearing of the ceaseless genocide that marked his century than his contemporaries could.

It is we who have suppressed it. We do not want to remember. We want genocide to have begun and ended with Nazism. That is what is most comforting.

I am fairly sure the nine-year-old Adolf Hitler was not in the Albert Hall when Lord Salisbury was speaking. He had no need to. He knew it already. The air he and all other Western people in his childhood breathed was soaked in the conviction that imperialism is a biologically necessary process, which, according to the laws of nature, leads to the inevitable destruction of the lower races. It was a conviction which had already cost millions of human lives before Hitler provided his highly personal application.

LEBENSRAUM, TODESRAUM

*"das Recht der stärkeren Rasse,
die niedere zu vernichten"*
[*The right of the stronger race to annihilate the lower*]

136

In the mid-nineteenth century, the Germans had still not exterminated any people, so were able to look more critically on the phenomenon than did other Europeans. The most thorough investigation into people threatened with extermination was made by the
German anthropologist Theodore Waitz, in *Anthropologie der
Naturevölker* (Anthropology of Primitive Peoples) (1859–62),
which summarizes and analyzes information from reports by traveling scholars. His pupil, Georg Gerland, took up the problem of
extermination in *Über das Aussterben der Naturvölker* (On the
Extinction of Primitive Peoples) (1868).

Gerland goes through and evaluates every conceivable reason
named in the debate: primitive peoples' lack of care of their own
bodies and of children, taboos about certain foods, features of personality such as indolence, rigidity, and melancholy, sexual deprav-
ity and inclination to addiction to intoxicants, tribal warfare, can-
nibalism and human sacrifices, frequent capital punishment, an
inhospitable environment, and finally influences from higher cultures and the whites' treatment of colonized peoples.

He concludes that the diseases of the whites have often been
decisive exterminating factors. Even healthy whites can be infec-
tious as they carry a "miasma," a "dust of disease," which was the
name in those days for what we would call bacteria and viruses.

The miasma works more powerfully the further away and more
free of this dust a people has previously lived. The Europeans have
slowly acquired a resistance to miasmas which peoples living in
nature lack. So they die.

But an even more decisive factor is the hostile behavior of the whites, constituting one of the blackest chapters in the whole history of mankind. What could be called "cultural violence" is even more efficacious than physical violence, Gerland says.

The way of life of primitive peoples is so wholly adapted to climate and nature that sudden changes, however innocent and even useful they may seem, are devastating. Radical changes such as the privatization of land that had previously been public property, disturb the basis of a whole way of life. Europeans destroy out of rapacity or lack of understanding the basis of everything the natives thought, felt, and believed. When life loses its meaning for them, they die out.

Physical force is the clearest and most tangible factor in extermination. The bloodthirstiness of the whites is especially frightening as it is exercised by intellectually highly developed people. It cannot be said that violence is taken to only by individuals who could be made individually responsible — no, "the cruelties have been carried out fairly uniformly by whole populations in the colonies or anyhow have been approved by them; yes, even today violence is not always condemned."

It is no law of nature that primitive people must die out. Hitherto only a few peoples have been completely exterminated. Nowhere have we found any physical or mental inability to develop among them, Gerland ends. If the natural rights of the natives are respected, they will live on.

Darwin read this book and refers to it in *The Descent of Man* (1871).[68] But he was more influenced by Lyell and Wallace and Greg and Galton, who had already drawn "Darwinian" conclusions for man and society from *Origin of Species* (1859). Darwin was forestalled by those who parroted him, and he seems to have been seduced by their higher bids.

At the turn of the century, the German authority in this field was Friedrich Ratzel. He devotes the tenth chapter of his *Anthropogeographie* (1891) to "the decline of peoples of inferior cultures at contact with culture."

It has been, he writes, a deplorable rule that low-standing peoples die out at contact with highly cultivated people. This applies to the vast majority of Australians, Polynesians, northern Asians, North Americans, and many peoples in South Africa and South America. "The theory that this dying out is predestined by the inner weakness of the individual race is faulty," Ratzel writes. It is the Europeans who cause the destruction; as "the superior race" is in a minority, it must weaken the natives in order to gain domination. The natives are killed, impoverished, and driven away, their social organization destroyed.

The basic feature of white policies is the assault of the strong on the weak, the intention to take their land from them. This phenomenon has taken its most grandiose form in North America. Land-hungry whites crowd in between the weak and partly decayed settlements of the Indians. In Ratzel's day, the still increasing immigration into native lands was contrary to treaties and one of the main reasons for the extinction of the Indians.

That far, Ratzel sounds just like Gerland. Since Waitz's day this had been the standpoint of German anthropology. After all, the Germans had no colonies.

138

However, at the beginning of the 1890s, colonial ambitions had also begun to arise in Germany. The same year that Ratzel published his *Anthropogeographie*, he became a founding member of the Pan-German League, a radical right-wing organization that had the creation of a German colonial empire highest on its agenda.

This gives rise to some contradictions in Ratzel's view on the extinction of the lower races.

The question is whether this "deplorable process" is not after all driven on by a certain "demonic necessity," he goes on. Violence and the theft of land are indeed the main reasons for the decline of native peoples, but the logic that this is precisely why they die out would be far too simple.

Anyone looking more deeply will see that the European assaults really only intensify an already existing evil. In peoples with little culture there are inner forces of destruction that are released for the slightest reason. Their decline can therefore not be seen only as a result of attacks by more advanced peoples.

No, those with little culture have fundamentally passive characters. They seek to endure rather than overcome the circumstances that are reducing their numbers. Contact with Europeans simply hastens an extinction already underway. Many peoples at lower cultural levels have died out for internal reasons, with no assaults from the outside.

Thus Ratzel has gone full circle. He now maintains what he began by denying. For a future empire builder, the new standpoint was undeniably more comfortable.

139

The Jews could not really be regarded as "a people of inferior culture" in the sense Ratzel meant. A standard accusation against them was the opposite, that their position in German cultural life was far too dominating. But in his book *Politische Geographie* (1897), Ratzel nevertheless is able to pair them with people who, according to him, are condemned to annihilation. Jews and gypsies are brought together with "the stunted hunting people in the African interior" and "innumerable similar existences" into the class of "scattered people with no land." [69]

Land with no peoples, on the other hand, no longer exists. Not even the deserts can today be regarded as ownerless empty spaces. So a growing people needing more land has to conquer land, "which through killing and displacement of the inhabitants is turned into uninhabited land."

Pericles depopulated the island of Aegina to prepare room for Attic settlers. Rome carried out the same transplantations. Since then these have become increasingly necessary as uninhabited land became rarer and, finally, nonexistent. "Colonization has long since become displacement."

The history of American colonization provides a great many examples of people being removed and displaced. "The higher the culture of the immigrants stands above that of the original inhabitants, the easier the process. . . ." The United States is the best example of swift spatial expansion: from 1.8 million square kilometers in 1783 to 4.6 million in 1803 and 9.2 million in 1867.

Europe is the most thickly populated continent and the one whose population is growing fastest. So colonies are for Europe a necessity.

But it is a mistake to think that colonies have to be on the other side of the oceans. Border colonization is also colonization. Occupations near at hand are more easily defended and assimilated than distant ones. Russia's spread into Siberia and Central Asia is the most important example of this type of colonization, Ratzel maintains.

Hitler was given Ratzel's book in 1924, when he was in Landsberg prison writing *Mein Kampf*.

140

There are toads for dinner. Live toads. I wake just as I am to bite the head off a toad. It is still throbbing in my hand.

What about international law, then? The British had always regarded their expansion as a self-evident right. The French expansion in Northern Africa and the Russian in Central Asia, on the other hand, they regarded as reprehensible aggressive acts. And that German expansion was the height of immorality—on that point, the French, Russians, and British were all in agreement.

Robert Knox drew the conclusion that might is right: "Whilst I now write, the Celtic race is preparing to seize Northern Africa by the same right as we seized Hindostan—that is might, physical force—the only real right is physical force." [70]

The British are now appalled by the French invasion and regard it as ruthless aggression. We forget, says Knox, that "laws are made to bind the weak, to be broken by the strong." Could we really expect mighty France to be content to be "cabin'd, cribb'd, confin'd" and stay within the borders that chance and fortunes of war had handed her? No, of course not.

And this even if France is regarded simply as a nation! If we look on it from a more elevated viewpoint and remind ourselves that France represents a race, then we realize that the French claims are fully justified. "The Celtic race of men demand for their inheritance a portion of the globe equal to their energies, their numbers, their civilization, and their courage," Knox wrote in 1850. The same argument was now used in German as a motive for German expansion eastward.

As lecturer in German at Glasgow (1890–1900), Alexander Tille became familiar with British imperial ideology. He "Germanized" it by linking Darwin's and Spencer's theories to Nietzsche's superman morality into a new "evolutionary ethic."

In the field of international law, this evolutionary ethic entails that the stronger are right. By displacing the lower races, man is only doing what the better organized plants do with the less well organized, and what more highly developed animals do to the less developed. "All historical rights are invalid against the rights of the stronger," writes Tille in *Volksdienst* (Service to the people) (1893).

In nature, the higher are everywhere victorious over the lower. The weaker races die out even if no blood flows. It is "the right of the stronger race to annihilate the lower." Tille further argues that "when that race does not maintain its ability to resist then it has no right to exist, for anyone who cannot maintain himself must be content to go under."[71]

These iron "laws" were so generally worded by Tille that they could easily be applied not only to primitive peoples on other continents but also to the economically less successful peoples of Europe.

The Pan-German League paper *Alldeutsche Blätter* in the following year, 1894, stated that the conditions of life for the German race could be assured only through "elbow room" stretching from the Baltic to the Bosphorus. In that process one should not allow oneself to be hindered by the fact that inferior peoples such as Czechs, Slovenes, and Slovaks would lose their existence, anyhow worthless to civilization. Only "peoples of higher culture" have the right to a nationality of their own.[72]

143

When the big boys go into attack, I entrench myself on the upper floor of my childhood home. I confront them on the stairs and defend myself by breaking off large bits of the banisters and the rail to use as weapons. But they are light and brittle as meringue and at once fall to pieces. I am overwhelmed in a flash.

Then the wallpaper comes away from the walls of my parents' bedroom and slips to the ground. Not that I have ever been particularly fond of that showy large-flowered pattern, but nonetheless it is frightening that it is falling off. A pattern is a kind of skeleton even if it is on the outside. An entire architecture of life has collapsed, leaving behind the bare walls.

144

In Southwest Africa in 1904, the Germans demonstrated that they too had mastered an art that Americans, British, and other Europeans had exercised all through the nineteenth century—the art of hastening the extermination of a people of "inferior culture."

Following the North American example, the Herero people were banished to reserves and their grazing lands handed over to German immigrants and colonization companies. When the Hereros resisted, General Adolf Lebrecht von Trotha gave orders in October 1904 for the Herero people to be exterminated. Every Herero found within the German borders, with or without weapons, was to be shot. But most of them died without violence. The Germans simply drove them out into the desert and sealed off the border.

"The month-long sealing of desert areas, carried out with iron severity, completed the work of annihilation," the General Staff writes in the official account of the war. "The death rattles of the dying and their insane screams of fury . . . resounded in the sublime silence of infinity." The General Staff's account further reports that "the sentence had been carried out" and "the Hereros had ceased to be an independent people." [73]

This was a result the General Staff was proud of. The army earned, they stated, the gratitude of the whole fatherland.

When the rainy season came, German patrols found skeletons lying around dry hollows, twenty-four to fifty feet deep, dug by the Hereros in vain attempts to find water. Almost the entire people—about eighty thousand human beings—died in the deserts. Only a few thousand were left, sentenced to hard labor in German concentration camps.

Thus the words "concentration camp," invented in 1896 by the Spaniards in Cuba, anglicized by the Americans, and used again by the British during the Boer War, made their entrance into German language and politics.[74]

145

The cause of the rebellion was "the Hereros's warlike and freedom-loving nature," the General Staff stated.

The Hereros were not particularly warlike. Their leader, Samuel Maherero, over two decades had signed one treaty after another with the Germans and ceded large areas of land to avoid war. But just as the Americans did not feel themselves bound by their treaties with the Indians, equally, the Germans did not think that as a higher race they had any need to abide by treaties they made with the natives.

As in North America, the German plans for immigration at the turn of the century presupposed that the natives were to be relieved of all land of any value. The rebellion was therefore welcomed as an opportunity to "solve the Herero problem."

The arguments the English, French, and Americans had long used to defend genocide were now also put into German: "Existencies, be they peoples or individuals who do not produce anything of value, cannot make any claim to the right to exist," wrote Paul Rohrbach in his best-seller *German Thought in the World* (1912). It was as head of German immigration in Southwest Africa that he had learned his colonial philosophy:

> No false philanthropy or racial theory can convince sensible people that the preservation of a tribe of South Africa's kaffirs . . . is more important to the future of mankind than the spread of the great European nations and the white race in general.
> Not until the native learns to produce anything of

value in the service of the higher race, i.e. in the service
of its and his own progress, does he gain any moral
right to exist.

146

From my place on the hotel roof terrace, I look down over the
market place in Agadez. A black man is walking along wearing
shiny reflector sunglasses and a gray corduroy suit. Has he any
right to exist?

And that man in the black trench coat? Or him over there in a
red jogging suit with white reveres? Everything suits a beauty, it is
said, but that should be: everything suits a pride. These people
move like kings, most of all the men of white shirts and flapping
cloaks with turbans like eagle's nests on their heads. They often
walk hand in hand. They carry nothing except possibly a tooth-
brush in their mouths or a sword at their sides.

Their way of life is threatened. The nomads are attacked from
one direction by the assailing deserts, from the other by cultiva-
tors' fields, which today go right up to the borders of the desert.

When drought strikes, when the grazing vanishes and the wells
dry, the nomads make their way to Agadez. Some return when the
drought is over, but most remain—far too impoverished to take up
the struggle against the desert again. They live in a circle around
Agadez, crammed into small round tents of raffia mats, and have
already tripled the population of the town.

They meet in the camel market. I sometimes go there when the
dust has made it impossible to continue the day's work. The strong
evening wind sweeps people and animals into a fog of dust. In this
haze, heavily veiled men stand looking at each other's camels.

The camels protest against every change, with loud complaining screams. Their mouths are ash gray and evil smelling, their
tongues as pointed as wedges. They hiss like dragons, strike like
snakes, inflict hideous bites, and rise reluctantly on tall wobbling

legs to stand there like some kind of outsized greyhounds with swollen stomachs and wasp waists at their loins, superciliously looking down on the world around them, their eyes filled with unspeakable contempt.

The same arrogance marks their masters. They often cannot even imagine abandoning their lifestyle. But nor can they live by selling their camels to each other. Nor can they live by transporting homemade desert salt from Bilma or Tueggidam in caravans, when one single truck carries a larger load than a hundred camels.

Tuaregs are not hunted as are the natives in the Amazon or the jungles of Borneo, but the basis of their life is disappearing like a melting ice floe. Many succeed in jumping over to other floes. The old camel yards have become repair workshops and diesel stations. As drivers, the Tuaregs find a use for their knowledge of the desert. Others despise such change or cannot cope with it.

147

A German schoolmaster is sitting on the roof this evening. For seven years he has spent his vacations in the Sahara and his idea of sport is to get as far south as possible before he has to return. Tomorrow he is to take the bus to Niamey, then fly back to Germany, where the neo-Nazis are attacking some refugee camps almost every night, his crackling transistor tells us. In Sweden, too, refugee quarters have been set on fire. In Paris, Le Pen is speaking on May Day.

"I've heard him," says a French engineer working for Michelin in Nigeria. "I thought that when Fascism came back, it would be disguised in bright friendly colors, so that it would be difficult to recognize. I didn't think it would come in a brown shirt and black leather. I didn't think it would be shaven heads, swastikas, boots, and officer's shoulder belts. I didn't think it would call itself 'national and socialist.'"

But just as recognizably, it is coming, swaggering with its heritage from Nazism. The same roar after every sentence when the leader speaks. The same hatred of aliens. The same preparedness for violence. The same wounded manhood.

"And the same soil," says the German. "After the war, *everyone* was afraid of unemployment. Everyone knew where that had led to and could do so again. That insight lasted for twenty-five years. Then it was forgotten."

The advantages are tempting. Unemployment rates of 5,10,15, or 20 percent give the employer a wonderful upper hand. The workforce stands on tiptoe, longing to be exploited.

And this is just the beginning. The great mass of unemployed are on the other side of Europe's Rio Grande, in Asia and Africa. Just wait until they come flooding in, said the German. Wait until the border falls just like the Wall fell and everything will be one great labor market. Who will then win elections?

148

The Pan-German League's "elbow room" was given wings when Friedrich Ratzel renamed it *Lebensraum* at the turn of the century.

The geographer Ratzel was originally a zoologist. In the concept of *Lebensraum*, he linked the biological theory of life with the geographical theory of space, into a new theory, charged with political dynamite.

Between the never-ending movement of life and the unalterable space of the earth lies a contradiction that always and everywhere gives rise to struggle, Ratzel writes in *Der Lebensraum* (1901, in book form 1904). Since life first reached the limits of space, life has been fighting with life for space.

What is called the struggle for existence is really a struggle for space. True "lack of space" we see most clearly in animals living together in colonies. The first to arrive take the best places, those who come later have to be content with the worst. Among them, infant mortality is greatest, and corpses lie scattered over the ground.

Similar courses of events arise in human life, says Ratzel. His readers knew what he was aiming at. Germany was one of the last to arrive among the European nations. In a world the colonial powers had already divided up between themselves, Germany had to be content with the worst places. This was why the children of the unemployed were dying in Berlin and Hamburg—that was the conclusion the reader was expected to draw.

As a young man, Ratzel had traveled in North America and seen the way whites and Indians fought over lands. This struggle became for him a paradigm, which he constantly returned to.

A few hundred thousand Indians, degraded and removed to unfavorable areas, had seen their continent Europeanized as to people, animals, and plants. The Spaniards built towns and ruled the crop-growing Indians. The Germanic and French settlers in North America took over the land from the natives in order to cultivate it themselves. "The result was an annihilating struggle, the prize for which was the land, the space."

This struggle is not only over *Lebensraum*, as when a bird builds its nest. It concerns the much larger *Lebensraum* needed to earn a livelihood. To conquer and hold sufficient *Lebensraum*, others have to be displaced, that is, lose space—which often entails the species weakening and dying out, leaving the space completely.

The shortage of living space on this earth makes it necessary for an old species to disappear to open the space for a new species to evolve. Extinction is a presupposition for creation and progress. "The history of primitive peoples dying out on the appearance of a people of higher culture provides many instances of this."

How much of the loss of space by the old species is due to inner reasons, such as declining life force, and how much due to the victorious progress of the new species is still an open question. What is certain is that the decline of a species is always expressed by it being crowded together into an increasingly smaller space.

One of the greatest riddles in the history of evolution is that some of the oldest and largest animal groups died out on the threshold of the Tertiary period. The reptiles dominating land

and water during the Triassic, Jurassic, and Cretaceous periods died out in the Tertiary period and were replaced by mammals and birds.

We do not know why. From our starting point, Ratzel says, it is enough to establish what happened: an animal species replaced another in the space. Extinction is often preceded by a decline in numbers, which also suggests a reduction of the space.

Ratzel did not have to draw the conclusion himself. It was already clear: a people that does not wish to share the fate of the dinosaurs must constantly increase its living space. Territorial expansion is the safest, indeed fundamentally the only real sign of the vitality of the nation and the race.

149

Ratzel's theories were a good summary of what had happened during the nineteenth century. The spread of Europeans over four continents, the growth of the British, French, and Russian empires, such examples seemed to demonstrate that territorial expansion was necessary and favored the conquerors. A stagnant territory was considered as abnormal and as ill-omened as a stagnant economy is considered today.

But even in 1900, when the concept of *Lebensraum* was born, that approach was outmoded. Size of territory had been decisive for agricultural states, but for industrial states, other factors were much more important. Geographically insignificant, Germany developed her economy at the end of the 1800s as rapidly as the huge United States and considerably more quickly than the British Empire. Technology and education were already more important economic driving forces than spatial size.[75]

So the *Lebensraum* theory was backward-looking. Perhaps just because of that it became an enormous success. It appealed to the major power that had arrived last to imitate its predecessor. "The loser from 1870," as France was called in Germany, had since then built up the second largest colonial empire. Why not Germany? The Germans had lagged behind. Germany must catch up.

The *Lebensraum* theory urged Germany to use the strength the country had gained through new means of production (industry) to acquire more of the old means of production (land), roughly like the new industrial barons showing off their power by displacing the old nobility from their manors and estates.

An expanding people needs space, it was said. A people who cannot "feed itself" is doomed to die out. Why? No answer.

Hitler started the war to acquire more agricultural land a few decades before all the states of Europe began to pay their farmers to reduce cultivation.

150

When Adolf Hitler entered politics, one of the opportunities for Germany to expand had been closed. The British Navy ruled the seas and stopped every attempt to conquer new lands in the colonies.

There remained the continent. In *Mein Kampf* (1925–27) Hitler describes how Germany and England are to divide up the world between them. Germany is to expand eastward just as England had already expanded westward in America and south in India and Africa. The culmination of Hitler's policy of eastward expansion was the invasion of the Soviet Union in June 1941.[76]

German propaganda portrayed the war as an anti-Communist crusade. In that way, Hitler hoped to win sympathy among all those in western Europe and the United States who hated communism. But the crusade would never have come about if there had not also been economic reasons for it.

In the short term, by conquering the agricultural areas of the western Soviet Union, Hitler wanted to improve the food situation in wartime Germany. In this way an unknown number of millions of people (*zig Millionen Menschen*) in the Soviet Union were to die of starvation, which would also be a long-term advantage.

In the long term, Hitler intended to incorporate these agricultural areas into the German *Lebensraum*. The land, "which through killing and displacement of the inhabitants is turned into uninhabited land" (cf. Ratzel), would come into German possession. The decimated Slavic population, like the Hereros in Southwest Africa, would be the servants and workers of their German masters.

151

On the night of September 18, 1941, Hitler painted for his collaborators a rosy future in which the Ukraine and the Volga basin had become the bread basket of Europe. There, German industry would exchange grain for cheap utility goods. "We'll send to the Ukraine kerchiefs, glass beads, and other things colonial peoples like." [77]

Of course, he was joking. But to understand Hitler's campaign to the east it is important to realize that he considered he was fighting a colonial war. For wars of that kind, special rules applied — those already laid down in *Politik* (1898) by the German extreme right's most beloved political scientist, Heinrich von Treitschke: "International law becomes phrases if its standards are also applied to barbaric people. To punish a Negro tribe, villages must be burned, and without setting examples of that kind, nothing can be achieved. If the German Reich in such cases applied international law, it would not be humanity or justice but shameful weakness."

Treitschke was only putting into words the practice European states had long applied and which Hitler now used against his future "colonial peoples" in the east.

In the war against the western powers, the Germans observed the laws of war. Only 3.5 percent of English and American prisoners of war died in captivity, though 57 percent of Soviet prisoners of war died.

Altogether, 3.3 million Russian prisoners of war lost their lives, two million of them in the first year of the war, through a combination of starvation, cold, disease, execution, and gassing. The first to be gassed in Auschwitz were Russians.

There is a crucial difference between these killings and the murders of Jews. Of non-Jewish Russians, only certain categories — first and foremost intellectuals and Communists — were totally exterminated. Among other Russians, according to the plans, some ten million or so were to be weeded out, but the remainder were to live on as a slave labor force under German command. On the other hand, the Jewish people as a whole were to be exterminated.[78]

In that, the Holocaust was unique — in Europe. But the history of Western expansion in other parts of the world shows many examples of total extermination of whole peoples.

152

My stomach is being filled with a great blood blister. My whole belly is full of black blood.

Just as a toenail blackens and falls off when the blood has coagulated under it, my body blackens and drops off.

All that is left is the throbbing blood beneath its membrane, thin and shimmering like a soap bubble.

An immense drop of black blood, for a moment still held together by its surface tension — that is me, before I burst.

153

"Many of the most horrendous of Nazi actions (especially the massacre of the Jews) . . . had comparatively little to do with the imperialist parts of the Nazi program," writes Woodruff D. Smith in *The Ideological Origins of Nazi Imperialism* (1986).

Smith is a great specialist in this field, but in my opinion he is wrong. Imperialist expansion gave the Nazis the practical opportunity and economic reasons to exterminate the Jews. The extermination project's theoretical framework, the *Lebensraum* theory, is part of imperialist tradition. To the same tradition belongs the historical model of extermination of Jews: genocide in the colonies.

When the mass murder of Jews began, there were only a quarter of a million Jews left in Germany. The rest had either fled or been banished. The great Jewish populations were in Poland and Russia. Hitler had the practical possibility of eradicating them only by attacking and capturing these areas.

The main intention behind the conquest was not to murder Jews, just as the Americans did not advance westward in order to murder Indians. The intention was to expand Germany's own *Lebensraum*. The Russian Jews lived in just those areas Hitler was after, making up 10 percent of the total population there and up to 40 percent of the urban population.

To faithful Nazis, the killing of Jews was a way of implementing the most central point of the party program. For those less faithful, it was a practical way of reducing the consumption of food and making room for the future German settlement. German bureaucracy spoke of "de-Jewishing" (*Entjudung*) as a way of clearing out "superfluous eaters" (*überzähligen Essern*) and in that way creating a "balance between population and food supply."

Hitler himself was driven throughout his political career by a fanatical anti-Semitism with roots in a tradition of over a thousand years, which had often led to killing and even to mass murder of Jews. But the step from mass murder to genocide was not taken until the anti-Semitic tradition met the tradition of genocide arising during Europe's expansion in America, Australia, Africa, and Asia.

According to the *Lebensraum* theory, the Jews were a landless people, like the stunted hunting people of the African interior. They belonged to an even lower race than Russians and Poles, a race which could not lay claim to the right to live. It was only natural that such lower races (whether Tasmanians, Indians, or Jews) should be exterminated if they were in the way. The other Western master races had done just that.

The Nazis gave the Jews a star on their coats and crowded them into "reserves"—just as the Indians, the Hereros, the Bushmen, the Amandabele, and all the other children of the stars had been crowded together. They died on their own when the food supply to the reserves was cut off. It was a sad rule that low-standing people died out on contact with highly cultivated people. If they did not die fast enough, then it was merciful to shorten their suffering. They were going to die anyhow.

154

Auschwitz was the modern industrial application of a policy of extermination on which European world domination had long since rested.

155

The Nazi slaughter of the Jews, like every other event, however unique it may be, has to be seen in its historical context.

Arno J. Mayer, in his controversial book *Why Did the Heavens Not Darken? The "Final Solution" in History* (1988), goes right back to the horrors of the Thirty Years' War, the storming of Magdeburg on May 10, 1631, when thirty thousand men, women, and children were murdered, and even further back to the mass murder by the Crusaders of eleven hundred innocent inhabitants of Mainz in 1096, to find equivalents to the mass murders of Jews during World War II.[79]

On the other hand, there is no mention of the European slave trade, which forcibly moved fifteen million Negroes between continents and killed perhaps just as many. Nor are the nineteenth-century European colonial wars or punitive expeditions mentioned. If Mayer had as much as glanced in that direction, he would have found so many examples of brutal extermination based on clearly racial convictions, that the Thirty Years' War and the Crusades would seem to lie unnecessarily far back.

On my journey through the Sahara alone, I have been in two Mainzes. One is called Zaatcha, where the entire population was wiped out by the French in 1849. The other is Laghouat, where on December 3, 1852, after the storming, the remaining third of the population, mainly women and children, was massacred. In one single well, 256 corpses were found.

That was how one mixed with the inferior races. It was not considered good form to talk about it, nor was it anything that needed concealing. It was established practice. Only occasionally was there any debate—for instance, over the events taking place while Joseph Conrad was writing *Heart of Darkness* and the Central African Expedition was on its way toward Zinder.

<h1 style="text-align:center">156</h1>

The bus to Zinder leaves at 7:30. At dawn I find a man with a wheelbarrow to help me wheel away my word processor and suitcase. It is a windy and cold morning, some fires flickering over by the stalls across the street, a few lamps glowing faintly, overcome by the morning light.

After half an hour, the driver arrives and starts washing the windows of the big white Renault truck that has been converted into a bus. On the sides it says in giant red letters: SOCIETE NATIONALE DE TRANSPORT NIGERENNE.

Vendors of loose cigarettes and sticky lollipops start assembling. A shivering man is carrying round red nuts, already shelled and indecently naked on his tray. A bright yellow baby's cap frames his anthracite black face.

Toward half-past eight, the blind women come, all of them at once, all singing, all begging, all led by children, some of the women with newborn babies on their backs.

At nine, the passengers are called out according to the passenger list and each given a small piece of paper, which after another roll call is exchanged for the ticket already booked and paid for the day before yesterday.

A man stands on a barrel and flings the luggage up to the driver, who stows it on to the roof of the bus. After that the station supervisor gets into the bus and, standing inside where he is very difficult to hear, starts the third and determining roll call. It is not easy to predict how a name like mine will sound. I miss the name and thus lose my booked seat in the front of the bus. Only the seats at the back are left.

I can still change my mind. I can still jump off. Here at the far back I will never cope with the jolts. And once out in the desert there is no return. One has to go on, for eight hours, whatever happens. It is now, at this moment, and only now, I still have a chance to get off.

Always the same alloy of panic and joy at the moment of departure. It is like losing your foothold in a great love affair. What will happen now? I have no idea. All I know is that I have just thrown myself out into it.

157

At the head of the 1898 Central African Expedition was Captain Voulet and Lieutenant Chanoine.[80]

Paul Voulet, the thirty-two-year-old son of a doctor, had, according to his officer colleagues, "a true love of blood and cruelty coupled with a sometimes foolish sensitivity." He was, it was said afterward, a weak character dominated by two evil people, his black mistress and Chanoine.

Charles Chanoine, the son of a general, was described as impulsive, ruthless, and cruel—"cruel out of cold-bloodedness as well as for pleasure." Two years previously, in 1896, the two friends had conquered Ouagadougou in what is now Burkina Faso, and had shown themselves to be skilled at burning down villages and murdering natives. Faced with this new expedition, Voulet boasted to the governor of Sudan of how he would crush resistance by letting the villages burn.

So despite, or perhaps thanks to, his reputation, Voulet was appointed head of an expedition that was to explore the area between the Niger and Lake Chad and place it, as was said, "under French protection."

Otherwise his orders were vague in the extreme. "I don't pretend to be able to give you any instructions on which route to choose or how you are to behave toward the native chieftains and peoples," wrote the minister for the colonies modestly.

Voulet was given a free hand to use the methods for which he had made himself notorious.

158

It is 270 miles from Agadez to Zinder—270 miles of washboard, sanded over by high wandering dunes that lift the bus and throw it down with fierce, stunning jolts.

The driver maintains a good speed in order to get there before sunset. It is like sitting on a leaping compressed air drill. The fat in my blood ought to be churned to butter by the vibration.

At the same time you have to be constantly prepared to rise in the saddle and receive the great jolts with your thigh and arm muscles instead of your spine. But I miss every fourth or every tenth one, not noticing in time that the driver has taken his foot off the accelerator, and I am suddenly hurled with full force down toward the center of the earth. All my vertebrae come tumbling down and the disks in my spine have to take the whole jolt.

For the first hours the wind is very strong. The dust turns day into white night, and the sand sweeps over steppe and savanna. The white steppe grass drowns, the bushes ride in despair on the waves of sand. The occasional tree is glimpsed in the blurred murkiness of the sand, and misty human figures struggle on, whipped by the sand in the air.

The sand seems to be the attacker when the desert comes, but it is the dryness that kills. Dead plants can no longer bind and stop the sand. We drive for hours through sparse forest where only every hundredth tree is alive. White tree trunks lie like distorted skeletons on the ground.

After five desert hours we are suddenly in among fields. The cultivation boundary has moved forward until it coincides with the boundary of the desert. The vulnerable living space the nomads once found between desert and field no longer exists.

159

Here on the edge of the desert, in 1898, marched the Central African Expedition. It consisted of nine French officers, seventy regular Senegal soldiers, and thirty interpreters and "agents." In addition, they had recruited four hundred "auxilliaries," Africans who went with the French and took part in the fighting for a chance to plunder. In Tombouctou, ninety Senegalese joined them, placed at the expedition's disposal by Lieutenant-Colonel Klobb.

Voulet took with him great quantities of arms and ammunition, but had not taken any means of paying the bearers. His men simply seized eight hundred black men and forced them to be bearers. The latter were dressed for the hot climate prevailing where they were captured and suffered severely from the night cold in the desert. A dysentery epidemic broke out, and 148 bearers died during the first two months of the expedition. Chanoine set an example by having anyone who tried to escape shot.

They requisitioned food from the villages, naturally without payment. What with baggage and mistresses, the expedition had grown to sixteen hundred people and eight hundred animals. It moved on like a swarm of locusts through areas normally living on the edge of starvation. Neither of the two commanders had any experience of desert areas. The expedition cruised between the water holes, dominated by the necessity of supplying men and animals with forty tons of water a day.

160

Meanwhile Joseph Conrad was sitting at his Chippendale desk at Pent Farm in Kent, penciling out his story about Kurtz, the story of outrages committed in the name of Civilization and Progress. He could not have been influenced by contemporary events in French Sudan, as he knew nothing about them.

319

Not until January 29, when Conrad had almost finished his story, was one of the French officers, Lieutenant Peteau, sent back owing to "lack of discipline and enthusiasm." Not until February 5 did Peteau write a fifteen-page letter to his wife-to-be in Paris to tell her of some of the atrocities he had been involved in.

The forcibly recruited bearers were maltreated and refused medical attention during the dysentery epidemic, Peteau writes. Those who were unable to continue were beheaded. Twelve bearers were shot for trying to escape, the rest bound together with neck chains, in groups of five.

To recruit new bearers, the French sent out patrols, which surrounded the villages at dawn and shot anyone trying to escape. As evidence that they had carried out their orders, the soldiers took the heads back with them. Voulet had the heads impaled on stakes and placed out to frighten the population into submission.

In Sansan-Hausa, a village already under French "protection," Voulet had given orders that thirty women and children were to be killed—with bayonets, to save ammunition. According to the chieftain, Kourtey, there were even more victims. "I had done nothing to them," he said. "I gave them everything they asked for. They ordered me to hand over six horses and thirty head of cattle within three days. I did so. And yet they killed everyone they could get hold of. A hundred and one men, women, and children were massacred."

161

Peteau's fiancée sent his letter to her deputy in parliament, and in the middle of April, the government intervened. The governor of Sudan gave orders to Lieutenant-Colonel Klobb in Tombuoctou to find Voulet and remove from him his command of the expedition.

Just as in Conrad's novel Marlow set off into the interior to find Kurtz, Klobb took up the hunt for Voulet. His tracks were easy to follow; they consisted of ruins and corpses, which increased in number appallingly the closer Klobb came.

Klobb found guides who had displeased Voulet and had been strung up alive, low enough for hyenas to eat their feet, while the rest of the bodies were left to the vultures. Outside the burned-out village of Tibiri, 120 miles west of Zinder, Klobb found the bodies of thirteen women hanging in the trees. Outside Koran-Kaljo, nearer to Zinder, hung two corpses of children.

On July 10, 1899, Klobb arrived at the little village of Damangara to be told that Voulet was only a few hours' march away.[81]

162

In the middle of the night, my father telephones. Surprised and confused, I rush across the hotel yard in the dark to take the call in Reception. When I lift the receiver I can hear nothing but a hollow crackling.

Nor could I expect anything else, I realize when I wake up. After all, Father is dead.

The heat enfolds me in its moist embrace. The heat in the Sahara stings like a whiplash, but only where the searchlight of the sun fell; in the shade it was cool, at night cold. Here in Zinder the summer temperature seldom goes below 105°F.

Your veins swell and snake along under your skin, pumping, throbbing, ready to burst. Hands and feet swell, the soles of your feet sting, fingers resemble small clubs, your skin is not large enough. Your face swells up, becomes porous and opens. Sweat spurts out through the pores, suddenly, just as when a heavy raindrop strikes your skin.

I can feel a burning heat on the inside of my lower arm and notice it is brushing my stomach. I have burned myself on my own body.

All flesh thickens, overflows, starts running. A movement and your body is soaked all over. Keep still and nonetheless you are soaked.

I drink so much, the salt balance in my body is disturbed. Then I eat salt, become thirsty, and have to drink even more. My belly swells, my body slops about, nothing helps.

Next morning I am sitting as usual in the library of the French Institute reading Klobb's journal.[81] But my mind stiffens like coagulated blood in my head, and the afternoons start earlier and earlier, sinking deeper and deeper into a hot torpor.

In the evening as I sit waiting for the news on the hotel owner's radio, I hear a sea moving in the rise and fall of the interference. Above me, filled with a wonderful cool, roll the huge roaring breakers of space.

163

The meeting between Klobb and Voulet was even more dramatic than the meeting between Marlow and Kurtz in Conrad's novel, by then already finished and published in *Blackwood's* magazine. Marlow did not after all have to make Kurtz come back with him. Kurtz was seriously ill and went with him after some persuasion. Voulet did not.

Klobb sent a sergeant and two soldiers with a letter that briefly and curtly told Voulet he had been removed from his command and was to return home immediately. Voulet replied that he had six hundred rifles against Klobb's fifty and would open fire if Klobb approached.

On July 13, Voulet had a hundred and fifty women and children executed as punishment for the death of two of his soldiers during an attack on a nearby village. On the same day, he once again wrote to Klobb and warned him not to come any nearer.

Klobb was convinced that neither Senegalese soldiers nor French officers would bring themselves to shoot at a superior officer. He counted on the ninety soldiers he had lent the expedition preferring to obey him rather than Voulet. What he did not know was that Voulet and Chanoine had kept his letter secret from the other whites and had sent them all out on various assignments in the vicinity, keeping with them only the black troops personally loyal to them.

On July 14, Bastille Day, Klobb's and Voulet's troops stood facing each other. Klobb gave his men strict orders not to open fire under any circumstances. Then he started slowly walking toward Voulet, who had his soldiers fire two salvos into the air. When Klobb was within earshot, he stopped and started speaking directly to the soldiers.

Voulet was furious and, threatening them with a pistol, forced his men to fire at Klobb. Klobb was wounded and fell—still calling on his men not to answer fire. The next salvo killed him.

164

Naturally, Voulet had not read Conrad's recently published story about Kurtz, the white man who, with terror and magic, had made himself king over a black realm in the heart of the continent.

But when the white officers returned that evening, Voulet told them what had happened and suggested a solution of exactly that kind: they would continue to Lake Chad and there set up their own kingdom, "a strong and impenetrable empire, surrounded by a waterless desert."

"I am no longer a Frenchman. I am a black chief," said Voulet.

The following day, the black sergeants decided to mutiny. Voulet was warned by an interpreter, who was immediately shot for not warning him earlier. Voulet mounted his horse and, with Chanoine, addressed the soldiers, firing at them at the same time. The soldiers answered fire and killed Chanoine. When Voulet tried to approach the camp the following morning, he was also shot.

The French officers held a council of war and decided to continue the expedition. They marched toward Zinder and captured the town.

The hotel owner sits all day in the yard talking to his parrot, his voice caressing and loving, quite different from the brusque commanding tone he otherwise uses in his contact with the outside world.

Sometimes he brings his two dogs here and exercises them in the yard. An adopted son takes up a middle position, a handsome black boy, son of his dead housekeeper.

I am the only guest.

I am engrossed in the history of Zinder. It turns out that a much larger French expedition, which had just crossed the Sahara in the summer of 1899, was on its way to Zinder. So it was quite superfluous for other Frenchmen to capture the town.

But the remains of the Central African Expedition got there first. These were the troops to gain everlasting glory by occupying Zinder, the expedition's officers hoping their crimes would be forgotten.

They were right.

When the murder of Klobb became known in Paris, an official inquiry was set up on August 23. After having accumulated three huge cardboard boxes of statements and documents, they found only one conceivable explanation: the climate. Voulet must have gone mad in the African heat.

The crimes of the others were excused and forgotten, and France kept her captured possessions.

The French left wing took over in government in 1899 and had little interest in digging any further into the affair. The right wing had even less. The ugly truth stayed in the inquiry's cardboard boxes.[82]

166

Eventually the facts trickled out. Of course, educated Frenchmen knew roughly, or even quite precisely, by what means their colonies were captured and administered.

Just as educated Frenchmen in the 1950s and 1960s knew what

their troops were up to in Vietnam and Algeria.

Just as educated Russians in the 1980s knew what their troops did in Afghanistan, and educated South Africans and Americans during the same period knew what their "auxilliaries" were doing in Mozambique and Central America respectively.

Just as educated Europeans today know how children die when the whip of debt whistles over poor countries.

It is not knowledge that is lacking. The educated general public has always largely known what outrages have been committed and are being committed in the name of Progress, Civilization, Socialism, Democracy, and the Market.

167

At all times it has also been profitable to deny or suppress such knowledge. Even today there are readers of Conrad's story who maintain it lacks universal application.

It has been said that the circumstances in the Congo of the Belgian monarch were unique. The novel cannot be seen as an accusation against the whole of the civilized world, as the oppressive Belgian regime in the Congo was a one-of-a-kind phenomenon already condemned by most reasonable people.

But during just those months when Conrad was writing the book, similar or even worse events were occurring by another river, the Niger, on the way to another chamber of the same dark heart.

No, the Belgians were not unique, nor were the Swedish officers in their service. Conrad would have been able to set his story using any of the peoples of European culture. In practice, the whole of Europe acted according to the maxim "Exterminate all the brutes."

Officially, it was, of course, denied. But man to man, everyone knew. That is why Marlow can tell his story as he does in Conrad's novel. He has no need to count up the crimes Kurtz committed.

He has no need to describe them. He has no need to produce evidence. For no one doubted it.

Marlow-Conrad was able to assume quite calmly that both the listening gentlemen on the yacht, the *Nellie*, and the readers of *Blackwood's* silently knew quite enough to understand the story and in their own imaginations develop details the novel only implied. This knowledge is a fundamental prerequisite of the book.

This knowledge could be expressed in general and scholarly language. Imperialism is a biologically necessary process that, according to the laws of nature, leads to the inevitable destruction of the lower races. Things of that kind could be said. But the way it actually happened, what it really did to the exterminators and the exterminated, that was at most only implied.

And when what had been done in the heart of darkness was repeated in the heart of Europe, no one recognized it. No one wished to admit what everyone knew.

168

Everywhere in the world where knowledge is being suppressed, knowledge that, if it were made known, would shatter our image of the world and force us to question ourselves—everywhere there, *Heart of Darkness* is being enacted.

169

You already know that. So do I. It is not knowledge we lack. What is missing is the courage to understand what we know and draw conclusions.

NOTES

See generally Ian Watt, *Conrad in the Nineteenth Century* (London, 1980) and Patrick Brantlinger, *Rule of Darkness* (Ithaca: Cornell University Press, 1988). This English edition of "*Exterminate All the Brutes*" is a translation of the second Swedish edition.

1. The most recent geological period, which began at the end of the Ice Age.
2. Kim Naylor, *Guide to West Africa* (London, 1986), p. 193.
3. John Aubrey, *Brief Lives* (1949), p. 157.
4. Joseph Conrad, "An Outpost of Progress" (1897).
5. B. W. Sheehan, *The Seeds of Extinction, Jeffersonian Philanthropy, and the American Indian* (Chapel Hill, 1973). S. M. Stanley, *Extinction* (New York, 1987).
6. R. C. Lewontin, *New York Review of Books* (14 June 1990).
7. Margaret T. Hodgen, *Early Anthropology in the Sixteenth and Seventeenth Centuries* (Philadelphia, 1964), p. 410.
8. Herbert Spencer, *Social Statistics* (1850), p. 416.
9. Eduard von Hartmann, *Philosophy of the Unconscious*, vol. 2, p. 12. Quoted in J. E. Saveson, *Modern Fiction Studies*, vol. 16, no. 2 (1970).
10. Ernst Nolte in *Historikerstreit: Die Dokumentation der Kontroverse um die Einzigartigkeit der nationalsozialistischen Judenvernichtung* (Munich, 1987), p. 33. See also Frank Chalk and Kurt Jonassohn, *The History and Sociology of Genocide* (New Haven, 1990) and Ervin Staub, *The Roots of Evil: The Origins of Genocide and Other Group Violence* (Cambridge, 1989). None of these authors saw the connection between genocide by Hitler and European imperialism. However, Richard L. Rubenstein has done so in *Genocide and Civilization* (1987). I am grateful to

Professor Sverker Sörlin, who drew my attention to Ruben-stein's writing and to Helen Fein's bibliography, *Genocide: A Sociological Perspective in Current Sociology*, vol. 1 (1990).

11. K. Lange, "Der Terminus 'Lebensraum' in Adolf Hitler's *Mein Kampf*," *Vierteljahreshefte für Zeitgeschichte* 13, 1965, pp. 426–37.

12. Edgar Sanderson, *The British Empire in the Nineteenth Century: Its Progress and Expansion at Home and Abroad* (London, 1898). James Morris, *Pax Britannica: The Climax of an Empire* (London, 1968), chap. 1. Aaron L. Friedberg, *The Weary Titan: Britain and the Experience of Relative Decline, 1895–1905* (Princeton, 1988).

13. Keyaerts mentioned in Najder, *Joseph Conrad*, p. 135.

14. *The Century Magazine* (September 1897).

15. Neal Ascherson, *The King Incorporated* (London, 1963).

16. David Lagergren, *Mission and State in the Congo* (Uppsala, 1970).

17. *Regions Beyond* (May 1896), pp. 253f.

18. Charles Dilke, "Civilization in Africa," in *Cosmopolis* (July 1896) cited in H. Zin, *Joseph Conrad and Africa* (Nairobi, 1982).

19. Leonard Courtney, *Journal of Royal Statistical Society*, vol. 61, no. 4 (1898), p. 640.

20. C. Lô, *Les foggaras du Tidikelt, Traveaux de l'Institut de recherches sahariennes* (Algiers, 1953), p. 139ff, (Algiers, 1954), pp. 49ff.

21. Ian R. Smith, *The Emin Pascha Relief Expedition, 1886-1890* (Oxford, 1972). See also Richard Hall, *Stanley* (London, 1974) and Frank McLynn, *Stanley: Sorceror's Apprentice* (London, 1991).

22. Philip Magnus, *Kitchener: Portrait of an Imperialist* (London, 1958). See also Trevor Royle, *The Kitchener Enigma* (London, 1985); Philip Warner, *Kitchener* (London, 1985); and P. M. Holt, *The Mahdist State, 1881-1898: A Study of Its Origins, Development, and Overthrow* (Oxford, 1970).

23. The execution of the wounded was defended in the *Saturday*

Review (3 September 1898, 10 September 1898).

24. Geoffry Parker, *The Military Revolution: Military Invention and the Rise of the West, 1500-1800* (Cambridge, 1988).

25. Daniel R. Headrick, *The Tools of Empire: Technology and European Imperialism in the Nineteenth Century* (Oxford: Oxford University Press, 1981). See also W. Broadfoot, "The Lee Metford Rifle," *Blackwood's Magazine* (June 1898).

26. Martin Reuss, "The Disgrace and Fall of Carl Peters," *Central European History*, vol. 14 (1981), pp. 110ff. See also *The Times* (26-27 April 1897). For other German examples, see Lionel Decle, *Three Years in Savage Africa* (London, 1900).

27. William Tordoff, *Ashanti Under the Prempehs, 1888-1935* (London, 1965). Richard Austin Freeman, *Travels and Life in Ashanti and Jaman* (Westminster, 1898).

28. Michael Rosenthal, *The Character Factory* (London, 1986) and Tim Jeal, *The Boy-Man: The Life of Lord Baden-Powell* (New York,1990). Robert S. S. Baden-Powell, *The Downfall of Prempeh* (London, 1896).

29. Philip A. Igbafe, *Benin Under British Administration* (Longman, 1979). See also Felix von Luchan, *Die Altertümer von Benin: Veröffentlichungen aus dem Museum für Völkerkunde* (Berlin & Leipzig, 1919); R. H. Bacon, *Benin: The City of Blood* (London, 1898); and M. M. Mahood, *The Colonial Encounter* (London, 1977).

30. Robert S. S. Baden-Powell, *The Matabele Campaign* (London, 1897, 1901), p. 63.

31. T. O. Ranger, *Revolt in Southern Rhodesia, 1896-97: A Study in African Resistance* (London, 1967), p. 121.

32. Darrel Bates, *The Fashoda Incident* (Oxford: Oxford University Press, 1984).

33. Norman Page, *A Kipling Companion* (London, 1984). See also Charles Carrington, *Rudyard Kipling* (London, 1955).

34. Nicholas Delblanco, *Group Portrait: A Biographical Study of Writers in Community* (New York, 1984). See also Iain Finlayson, *Writers in Romney Marsh* (London, 1986) and

Miranda Seymour, *Henry James and His Literary Circle, 1895-1915*, chap. 5.

35. *Chambers's Journal* (30 September 1893). Bernard Bergonzi, *The Early H. G. Wells* (Manchester, 1961). Wells and Conrad: literary survey in *Journal of Modern Literature* (1986), p. 37ff.

36. R. B. Cunningham Graham, *Mogreb-el-Acksa* (1898), pp. 25, 43f.

37. R. B. Cunningham Graham, "Higginson's Dream," *Saturday Review*, vol. 1, no. 10 (1898). See also Cedric Watts, *Cunningham Graham: A Critical Biography* (Cambridge, 1979).

38. *Mémoires de l'Institut national des sciences et des arts, Sciences mathématiques et physiques*, tome 2 (Paris, 1799). See also Georges Cuvier, *Discours sur les révolutions de la surface du globe* (1812, 1985), and Dorinda Outram, *Georges Cuvier* (Manchester, 1984).

39. Stanley, *Extinction*, p. 2 and passim. See also George G. Simpson, *Fossils and the History of Life* (New York, 1983), chap. 1 and 5.

40. Cuvier, *Discours sur les révolutions de la surface du globe* (1985), preface and afterword.

41. William Coleman, *Georges Cuvier, Zoologist* (Cambridge, Mass.: Harvard University Press, 1964), pp. 143-165.

42. Hodgen, *Early Anthropology in the Sixteenth and Seventeenth Century*, pp. 408ff, 418ff.

43. Charles White, *An Account of the Regular Graduations in Man* (1799), p. 135.

44. Erik Nordenskiöld, *History of Biology*, vol. 2, p. 45ff.

45. Charles Darwin, *The Voyage of the Beagle* (9 January–13 April 1834).

46. W. Bölsche, *Ernst Haeckel* (Leipzig, 1900), chap. 9.

47. Coleman, *Georges Cuvier* (1964), pp. 174ff.

48. Charles Darwin, *The Origin of Species*, chap. 9.

49. Letter to Lyell quoted in *Journal of the History of Biology*, vol. 10, no. 19 (1977). See also George W. Stocking, *Race, Culture and Evolution: Essays in the History of Anthropology*

(New York, 1968), pp. 113ff.

50. Alfred W. Crosby, *Ecological Imperialism: The Biological Expansion of Europe, 900-1900* (Cambridge, 1986), chap. 4.

51. Alfred W. Crosby, *The Columbian Exchange: Biological and Cultural Consequences of 1492*. See also Woodrow Borah, *New Spain's Century of Depression* (Berkeley, Calif.: University of California Press, 1951); Russell Thornton, *American Indian Holocaust and Survival: A Population History Since 1492* (Norman, 1987); Mörner Magnus, *History of Latin America* (Stockholm, 1969); and Lewis Hanke, *Aristotle and the American Indian: A Study in Race Prejudice in the Modern World* (London, 1959).

52. Adam Smith, *The Wealth of Nations* (1776), chap. 8.

53. Philip D. Curtin, *The Image of Africa: British Ideas and Action, 1780-1850* (Wisconsin, 1964), pp. 363ff, 373.

54. Darwin, *The Voyage of the Beagle*, chap. 5.

55. James R. Scobie, *Argentina: A City and a Nation* (1964), chap. 1.

56. James Bonwick, *The Last of the Tasmanians* (1870) (London, 1970). See also Robert Travers, *The Tasmanians: The Story of a Doomed Race* (Melbourne, 1968) and George W. Stocking, *Victorian Anthropology* (1987), pp. 274ff.

57. *Edinburgh New Philosophical Journal*, vol. 28 (1839), pp. 166-170.

58. D. Coates, et al., *Evidence on Aborigines* (London, 1837).

59. Adrian Desmond and James Moore, *Darwin* (London, 1991), p. 26.

60. Curtin, *The Image of Africa* (1964), pp. 377ff, 364. "In time, the new racism was to become the most important cluster of ideas in British imperial theory. . . ."

61. Reade is also quoted in Zin, *Joseph Conrad and Africa*, p. 186.

62. *Journal of the Anthropological Society of London*, vol. 165 (1864). Reprinted in A.R. Wallace, *Natural Selection and Tropical Nature* (1878).

63. John C. Greene, "Darwin as a Social Evolutionist," *Journal of the History of Biology*, vol. 10 (1977).

64. *Transactions of the Ethnological Society of London* (1867), p. 120.

65. Greene, "Darwin as a Social Evolutionist."

66. Howison and Merivale, see sections 115 and 116.

67. J. A. S. Grenville, *Lord Salisbury and Foreign Policy: The Close of the Nineteenth Century* (1964), pp. 165f.

68. Darwin, *The Descent of Man*, chap. 7. See also Woodruff D. Smith, *Politics and the Science of Culture in Germany, 1840-1920* (1991). This was not accessible to me until my own work was completed.

69. Friedrich Ratzel, *Politische Geographie* (1897), pp. 35, 119, 121.

70. Robert Knox, *The Races of Mankind: A Fragment* (1850), pp. 149, 198.

71. *Volksdienst* (1893), pp. 21f.

72. *Alldeutsche Blätter* quoted in Lange, "Der Terminus 'Lebesraum' in Hitler's *Mein Kampf.*"

73. *Die Kämpfe der deutschen Truppen in Südwestafrika. Auf Grund amtlichen Materials bearbeitet von der kriegsgeschichtlichen Abteilung I des großen Generalstabes. Erster Band. Der Feldzug gegen die Hereros.* (Berlin, 1906). Quote from preface and report by Oberleutnant Graf Schweinitz. K. Schwabe, *Der Krieg in Deutsch Südwestafrika, 1904-1906* (Berlin, 1907). See also Woodruff D. Smith, *The German Colonial Empire* (Chapel Hill, N.C., 1978); Helmut Bley, *Kolonialherrschaft und Sozialstruktur in Deutsch-Südwestafrika, 1894-1914* (Hamburg, 1968); "Die Methoden der Menschenbehandlung haben auf das Mutterland zurückgewirkt," p. 314.

74. Andrej J. Kaminski, *Konzentrationslager 1896 bis heute* (Munich, 1990), chap. 2.

75. Paul Kennedy, *The Rise and Fall of the Great Powers*, chaps. 5-6.

76. Eberhardt Jäckel, *Hitler's Weltanschauung* (Tübingen, 1969). See also Reinhard Rurüp, *Der Krieg gegen die Sowjetunion, 1941-1945* (Berlin, 1991) and R. D. Müller, *Hitler's Ostkrieg und die deutsche Siedlungspolitik* (Frankfurt am Main, 1991).

77. Werner Jochmann (ed.), *Monologe im Führerhauptquartier*

1941-1944 (Hamburg, 1980), pp. 58f.

78. Gerd R. Überschär, et al., *Der deutsche Überfall auf die Sowjetunion* (Frankfurt am Main, 1991); Götz Aly and Susanne Heim, *Vordenker der Vernichtung* (Hamburg, 1991), pp. 115ff, 123; and Eberhard Jäckel and Jürgen Rohwer (eds.), *Der Mord an den Juden im zweiten Weltkrieg* (Frankfurt am Main, 1987).

79. Arno J. Mayer, *Why Did the Heavens Not Darken: The "Final Solution" in History* (1988), prologue.

80. J. F. Rolland, *Le grand capitaine* (Paris, 1976). See also Douglas Porch, *The Conquest of the Sahara* (Oxford, 1984); A. S. Kanya-Forstner, *The Conquest of the Western Sudan: A Study in French Military Imperialism* (Cambridge, 1969); M. Mathieu, *La Mission Afrique Centrale,* thesis, (Université de Toulouse-Mirail, 1975), pp. 40, 102, 151; *Documents pour servir à l'histoire de l'Afrique Occidentale Française de 1895 à 1899* (Paris); General Jolland, *Le drame de Dankori* (Paris, 1930); P. Vigné d'Octon, *La Gloire de sabre* (1900) (Paris, 1984); and debates in chambre des députés (21 June, 23 November, 30 November, and 7 December 1900).

81. Klobb, *Dernier carnet de route* (Paris, 1904).

82. Cardboard boxes now in *Depôt des archives d'outre mer*, Aix en Provence.